IFIP Advances in Information and Communication Technology 742

Editor-in-Chief

IFIP Advances in Information and Communication Technology

The IFIP AICT series publishes state-of-the-art results in the sciences and technologies of information and communication. The scope of the series includes: foundations of computer science; software theory and practice; education; computer applications in technology; communication systems; systems modeling and optimization; information systems; ICT and society; computer systems technology; security and protection in information processing systems; artificial intelligence; and human-computer interaction.

Edited volumes and proceedings of refereed international conferences in computer science and interdisciplinary fields are featured. These results often precede journal publication and represent the most current research.

The principal aim of the IFIP AICT series is to encourage education and the dissemination and exchange of information about all aspects of computing.

More information about this series at https://link.springer.com/bookseries/6102

Lynette Drevin · Wai Sze Leung · Suné von Solms
Editors

Information Security Education

Empowering People Through Information Security Education

17th IFIP WG 11.8 World Conference, WISE 2025
Maribor, Slovenia, May 21–23, 2025
Proceedings

Springer

Editors
Lynette Drevin
North-West University
Potchefstroom, South Africa

Wai Sze Leung
University of Johannesburg
Johannesburg, South Africa

Suné von Solms
University of Johannesburg
Johannesburg, South Africa

ISSN 1868-4238 ISSN 1868-422X (electronic)
IFIP Advances in Information and Communication Technology
ISBN 978-3-031-94923-4 ISBN 978-3-031-94924-1 (eBook)
https://doi.org/10.1007/978-3-031-94924-1

This Springer imprint is published by the registered company Springer Nature Switzerland AG
The registered company address is: Gewerbestrasse 11, 6330 Cham, Switzerland

Preface

Welcome to the proceedings of the 17th World Conference on Information Security Education (WISE 2025), co-located with the 40th IFIP TC-11 International Information Security and Privacy Conference (SEC 2025) on May 21–23, 2025.

Organized by the IFIP Working Group 11.8, which comprises dedicated professionals from academia, government, and private organizations who volunteer their time and effort, WISE 2025 reflected a longstanding dedication to advancing information security through education. With nearly two decades of history, WG 11.8 has been shaping the landscape of information security and ensuring its relevance in a dynamic digital age.

Under the theme "Empowering People through Information Security Education", WISE 2025 received 30 submissions from around the world.

Prior to the assignment of reviewers to the submissions, members of the International Program Committee (IPC) were asked to indicate their conflicts of interest with submissions. This was further checked by the committee to ensure that any conflict of interest and potential bias was adequately managed. Each paper was then subject to double-blind review by at least three members of the IPC over a review period of 14 days. Where deemed necessary, additional reviewers with the necessary expertise to assess the submissions appropriately were identified to assist with assessing the quality of the work. Papers were reviewed according to a set of criteria which included: relevance, novelty and originality, technical strength, discussion of related work, the quality of the design and methodology, and the paper's plausibility. After careful consideration, the committee decided to accept 13 full papers. The acceptance rate for the conference was 43%. A further two papers which were submitted to the SEC 2025 Conference and reviewed by the SEC 2025 IPC, and which better fit the theme of WISE, have been included in this volume.

We extend our heartfelt gratitude to the TC-11 members for their continued support, enabling us to serve the working group and organize the WISE conferences. Our sincere appreciation also goes to the members of the Program Committee, the external reviewers, and to the authors who trusted us with their intellectual work. We are grateful for the support of the WG 11.8 Officers: Erik Moore, Jacques Ophoff, and Matt Bishop. In addition, we would like to thank the SEC 2025 general chair, Tatjana Welzer, the organizing chair, Marko Hölbl, and their team for their efforts in helping us to host WISE 2025.

Finally, we wish to acknowledge the Microsoft conference management system which was used for managing the submissions and reviews of WISE 2025 papers. As for the preparation of this volume, we sincerely thank our publisher Springer for their assistance.

May 2025

Lynette Drevin
Wai Sze Leung
Suné von Solms

Organization

TC11.8 Chair

Erik Moore	Seattle University, USA

WISE 2025 Conference Chair

Jacques Ophoff	Abertay University, UK

WISE 2025 Program Chairs

Lynette Drevin	North-West University, South Africa
Erik Moore	Seattle University, USA

WISE 2025 Conference Secretariat

Matt Bishop	University of California, Davis, USA

WISE 2025 Publication Chairs

Wai Sze Leung	University of Johannesburg, South Africa
Suné von Solms	University of Johannesburg, South Africa

WISE 2025 Web Chair

Jacques Ophoff	Abertay University, UK

Program Committee

Stefan Alfredsson	Karlstad University, Sweden
Maria Bada	Queen Mary University of London, UK

Matt Bishop	University of California, Davis, USA
Nathan Clark	University of Plymouth, UK
Michael de Jager	North-West University, South Africa
Lynette Drevin	North-West University, South Africa
Steven Furnell	University of Nottingham, UK
Paul Haskell-Dowland	Edith Cowan University, Australia
Ram Herkanaidu	University of Plymouth, UK
Sokratis Katsikas	Norwegian University of Science and Technology, Norway
Konstantin Knorr	Trier University of Applied Sciences, Germany
Wai Sze Leung	University of Johannesburg, South Africa
Dan Likarish	Regis University, USA
Sascha Löbner	Goethe University Frankfurt, Germany
Leonardo Martucci	Karlstad University, Sweden
Herbert Mattord	Kennesaw State University, USA
Stig Mjølsnes	Norwegian University of Science and Technology, Norway
Erik Moore	Seattle University, USA
Noluntu Mpekoa	University of Johannesburg, South Africa
Jacques Ophoff	Abertay University, UK
Jarred Orfao	University of Johannesburg, South Africa
Suzanne Prior	Abertay University, UK
Kai Rannenberg	Goethe University Frankfurt, Germany
Carlos Rieder	isec ag, Switzerland
Léo Robert	LIMOS, Université Clermont Auvergne, France
Rudi Serfontein	North-West University, South Africa
Chien-Chung Shen	University of Delaware, USA
Alireza Shojaifar	University of Applied Sciences and Arts Northwestern Switzerland, Switzerland
Frederic Tronnier	Goethe University Frankfurt, Germany
Manfred Vielberth	University of Regensburg, Germany
Suné von Solms	University of Johannesburg, South Africa
Susanne Wetzel	Stevens Institute of Technology, USA
Stephen Wolthusen	Royal Holloway, University of London, UK

Contents

Workforce and Curriculum Development

INFER: Enhancing Digital Forensics Education Through Ready-to-Use Hands-on Labs with Portable Operating Environments

Tran Ngoc Bao Huynh, Haowen Xu, Brian Almaguer, Jun Dai, and Xiaoyan Sun(✉)

Worcester Polytechnic Institute, Worcester, MA 01609, USA
{nhuynh1,hxu4,baalmaguer,jdai,xsun7}@wpi.edu

Abstract. As cybercrime increases annually, digital forensics, a subsection of cybersecurity that involves identifying, preserving and analyzing digital evidence, has seen a surge in demand over the years. Despite the need, there is a large shortage in the cybersecurity workforce, including digital forensics. Meanwhile, the community also faces a lack of free, interactive, and quality instructional resources for digital forensics education. In this paper, we introduce INFER (INstructional Forensics Education Resource), which develops a set of hands-on labs for digital forensics education. These labs were designed on different and essential topics from the basic to advanced levels. The hands-on activities are portable, comprehensive, expandable, adjustable, and easy to follow with step-by-step instructions and accompanying lab environments. We evaluated the effectiveness of these labs through students' surveys. A faculty development workshop was also hosted to disseminate the INFER materials and assess the usability. Based on the evaluation results, INFER is a valuable resource for providing quality digital forensics education.

Keywords: Digital Forensics Education · Hands-on Labs · Experiential Learning

1 Introduction

Digital Forensics (DF) is a subsection of cybersecurity that focuses on identifying, collecting, analyzing, and preserving digital evidence for various digital systems and platforms, including mobile devices, networks, databases, and IoT devices. DF is essential not only for recovering deleted or damaged files from disks and devices but also plays a crucial role in criminal investigations, particularly in cases involving cybercrime.

Despite the growing demand and potential, there is a significant shortage of professionals in the cybersecurity field. Digital forensics, being a specialized subset of cybersecurity, is also facing a growing need for experts in this area. In 2024, the global cybersecurity workforce gap is nearing 5 million professionals,

L. Drevin et al. (Eds.): WISE 2025, IFIP AICT 742, pp. 3–17, 2026.
https://doi.org/10.1007/978-3-031-94924-1_1

a 19.1% increase from 2023 [1]. This gap is expected to widen as new digital systems rapidly evolve. As society becomes increasingly reliant on technology and the threat of cyberattacks intensifies annually, the need for skilled cybersecurity professionals to defend against digital threats and investigate the cyber attacks has never been more critical.

Traditional training methods in digital forensics primarily emphasize theory and certifications. However, these approaches may not expose learners to sufficient practical exercises and hands-on experiences. High-quality digital forensics education stresses the importance of gaining practical experience with relevant forensics tools and platforms. Experiential learning, extensively studied in STEM fields, has demonstrated a positive impact on student learning outcomes. Yet, its effectiveness has not been thoroughly studied in the digital forensics field due to lack of systematic, comprehensive hands-on labs that are readily available and easily adaptable for in-depth research. As it stands, the most advanced hands-on training in digital forensics remains limited to a small audience.

Several recent digital forensics education projects [2–5] contribute to the field by developing specific courses (inherently a recipe of lectures and labs to fulfill learning outcomes) that cover one or more sub-branches (such as IoT forensics), or by pedagogically enhancing digital forensics education with specific technology (such as Augmented Reality). However, the lack of high quality labs remains a challenge. Besides, the impact of experiential learning in digital forensics education is still unclear.

Therefore, this paper presents a comprehensive instructional resource for digital forensics education and studies the impact of experiential learning based on a pool of newly developed hands-on labs. Specifically, this work develops an ***INstructional Forensics Education Resource (INFER)*** in the form of step-by-step hands-on labs with accompanying instructional operating environments, and research the labs' impact on student learning in digital forensics. The work in the paper answers the research question: *To what extent will the INFER labs impact student knowledge, skills, and attitudes regarding digital forensics?* More specifically, what is the impact towards the student learning outcomes in regards to the breadth of knowledge, skills, interest in forensics, and career readiness?

In this work, the designed INFER labs come with the required instructional operating environments so that instructors do not need to prepare them from scratch. The INFER labs are portable, comprehensive, expandable, and adjustable: 1) they systematically and comprehensively cover a number of forensics sub-areas in depth; 2) they are ready-to-use with the required lab environments and materials; and 3) they can be adopted for different levels of digital forensics education, such as the undergraduate and graduate level courses. Like SEED Labs [6], INFER can be adopted with proper adjustment by other courses in high school education and workforce development such as: summer academies or summer camps (e.g., GenCyber [7]); community college courses; and trainings for digital forensics practitioners, law enforcement personnel, and IT professionals from nonprofit organizations and government agencies.

2 Background and Related Work

2.1 Cybersecurity Education

There are several approaches to teach and introduce cybersecurity concepts to new learners, including courses, workshops, games, and cyber ranges. Traditional methods often rely on lectures focused on theoretical knowledge and the concepts of cybersecurity [8]. Cyber ranges are valuable tools for simulating real-time cyber scenarios [9–11]; however, they can be costly and often complex and challenging for beginners. Hands-on labs [6], workshops [12,13], and serious games [8,14,15] are effective tools for engaging new learners. These methods allow learners to gain practical experience through real-world use cases, fostering deeper engagement with the material, skill development, and a better understanding of core concepts. While games offer interactive and visually appealing experiences, they often lack the depth necessary to build proficiency with the tools used in the field. For all the above mentioned methods, most of them are for general cybersecurity education and not directly designed for digital forensics education

2.2 Digital Forensics Education

There remains a notable lack of comprehensive curricular and teaching materials for digital forensics, particularly at the undergraduate and postgraduate levels. While some efforts have been made to enhance digital forensics education through hands-on labs and activities [16–19], they might have various limitations. Some works do not provide sufficient comprehensiveness or depth to cover the different topics in digital forensics. Some provides a limited set of forensics tools or platforms. Most do not provide a step-by-step instruction to guide students in the learning process. In addition, these labs often do not come with the accompanying environment that is already configured with proper operating systems, software, and required lab materials (such as acquired images of disks, text/audio/video files, etc.). Setting up the lab environment and creating the lab materials from scratch can often be very time consuming.

3 INFER Hands-on Labs for Forensic Education

3.1 Why

The absence of quality hands-on labs renders many digital forensics courses impractical and superficial. For example, students completing a course may understand the concept of data acquisition (acquiring evidence), but they may not know how to actually zero-out (completely wipe) a target disk, construct a brand-new file system on it, and then perform data acquisition in a Linux environment. Similarly, they may have learned the concept of file carving (recovering the files from unallocated areas), but they may not know how to manually locate the file fragments on the disk and reassemble them to recover the file. Hence, well-designed hands-on labs will be indispensable for helping students delve into digital forensics and gain practical experience. Moreover, the delivery of these labs can help strengthen our understanding of the distinctive impact of experiential learning in digital forensics education.

Therefore, the INFER labs are designed to address gaps in current digital forensics education by being portable, comprehensive, expandable, adaptable, and ready for use by anyone with the provided lab environments and materials. By creating a structured learning framework, we can effectively convey advanced concepts to new learners while keeping them engaged through practical, real-world applications and exercises.

3.2 How

Our work contains 18 step-by-step, hands-on exercises covering 12 essential topics in digital forensics. These topics are categorized and range from foundational concepts, such as data acquisition, to advanced and contemporary areas, including social network forensics, memory forensics, and reverse engineering. Foundational labs are estimated to take about an hour. Intermediate problems will require approximately two to four hours to complete, while advanced activities will take four hours or more. Most labs can be divided into multiple modules to alleviate complexity and allow students to work on a smaller task at a time.

Recognizing that students and learners are often highly motivated to explore the real-world role of a digital forensics investigator [20], we have designed many of the labs to be problem-based and centered around authentic digital forensics cases. As exemplified by Fig. 1, each lab includes detailed step-by-step instructions with corresponding screenshots so that students can work on the labs following these instructions, requiring minimum help or guidance from the instructors. The instructions and needed lab materials (virtual machine images, artifact files, etc.) are accessible through the project website [21] and GitHub [22].

To provide a comprehensive learning experience, the labs utilize CAINE, Windows, and Kali Linux operating systems (OS). This variety ensures learners are prepared to navigate different OS environments they may encounter in professional practice. Windows, as one of the world's most widely used desktop operating systems, is a critical platform for digital forensic investigations. Familiarity with its essential tools and mechanisms is indispensable for effective forensic analysis. Kali Linux is an open-source distribution specifically tailored for penetration testing, computer forensics, ethical hacking, and reverse engineering [23]. Similarly, CAINE (Computer Aided INvestigative Environment) is an open-source Linux distribution designed to support digital forensic investigations [24]. Both operating systems come equipped with an extensive array of pre-installed forensic tools, enabling tasks such as disk imaging, analysis, and memory forensics. These tools provide the foundational capabilities required for collecting and analyzing digital evidence.

In addition to the pre-installed tools, the labs incorporate other free and readily accessible software such as WinPMem, Ghidra, and FTK Imager. For tools requiring separate installation, we provide detailed installation links and setup instructions within the lab documentation.

Step 21: Start Sonic Visualiser program. Click on **File->Open** to open the carrysong-with secret message.wav file.

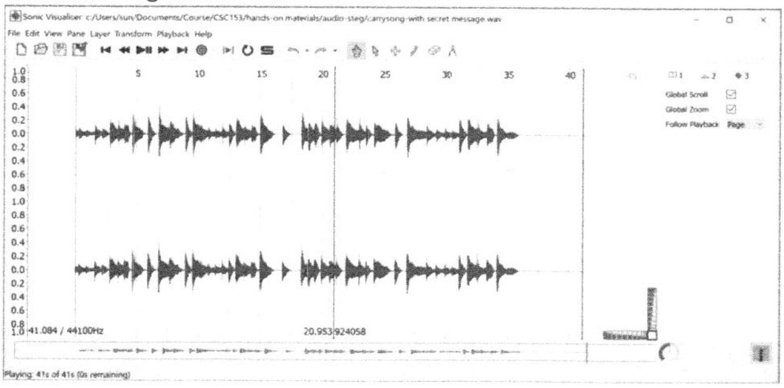

Step 22: Click on **Layer->Add Spectrogram-> carrysong-with secret message.wav: All Channels Mixed**.

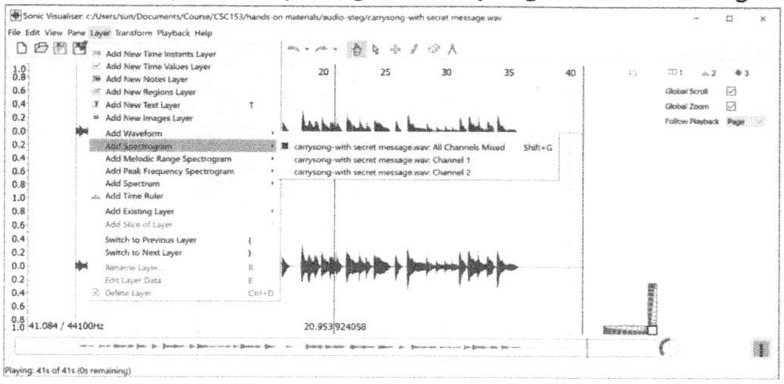

Step 23: You can move around to display the secret message.

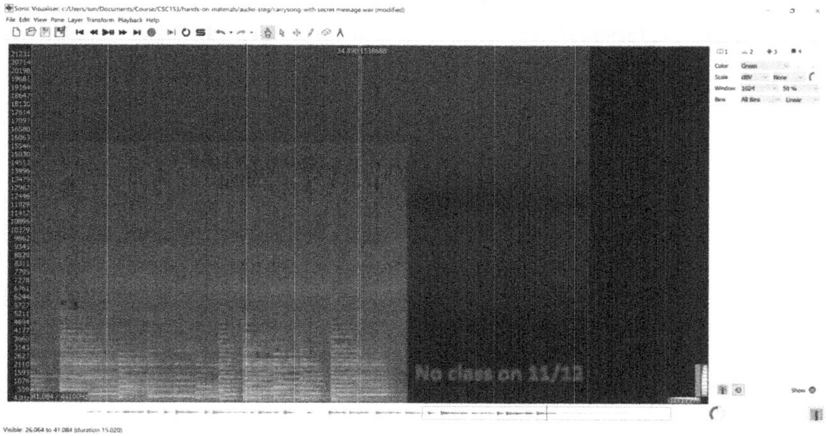

Fig. 1. An excerpt of step-by-step instructions from example INFER Lab: Steganography with Audio File.

Each lab directory in the GitHub repository contains comprehensive materials, including lab instructions, relevant files, and tools for practice. For instance, Fig. 2 highlights a steganography-focused repository. This repository includes a PDF file with lab instructions, input files such as "fun.bmp" and "lake.jpeg.cpt," and the tool "stegseek_06.1.deb" for practice. To reinforce learning, each lab concludes with review questions and optional bonus challenges. These challenges are designed to deepen the learner's understanding and encourage independent problem-solving. While step-by-step instructions are provided for the primary tasks, the bonus challenges require learners to apply the knowledge and skills gained during the lab to complete the tasks independently.

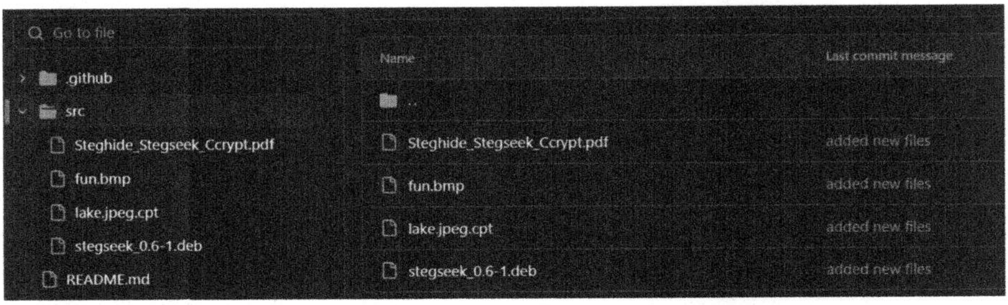

Fig. 2. Steganography hands-on repository.

4 Evaluation

4.1 Student Perspective

Studies were conducted towards students who used INFER labs to assess the impact of these labs on students' learning effectiveness and their attitude towards digital forensics. The participants were from digital forensics courses at different levels: the undergraduate level and the graduate level. The majority of the students are pursuing majors in computer science, cybersecurity, or related fields. Our data collection and processing procedures adhered to ethical guidelines for human subject research, and has obtained the Institutional Review Board (IRB) approval. We conducted different surveys with approximately 50 college students (ages 18 and older). This include the pre-course and post-course surveys that evaluate aspects such as students' level of knowledge, interest, confidence, and career readiness, and also surveys on each hands-on lab that they've work on to evaluate the effectiveness for each individual lab. Please note that the surveys for individual labs were conducted with only a subset of labs due to the limited time allocated for labs within the courses. It is not feasible to incorporate all the designed labs, as each course requires specific topics to be covered.

In the pre-course survey, students were asked to rate their interest in Digital Forensics on a scale from 1 (low) to 5 (high). We found that 98% of the students expressed interest in the topic. Over half of the students were considering or interested in pursuing a career related to digital forensics. However, most students were initially unfamiliar with the digital forensics and perceived it as a complex subject. When being asked about their confidence in their skills and career readiness in digital forensics, only 15 out of 51 students reported average or high confidence, with just 3 students selecting a rating of 4 or 5.

More than 60% of the students were unfamiliar with how to set up a Virtual Machine (VM) for a digital forensic workstation, a fundamental yet critical step in forensics and many other cybersecurity tasks. Most undergraduate students were unable to perform this task, while 60% of the graduate students were comfortable preparing a VM environment before the course. In all labs, we emphasize the importance of ensuring the integrity of the evidence data. Since the evidence data and devices might contain malware, opening them on the host machine is risky. Additionally, data on the investigator's host machine could interfere with the evidence, compromising its integrity. Therefore, understanding how to set up a sandbox, such as the VM environment, to handle potentially harmful data is essential in cybersecurity, as well as in digital forensics.

Only 15% of the students had experience with Linux or Windows data acquisition, the first and most crucial step in collecting and retrieving valid data. Unlike Network Forensics, which involves tools like Wireshark and is typically covered in Computer Network courses, most other topics in digital forensics were unfamiliar to the students.

In the surveys for individual hands-on activities, we gathered student feedback through rating scale questions and short-answer responses to assess the labs' impact on their learning in Digital Forensics. Specifically, we ask questions such as: *Do you feel Activity 6 was effective in helping you learn digital forensics concepts such as how to use Winhex to recover graphics files? Does Activity 6 make you interested in the topic of using Winhex to recover graphic files?*

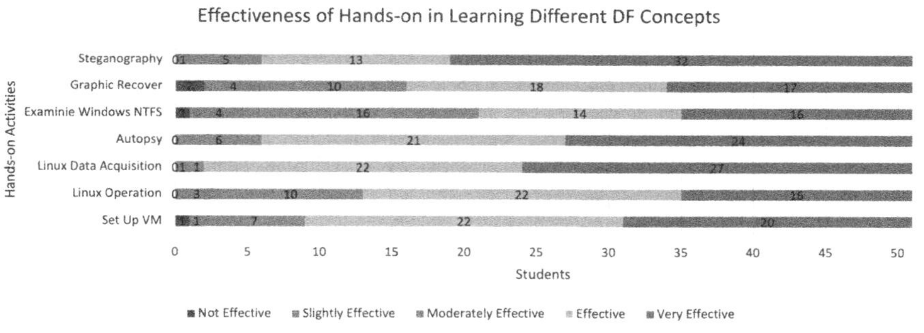

Fig. 3. Effectiveness of INFER labs for learning different DF concepts.

As shown in Fig. 3, when students were asked if the hands-on labs helped them effectively learn digital forensic concepts, most participants found the activities helpful. However, there were often students who ran into technical challenges for some labs. For example, some students encountered challenges during the "Set Up VM" task, particularly when setting up the virtual environment on Mac machines. Due to Apple's proprietary silicon chips, many x86_64 VM images are incompatible with Mac's unique architecture. We recognize this issue and have worked to develop additional instructions for these special cases. For Mac machines, alternative software and setup steps may be required. For example, VMware Fusion or Workstation can be used on Mac as alternatives to VirtualBox, which is no longer supported on mac OS. However, VMs must be compatible with Mac processors (i.e., ARM architecture) to run on Mac, even when using VMware. For VM images incompatible with Mac processors, the QEMU emulator [25] provides an effective solution. QEMU is a free, open-source software that is easy to install and can be managed efficiently through the command line in the terminal.

In addition to the "Set Up VM" activity, students who rated other tasks as "Not Effective" or "Slightly Effective" suggested the inclusion of instructional videos. While we indeed provide videos to instructors to better support the teaching, we encourage students to first attempt the exercises on their own. Working on the lab independently by following the instructions, addressing the technical challenges, and answering the lab questions can promote better comprehension and retention compared to simply replicating steps from a video.

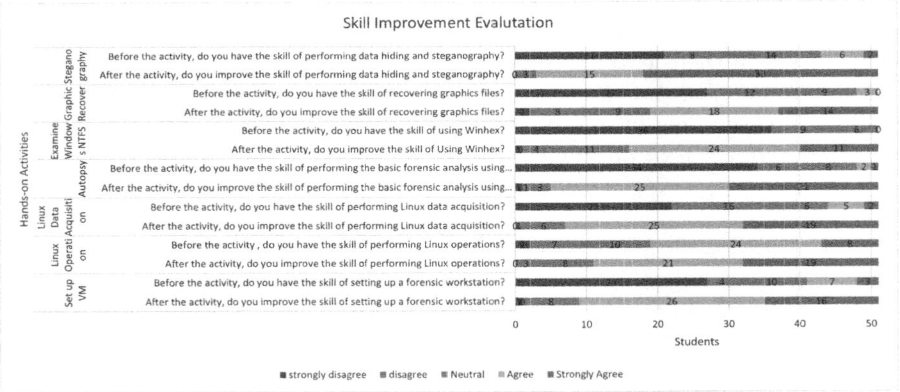

Fig. 4. Students' skill improvement through INFER labs.

The improvement in students' skills before and after participating in the activities is significant, as illustrated in Fig. 4. For instance, in the "Examine Windows NTFS" activity, none of the students initially possessed the skill to use WinHex. However, after completing the hands-on lab, this number surged to 35 students, reflecting an almost 70% improvement. Similarly, activities such as "Steganography" and "Set Up VM" demonstrated nearly 100% skill enhancement rates. Upon examining the cases where students reported no improvement in their skills, their short-answer feedback revealed that these instances were primarily due to technical issues with Mac machines, as previously explained.

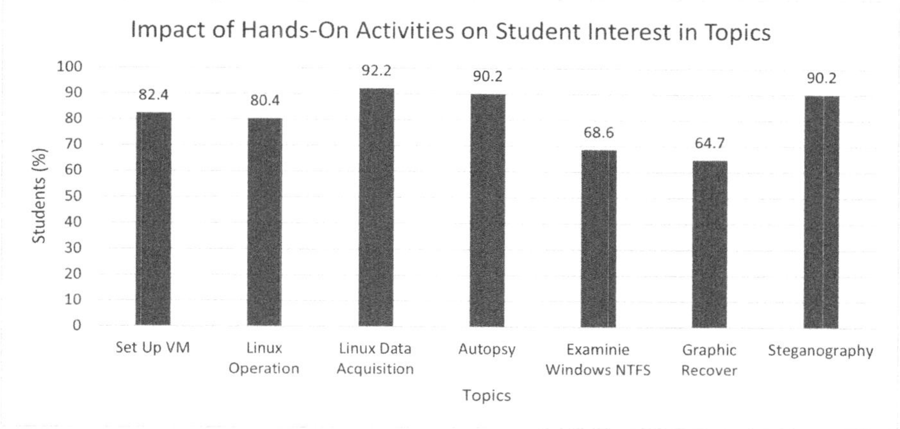

Fig. 5. Impact of INFER labs on student interest in learning DF.

As shown in Fig. 5, the INFER hands-on activities significantly boosted students' interest in digital forensics, while effectively enhancing their skills across various topics and tasks. Students were asked to rate their interest levels on a scale from 1 (Not Interested) to 5 (Very Interested) in response to whether the activities increased their capability of using the tools and performing digital forensic tasks. The activities that garnered the most interest included steganography, data acquisition, and real-world case-based autopsy labs. On the other hand, activities such as "Windows NTFS" and "Graphic Recovery" required extensive understanding and interaction with hex data files, which proved to be more challenging for many undergraduate students. Consequently, these topics received lower interest ratings among this group. However, the inspiration rates among graduate students for these two topics were notably higher, at 90% and 70%, respectively.

After completing the course, students also completed a post-course survey. As shown in Fig. 6, there was a significant increase in the number of students who somewhat agreed or strongly agreed that their ability to understand and perform digital forensic tasks had improved. Nearly all students were now able to set up their own VM for forensic investigations and perform data acquisition in both Windows and Linux, compared to just 10–20% at the start of the course.

For advanced topics such as "Android Forensics" and "Drone Forensics", none of the students had prior experience with the material before the course. This is partly due to the fact that many of the tools involved are not free, and not everyone has access to expensive smartphone or drone technology.

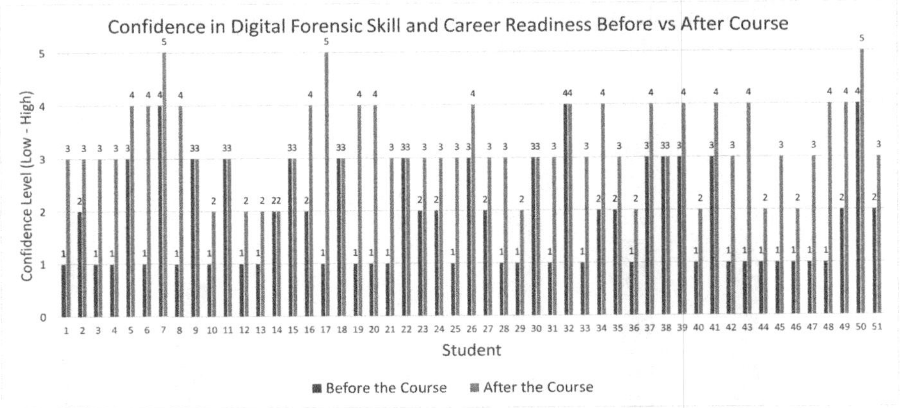

Fig. 6. Students' confidence in DF skill and career readiness before vs. after the course.

Additionally, we found that labs focusing on binary analysis or assembly code, such as "Reverse Engineering", as well as labs requiring a combination of various digital forensics skills and knowledge—such as "Social Network Forensics", "Memory Forensics", and "Drone Forensics"—proved to be more challenging for students. As a result, the understanding and confidence levels for these exercises were generally lower compared to those for other labs (Fig. 7).

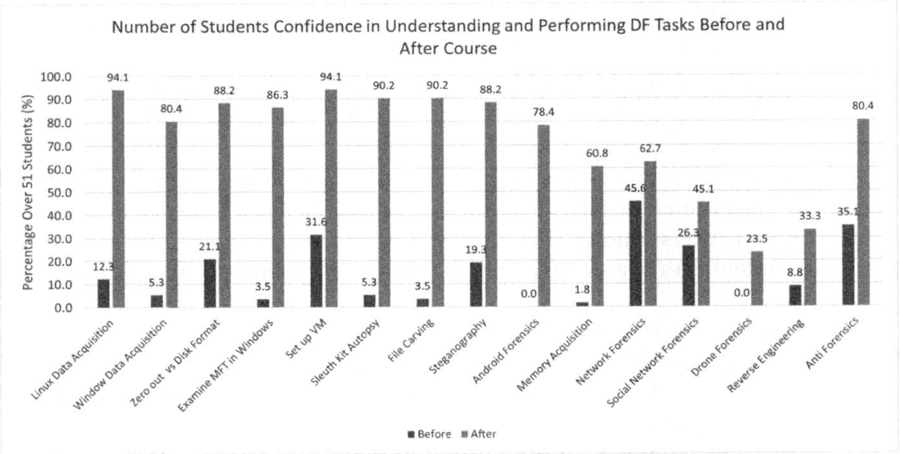

Fig. 7. Number of students confident in performing DF tasks before vs. after the course.

Nonetheless, the feedback we received from students after completing the hands-on tasks was largely positive. Below are some of the comments from students following the course and their hands-on lab experiences:

"It is a truly enriching experience to learn more about digital forensics through hands-on activities with different tools, such as how to recover deleted or hidden data and bypass security measures on Android."
"Much more interested now than I was before. May choose this as my career path. Thanks for the introduction!"
"This was a phenomenal experience. I look forward to implementing what I've learned in the future. I look to brush up on a few more concepts and skills before applying them to a job. This class is a wonderful stepping stone".
"Overall, a great and engaging class. Really enjoyed the activities and gained a greater knowledge in digital forensics".
"Very interesting and allows you to explore different areas of forensics".

4.2 Educator Perspective

This project was also evaluated from the educator's perspective by collecting feedback from two groups: K-12 teachers and college faculty. Two major efforts were made to gather their feedback: 1) we used the INFER labs in a graduate-level summer course in digital forensics for K-12 teachers (mostly high school teachers); 2) we hosted a 2-day faculty development workshop to disseminate the labs to college professors.

The graduate level summer course in digital forensics has approximately 20 teachers from K-12 schools (mostly high schools) nationwide. All participants were teaching or planning to teach courses in cybersecurity, or other courses related to computer science, engineering, or similar disciplines. Before participating in the hands-on labs, most teachers had little to no familiarity with digital forensics, with only about 30% having prior experience or confidence in the subject. Considering that most teachers were teaching at the high school level, the course used only a small subset of INFER labs as the hands-on activities: "Linux Data Acquisition", "Zero and Disk Formatting", "Setting Up Virtual Machines for Digital Forensics Investigations", and "Steganography". The feedback collected from teachers on confidence is presented in Fig. 8 below. Despite not covering all topics, hands-on lab practice based on INFER significantly improved participants' confidence, with 100% reporting confidence in performing Digital Forensics tasks by the end of the course. This indicates that the teachers gained sufficient technical background to teach their students in these topics confidently.

A two-day development workshop was also hosted for faculty from community colleges and four-year universities to disseminate the designed labs. The event brought together 11 faculty members and professors from various institutions across the United States. We provided an introduction of the INFER project and also a training on how to use the labs in digital forensics courses. Participants also received a in-depth guided walkthrough of five hands-on labs during the workshop, and then they were given the opportunity to work on the labs independently taking the students' role. These five labs, including "Linux Data Acquisition with Zero Out and Disk Formatting", "Sleuth Kit Autopsy", "Image Steganography", "Audio Steganography", and "Reverse Engineering", are

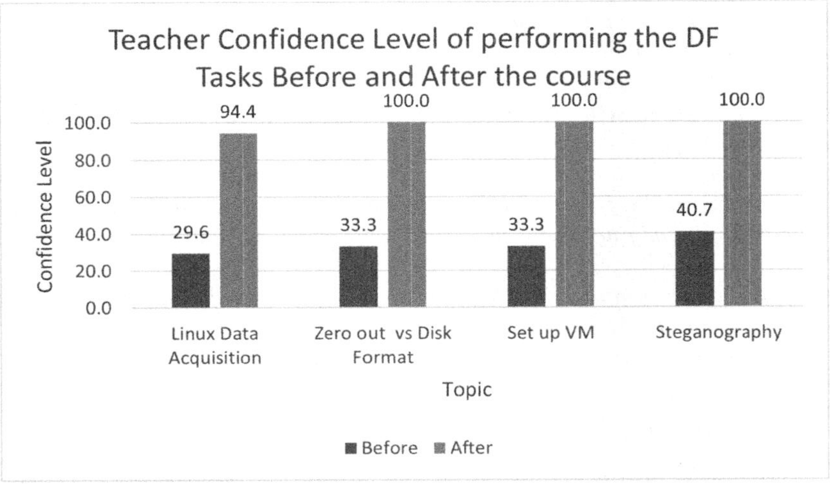

Fig. 8. Teachers' confidence level in performing DF tasks before vs. after the course.

examples demonstrating how the faculty can use them in their own class. With these examples, they also know how to access and use the materials for the remaining labs. At the end of the workshop, participant surveys were conducted to get the faculty's opinions on INFER labs' design and effectiveness. All participants (100%) found the INFER labs valuable and would recommend them to colleagues or friends teaching cybersecurity or digital forensics-related courses. Many of them have plans to adopt INFER labs in their own courses or start a digital forensics course in their institution.

Below are reflections and feedback from some teachers and professors who participated in the course and workshop:

> *"The synchronous instructions coupled with the hands-on labs offered the best of both worlds."*
> *"The hands-on labs are really useful in my teaching and research."*
> *"I really liked the accessibility of the labs and being able to continue to work with them outside of the workshop."*
> *"We would like to use the labs in our digital forensics courses."*
> *"The INFER labs offer multiple opportunities for advancing digital forensics (DF) research and education. We can create new courses for undergraduate and graduate students, integrating selected DF labs into these new courses as well as existing ones. Additionally, we can conduct DF research to develop new techniques that enhance current DF methodologies and skills."*

4.3 Limitations and Future Work

Keeping software up to date is essential for rapid technological advancements. For instance, Android, IoT, and drone software evolve very quickly, making some lab tools potentially obsolete for current or future applications. Continuous effort and dedicated human resources are required to track and update tools accordingly.

Additionally, some software, such as Belkasoft X and WinHex, offer limited-time free access or restrict advanced features in their free versions, which may hinder long-term learning and the ability to perform complex tasks. To enhance accessibility, we are working on extending lab instructions to Mac environments, particularly in preparing virtual machines and images, as several tools are not Mac-compatible and require alternative setup procedures.

For future work, we aim to integrate more real-world attack scenarios and case studies, as suggested by [18,20]. This will provide students with a more practical, engaging, and effective learning experience. We will periodically review and update the tools and software to ensure they remain up-to-date and accessible for use.

5 Conclusion

The demand for a highly skilled cybersecurity workforce, particularly in digital forensics, continues to grow. INFER labs aim to bridge this gap by offering a practical, interactive, comprehensive, and readily-available resource for digital forensic education. Survey results from students, teachers, and college faculty provided very positive feedback, reinforcing the project's usability, effectiveness, and potential to enhance digital forensics training. As INFER is free and open source, future collaborations and contributions can further expand and refine the materials, ensuring they remain practical and aligned with real-world applications.

Acknowledgment. Drs. Xiaoyan Sun and Jun Dai are supported by NSF DGE-2409851. Dr. Jun Dai is also supported by NSF DGE-1934285/2403603.

References

1. ISC2 Cyber Security Workforce Study: Global Cybersecurity Workforce Prepares for an AI-Driven World (2024). Accessed 27 Jan 2025
2. Cybersecurity Education Workshop 2019. CyberEd 2019. https://sceweb.sce.uhcl.edu/cybercorps/workshop.html. Accessed 1 Apr 2025
3. CFEAR: Cyber Forensics Education via Augmented Reality - NSF Award Research: SaTC-EDU: EAGER: CFEAR: Cyber Forensics Education via Augmented Reality. https://www.nsf.gov/awardsearch/showAward?AWD_ID=1500055&HistoricalAwards=false. Accessed 27 Jan 2025

4. Expanding Digital Forensics Education with Artifact Curation and Scalable - NSF Award Research: SaTC: EDU: Expanding Digital Forensics Education with Artifact Curation and Scalable, Accessible Artifact Exercises. https://www.nsf.gov/awardsearch/showAward?AWD_ID=1900210&HistoricalAwards=false. Accessed 27 Jan 2025
5. Online Digital Forensics Courses and Labs for Students and Professionals - NSF Award Research: SaTC: EDU: Online Digital Forensics Courses and Labs for Students and Professionals. https://www.nsf.gov/awardsearch/showAward?AWD_ID=1802701&HistoricalAwards=false. Accessed 27 Jan 2025
6. Du, W., Wang, R.: SEED: a suite of instructional laboratories for computer security education. J. Educ. Res. Comput. (JERIC) **8**(1), 1–24 (2008). https://doi.org/10.1145/1348713.1348716
7. GenCyber. https://public.cyber.mil/gencyber/. Accessed 27 Jan 2025
8. Friedl, S., Glas, M., Englbrecht, L., Bohm, F., Pernul, G.: ForCyRange: an educational for IoT cyber range for live digital forensics. IFIP WISE, June 2022. https://doi.org/10.1007/978-3-031-08172-9_6
9. Katsantonis, M.N., Manikas, A., Mavridis, I., Gritzalis, D.: Cyber range design framework for cyber security education and training. Int. J. Inf. Secur. **22**, 1005–1027 (2023). https://doi.org/10.1007/s10207-023-00680-4
10. Leitner, M., et al.: AIT cyber range: flexible cyber security environment for exercises, training, and research. In Proceedings of the 2020 European Interdisciplinary Cybersecurity Conference (EICC '20). Association for Computing Machinery, New York, NY, USA (2021). Article 2, 1–6. https://doi.org/10.1145/3424954.3424959
11. Oh, S. K., Stickney, N., Hawthorne, D., Matthews, S. J.: Teaching web-attacks on a Raspberry Pi cyber range. In Proceedings of the 21st Annual Conference on Information Technology Education (SIGITE '20), pp. 324–329. Association for Computing Machinery, New York, NY, USA (2020). https://doi.org/10.1145/3368308.3415364
12. Yuan, X., et al.: Developing faculty expertise in information assurance through case studies and hands-on experiences. In: 2014 47th Hawaii International Conference on System Sciences. IEEE (2014). https://doi.org/10.1109/HICSS.2014.606
13. Englbrecht, L., Pernul, G.: A serious game-based peer-instruction digital forensics workshop. In: Drevin, L., Von Solms, S., Theocharidou, M. (eds.) WISE 2020. IAICT, vol. 579, pp. 127–141. Springer, Cham (2020). https://doi.org/10.1007/978-3-030-59291-2_9
14. Friedl, S., Reittinger, T., Pernul, G.: Digital detectives: a serious point-and-click game for digital forensics. In: Drevin, L., Leung, W.S., von Solms, S. (eds.) Information Security Education - Challenges in the Digital Age, WISE 2024. IFIP Advances in Information and Communication Technology, vol. 707 (2024). https://doi.org/10.1007/978-3-031-62918-1_9
15. Pan, Y., Schwartz, D., Mishra, S.: Gamified digital forensics course modules for undergraduates. In: 2015 IEEE Integrated STEM Education Conference. IEEE (2015). https://doi.org/10.1109/ISECon.2015.7119899
16. Chi, H., Jones, E. L., Chatmon, C., Evans, D.: Design and implementation of digital forensics labs: a case study for teaching digital forensics to undergraduate students. In: Proceedings of the Conference, vol. 672, no. 057, p. 193 (2009)
17. Ward, P.: Development of a small cybersecurity program at a community college. Inf. Syst. Educ. J. **19**(3), 4–10 (2021)
18. Xu, W., Deng, L., Xu, D.: Towards designing shared digital forensics instructional materials. IEEE COMPSAC (2022). https://doi.org/10.1109/COMPSAC54236.2022.00025

19. Wang, X., Bhuse, V., Sutton, S.: The design and development of hands-on activities for digital forensics education. J. Colloquium Inf. Syst. Secur. Educ. **11**(1) (2024). https://doi.org/10.53735/cisse.v11i1.187
20. Wang, X., Bai, Y., Goda, B.: Project design and implementation for digital forensics education. In: Proceedings of the 20th Annual SIG Conference on Information Technology Education (SIGITE '19), pp. 33–38. Association for Computing Machinery, New York, NY, USA (2019). https://doi.org/10.1145/3349266.3351402
21. INFER Project Website. https://wp.wpi.edu/infer/. Accessed 2 Apr 2025
22. INFER Project Github Repository. https://github.com/WPI-LIONS-Group/INFER.git. Accessed 2 Apr 2025
23. Kali Linux. https://www.kali.org/. Accessed 21 Dec 2024
24. Caine. https://www.caine-live.net/. Accessed 21 Dec 2024
25. QEMU. https://www.qemu.org/download/. Accessed 27 Jan 2025

Expanding the Cybersecurity Workforce: Challenges, Current Practices and Future Directions in Attracting and Cultivating Multidisciplinary Talent

Christos Kallonas and Eliana Stavrou(✉)

Open University of Cyprus, Nicosia, Cyprus
christos.kallonas@st.ouc.ac.cy, eliana.stavrou@ouc.ac.cy

Abstract. As technology and digitalization rapidly advance, the demand for cybersecurity professionals continues to grow. The surge in cyber threats has further emphasized the necessity for skilled cybersecurity experts as organizations strive to secure their operations. This research paper undertakes a qualitative analysis of specific cybersecurity reports to identify employment-related concerns and prevailing practices within the cybersecurity sector. Specifically, the analysis seeks to un-cover obstacles hindering the recruitment of candidates from non-traditional disciplines, while also identifying effective strategies for attracting, retaining, and developing multidisciplinary cybersecurity talent.

Keywords: Cybersecurity skills · Cybersecurity professional development · Cybersecurity skills gap · Cybersecurity talent · Multidisciplinary skills · Transferable skills · Cybersecurity

1 Introduction

The fast growth of technology and the extended digitalization of several aspects of business and daily life have led to an increased demand for cybersecurity professionals. The rise of cyber threats, such as data breaches, ransomware attacks, and other malicious activities, has further highlighted the need for skilled cybersecurity professionals [1]. Although the demand for cybersecurity professionals has increased, supply cannot fulfil the labor market needs, adding to the existing problem of finding and retaining talent in cybersecurity. As indicated in recent cybersecurity workforce reports [2, 3], millions of cybersecurity specialists will still be needed globally in the next several years. This significant mismatch between supply and demand highlights the pressing need for practical approaches to attract, develop, and preserve talent in this critical area [4]. However, a fundamental question arises: who should be trained to meet these growing demands? Should efforts focus solely on individuals from traditional disciplines such as computer science, engineering, and cybersecurity? Or is it time to broaden the pool of potential candidates by educating and integrating professionals from diverse disciplines into cybersecurity roles?

Published by Springer Nature Switzerland AG 2026
L. Drevin et al. (Eds.): WISE 2025, IFIP AICT 742, pp. 18–30, 2026.
https://doi.org/10.1007/978-3-031-94924-1_2

Potential solutions should address barriers to entering the cybersecurity field, alongside challenges and misconceptions. Regarding the latter, the cybersecurity industry suffers from the misperception that professionals usually require a technical background in IT and/or cybersecurity discouraging non-technical candidates from pursuing a career in the field [5]. However, many technical skills required for cybersecurity roles can be acquired on the job with proper training and development [4, 6]. The explosion in demand for cybersecurity professionals is a clear opportunity to create skilled and long-term careers for people who have fallen outside of the formal education system or whose education was not in a technical subject.

Cybersecurity is a multidisciplinary domain. One approach to consider in addressing the skills gap is to attract people from other disciplines, e.g., engineering, business, psychology, political studies, law, etc., that can be related to cybersecurity. Although this approach has been discussed before as a solution to the skills gap problem, investigations are rather at an early stage, and more insights are needed towards this direction [7, 8]. Therefore, the aim of this study is to explore the challenges related to attracting talent in cybersecurity from different disciplines. Moreover, this study will focus on identifying good practices the industry might have adopted that can potentially contribute to attracting and retaining individuals from diverse backgrounds. To achieve the study's research aims, a qualitative analysis was conducted, utilizing ten latest cybersecurity workforce studies delivered by professional and governmental organizations. The analysis aimed to identify factors that might impede efforts to attract candidates from non-traditional disciplines, alongside good practices that organizations might be utilizing, and which can attract them to pursue a career in cybersecurity. Insights derived from this study are envisioned to inspire the design of new interventions to contribute to the skills gap by increasing the talent pool with candidates originating from different disciplines.

Section 2 provides the background and context of this work, while Sect. 3 provides a brief analysis of the methodology used in this research. Section 4 examines and analyses the collected data from the cybersecurity workforce studies, and Sect. 5 offers a critical discussion of the findings and potential future research directions. Section 6 presents concluding remarks.

2 Background and Context

Despite extensive efforts to address the cybersecurity workforce shortage, the skills gap remains a persistent and growing challenge [4, 5]. Reports from leading organizations such as ISACA, ISC2 and ENISA consistently highlight the increasing demand for cybersecurity professionals, and the limited supply of skilled workers [5]. This growing imbalance raises concerns about the long-term sustainability of the cybersecurity workforce, as existing measures appear insufficient to meet the sector's rapidly evolving needs [9].

One of the key deficiencies in current initiatives lies in their predominant focus on technical expertise. Many training programs emphasize technical skills such as penetration testing, network security, and incident response while overlooking the importance of interdisciplinary knowledge [10, 11]. Cybersecurity is not solely a technical field but rather a multidisciplinary field, encompassing a diverse range of knowledge areas beyond technical expertise. While traditionally perceived as a domain dominated by computer science, engineering, and information technology, cybersecurity increasingly requires insights from disciplines such as psychology, law, political science, and business [7, 10, 11]. The dynamic and evolving nature of cyber threats necessitates a broader approach that integrates these various perspectives to create more effective defense strategies, risk management frameworks, and security policies [8]. However, these aspects are often overlooked in education and training programs, limiting the industry's ability to attract a more diverse range of professionals. In addition, many cybersecurity job descriptions prioritize certifications and coding skills over critical thinking, policy expertise, or behavioral analysis, reinforcing a narrow talent pipeline [5]. This traditional approach overlooks the value of interdisciplinary collaboration in addressing modern cyber challenges, which extend beyond technical vulnerabilities to include human factors, legal considerations, and strategic decision-making [10]. Accessibility and visibility of entry points to cybersecurity remain a major challenge since traditional education pathways often fail to support career changers, individuals from underrepresented backgrounds, and those without formal technical training [12]. As a result, many potential candidates are excluded from cybersecurity career opportunities, further exacerbating the shortage [5].

The consequences of this skills gap extend beyond workforce limitations, affecting the well-being of professionals, the resilience of organizations, and broader national security [5]. The growing shortage places immense pressure on existing cybersecurity teams, leading to increased workloads, stress, and burnout [12]. Many professionals experience job dissatisfaction due to the overwhelming up taking of responsibilities due to the workforce shortage, which contributes to high turnover rates and an ongoing cycle of vacancies [5]. At the organizational level, the lack of skilled personnel undermines the ability to implement strong cybersecurity strategies, leaving businesses and institutions vulnerable to cyber threats [13]. Without adequate staffing, security teams struggle to proactively manage risks, detect and respond to incidents, and safeguard critical systems. This, in turn, elevates cybersecurity risks at a national and global level, as organizations in both the public and private sectors face escalating threats with insufficient human resources to mitigate them [9].

The continued gap suggests that current training approaches, while valuable, are not sufficient to meet the scale and complexity of the challenge [4, 5]. There is a growing need to rethink cybersecurity workforce strategies by embracing multidisciplinary approaches, expanding accessibility and visibility of entry points to cybersecurity, and ensuring that training efforts are more aligned with the realities of the evolving cyber threat landscape [10, 11].

3 Methodology

3.1 Selection of Reports

This study utilizes a selection of industry and policy reports that provide comprehensive insights into cybersecurity workforce challenges, skills gaps, and hiring trends. The reports analyzed include those published by ISC2 [3, 5], ISACA [2, 14], CIISec [12, 15], the UK government [16, 17], and the World Economic Forum [13, 18] over the past two years (2023, 2024). These reports serve as a foundation for understanding workforce development efforts at both national and global levels, offering perspectives from practitioners, employers, policymakers, and other key stakeholders. The insights gained from these reports will be critically examined to identify ongoing barriers to cybersecurity recruitment and explore innovative approaches to bridge the skills gap.

The selection of these reports is based on their scope, credibility, and relevance to cybersecurity workforce development. Each report is produced by an authoritative entity within the cybersecurity field, ensuring the data is derived from large-scale surveys, policy assessments, and industry insights. This allows for this study to incorporate empirical evidence and real-world perspectives, complementing academic research by highlighting the practical challenges and trends shaping the cybersecurity workforce. Additionally, these reports provide a broad and detailed view of workforce challenges across different regions and industry sectors.

3.2 Description of Codes Defined for the Qualitative Analysis

This study performed a qualitative analysis of selected reports. To facilitate a structured and in-depth qualitative analysis, a coding framework was developed to support the research objectives of this study. The codes for the qualitative analysis were developed using an inductive coding approach. Initially, an exploratory reading of the selected reports was conducted, during which recurring themes such as concerns and practices related to cybersecurity workforce development had been identified. The codes were selected based on their relevance to the central aims of the study, specifically, understanding the challenges, current practices and opportunities involved in attracting, cultivating, and retaining talent in cybersecurity from diverse disciplines.

The coding framework categorized key themes emerging from the selected reports, ensuring a systematic approach to analyzing workforce challenges, skills gaps, and potential solutions. The following codes were established to guide the analysis: a) **Talent Gap Identification:** This code is used to highlight findings related to current and anticipated shortages in the cybersecurity workforce, capturing insights into the extent of the talent gap. b) **Challenges and Limitations:** This code focuses on discussions concerning the barriers and limitations associated with current efforts to bridge the cybersecurity talent gap. It includes critiques of existing workforce development strategies, challenges in recruiting and retaining cybersecurity professionals, and limitations in traditional education and training models. Furthermore, it examines the obstacles faced by individuals from non-traditional disciplines who seek to transition into cybersecurity roles. c) **Multidisciplinary Skills Transferability:** Content categorized under this code explores the integration of skills from diverse disciplines into cybersecurity roles. This code also considers the extent to which existing workforce development initiatives recognize and facilitate interdisciplinary career transitions. d) **Technology Adoption and Impact:** This code assesses how emerging technologies—such as artificial intelligence (AI), machine learning, blockchain, and automation—are reshaping cybersecurity workforce demands and education and training programs. e) **Industry and Organizational Good Practices**: This code captures content related to effective workforce strategies, industry best practices, and organizational policies that facilitate the attraction and retention of cybersecurity talent from diverse backgrounds.

4 Critical Analysis and Findings

The primary goal of this critical analysis is to identify and discuss the employment-related concerns and prevalent practices within the cybersecurity sector concerning multi-disciplinary talent development and acquisition.

4.1 Talent Gap Identification

The cybersecurity workforce continues to face an expanding and persistent skills gap, with organizations globally struggling to find qualified professionals. The UK Cybersecurity Skills Report 2023 [16] revealed that 739,000 UK businesses (over 50%) lack staff with basic cybersecurity skills, while 487,000 (33%) report deficiencies in advanced capabilities, such as forensic analysis, penetration testing, security architecture, and interpreting malicious code. The global scale is equally concerning, with over 90% of organizations identifying skill shortages in one or more cybersecurity areas [5], and 67% of organizations reporting insufficient cybersecurity staff to manage security risks. This shortage is particularly pronounced in cloud security, AI security, and Zero Trust implementation, which have been identified as the top three areas with the highest workforce deficits.

Recent 2024 reports confirm that the situation has worsened. The ISC2 Cybersecurity Workforce Study 2024 [3] states that the global cybersecurity workforce gap has surged to 4.76 million, marking a 19.1% increase from 2023. Furthermore, the WEF Global Cybersecurity Outlook 2024 [18] highlights that 36% of organizations cite skills shortages as the primary barrier to achieving cyber resilience, with 78% admitting they lack sufficient in-house talent to meet cybersecurity demands. Smaller organizations are particularly vulnerable, with 31% of leaders from low-revenue businesses struggling to find cybersecurity talent, compared to only 11% in large corporations.

As cybersecurity threats continue to evolve, organizations are increasingly shifting their approach toward internal upskilling and alternative hiring strategies. The WEF 2024 report [18] highlights that 91% of organizations are now willing to fund cybersecurity training and certifications for their employees, recognizing that internal workforce development is a key solution. However, these measures alone have not yet translated into tangible workforce growth, as recruitment remains a challenge, and the demand for cybersecurity professionals continues to outpace supply. While larger organizations have begun investing in cybersecurity apprenticeships and internship programs, smaller firms struggle to provide similar opportunities due to budget constraints and concerns over employee retention that might leave an organization once they acquire more qualifications [2, 3].

4.2 Challenges and Limitations

The data collected under this code are particularly significant, as they provide a clear mapping of the organizational behaviors that contribute to cybersecurity workforce challenges. Understanding these challenges is crucial to identify the underlying causes of the skills gap and to address persistent issues in hiring, retention, career development, and economic constraints.

The demand for personnel possessing a blend of strong technical expertise and complementary skills within organizations remains notable and presents a significant challenge for organizations to find individuals with these skills [16]. This difficulty is reflected in some employers' perception that refer to these individuals with this unique combination of proficiencies as 'unicorns.' The scarcity of candidates with both deep cybersecurity knowledge and transferable skills such as critical analysis, problem-solving and communication skills is a significant limitation to workforce growth. Notably, this shortage persists across both cybersecurity generalist and specialist roles, indicating that these qualifications are essential either in roles that require a broad understanding of various cybersecurity areas or a deep specialization. The ISACA 2024 report [2] reinforces this issue, stating that 55% of organizations struggle to retain cybersecurity professionals, primarily due to higher salary offers elsewhere (50%) and workplace stress (46%).

The skills gap is not just about a lack of workers but also about mismatches between available talent and employer expectations. The ISC2 2024 Workforce Study [3] reports that 67% of cybersecurity professionals believe their teams are understaffed, and despite the rising demand for cybersecurity specialists, many organizations are struggling to hire due to strict job requirements that often exclude competent candidates. These include high experience requirements for entry-level roles, excessive certification demands, and a reluctance to hire candidates with non-traditional career paths.

One of the most persistent workforce issues is the lack of clearly defined career pathways, which presents challenges for both employers and job seekers. Many organizations fail to provide structured career progression models, leaving professionals without clear guidance on how to advance within cybersecurity. The ISC2 2024 Workforce Study [3] found that 66% of cybersecurity professionals believe the absence of defined career pathways is a major barrier to workforce development. The same finding is reported in UK Cybersecurity Skills Report 2023 [16]: "We currently are offering no career pathways in cyber roles and cannot offer any apprenticeships. You are expected to have the knowledge or experience already, and if a role becomes available, then apply for it.".

Cybersecurity hiring managers demonstrate a divided approach to recruitment, with approximately half of them reluctant to hire entry-level candidates, relying instead on degrees, certifications, or excessive job requirements [5]. The 2024 ISACA survey [2] found that many job postings require at least three years of experience for what should be entry-level roles, making it difficult for new professionals to transition into cybersecurity. Despite this, there is a growing trend of technically experienced professionals from non-cybersecurity backgrounds attempting to transition into the field [5]. However, many organizations remain hesitant to expand their hiring criteria, further contributing to the workforce shortage. This reluctance has prolonged the talent gap, as organizations overlook professionals who could successfully transition with additional training. Instead of hiring based on problem-solving ability, risk management skills, and adaptability, hiring managers continue to prioritize candidates with previous cybersecurity experience, even in areas where transferable skills from other fields would be equally valuable [5].

The current state of cybersecurity presents an alarming workforce shift, characterized by an aging workforce and limited entry-level hiring opportunities [14]. The ISACA 2024 study [2] found that, for the first time, the largest proportion of cybersecurity professionals are aged 45–54 (34%), surpassing the 35–44 age group (30%). At the same time, there has been no increase in younger professionals entering the field, raising concerns that the cybersecurity talent pipeline is not being replenished at a sustainable rate.

4.3 Multidisciplinary Skills Transferability

The insights obtained from the Multidisciplinary Skills Transferability code are particularly compelling, as they highlight the potential for bridging the cybersecurity skills gap, provided that clear multidisciplinary pathways are defined and supported. The evolving nature of cybersecurity necessitates diverse expertise, making it crucial for organizations to recognize and facilitate multidisciplinary career transitions.

Considering the evolving demands of the profession, it is apparent that cybersecurity offers a broad spectrum of roles, as evidenced by insights gathered from the evaluated reports (e.g. CIIS Security Profession Report [12]) and cybersecurity skill frameworks [19, 20]. These roles extend beyond purely technical skills to encompass non-technical competence areas such as compliance, law, and human aspects compliance specialists. This highlights the notion that cybersecurity is not an entirely technical discipline but rather an inclusive field that welcomes professionals from diverse backgrounds. However, ensuring favorable outcomes in multidisciplinary hiring requires addressing critical factors, including the definition of career pathways, targeted training programs, and strategic hiring approaches to attract professionals with skills in multidisciplinary knowledge areas such as risk management, law, compliance, business continuity, and leadership, all of which are increasingly valuable in the cybersecurity domain.

A critical question emerges: what is the primary requirement—more experienced personnel, skilled professionals in cybersecurity, or an inflow of entry-level graduates who can be trained on the job? An examination of the evaluated reports such as CIIS 2022/2023 Security Profession Report [12], reveals an interesting response: "... respondents believe that the industry is facing a shortage of skills, rather than people, and they believe this needs to be remedied with more skilled personnel than simply fresh recruits.". This indicates that fresh recruits might not be considered as a good option, and this can greatly hinder the efforts to increase cybersecurity talent. To strengthen the future cybersecurity workforce, emphasis should be placed across three directions: 1) recruit experienced professionals from different disciplines and upskill them in cybersecurity, 2) invest in upskilling existing IT/cybersecurity personnel, and 3) recruit graduates and/or professionals with little experience and accelerate their learning in cybersecurity.

According to the Department for Science, Innovation & Technology [16], a dedicated survey examined university graduates over three consecutive years who are currently employed in cybersecurity and IT roles across all degree pathways. The findings revealed an interesting insight, that nearly 30% of cybersecurity professionals had diverse educational backgrounds, spanning fields such as Science, Technology, Engineering, Mathematics, Accounting, Business, Economics, Finance, Humanities, and Social Sciences. This undeniably demonstrates that the cybersecurity talent pool can be enriched by professionals from various disciplines, reinforcing the importance of skill transferability [16]. The 2024 ISC2 Cybersecurity Workforce Study [3] further supports this by highlighting that hiring managers are actively seeking professionals with problem-solving, teamwork, and communication skills—skills that are highly transferable from other industries. Moreover, it is encouraging that professionals acknowledge that integrating professionals from non-technical fields can be beneficial and can help increase the talent pipeline: "Diverse backgrounds can help solve the talent gap. While IT remains a traditional entry point into cybersecurity, more professionals are transitioning from non-technical fields, bringing valuable perspectives and skills." [3]. In the 2024 ISC2 Cybersecurity Workforce Study, it is also noted that mid-career transitions are becoming a major source of cybersecurity talent, as professionals from engineering, project management, and risk management roles enter cybersecurity. The report states that 59% of hiring managers report an increase in job applications from professionals with technical experience but no prior cybersecurity background, with 51% actively adjusting their hiring requirements to attract candidates from non-cybersecurity fields.

The Multidisciplinary Skills transferability code analysis has indicated that cybersecurity is becoming a viable option for professionals looking for mid-career transitions, especially those with experience in IT, business strategy, data analytics, law, and finance. As the cybersecurity field grows, new pathways continue to emerge, reshaping the hiring practices and expectations of hiring managers. One of the most notable changes in hiring trends is the increasing preference for transferable skills over highly specialized technical expertise. The 2024 ISC2 Cybersecurity Workforce Study [3] found that hiring managers are now prioritizing non-technical skills such as problem-solving (31%), teamwork and collaboration (28%), and curiosity (26%) over highly specialized cybersecurity skills, as they considered that these transferable skills can be applied in various cybersecurity roles. This change is particularly significant given the anticipated impact of Artificial Intelligence (AI) on cybersecurity roles. With AI expected to automate certain technical functions, hiring managers are less focused on deep technical specialization and are instead emphasizing candidates with strong analytical, communication, and adaptability skills [3].

4.4 Technology Adoption and Impact

The code Technology Adoption and Impact gathered significant information on how emerging technologies impact the current skills gap within the cybersecurity workforce.

In 2022, for the first time, Artificial Intelligence (AI)/Machine Learning (ML) skills were ranked among the top five skills in terms of demand, underlining a significant upscaling from the previous years when they were near the bottom of the demands' list [3, 5]. As AI/ML assumes an emerging role in the cybersecurity skill set, employees find themselves less equipped to manage and effectively leverage its power compared to other cybersecurity competencies. A significant proportion of respondents (84%) admit having minimal to moderate knowledge of AI/ML. The skills gap in AI/ML trails just behind the gap in cloud computing security. Given the ongoing increase in demand for these skills among cybersecurity personnel, immediate access to more AI-based professional development is crucial [3]. In addition, given that AI/ML competences are cultivated across different disciplines, professionals originating from such disciplines could make a good fit for cybersecurity roles.

4.5 Industry and Organizational Good Practices

The Industry and Organizational Good Practices code provides insights into how current industry practices and organizational policies influence the attraction, retention, and upskilling of cybersecurity talent from diverse backgrounds. Moreover, this analysis sheds light on the varied approaches of the public and private sectors in addressing the persistent challenge of bridging the continuously growing cybersecurity skills gap.

Some of the organizations grappling with the extensive cybersecurity skills gap have begun reassessing their hiring criteria. A notable 2024 trend is the increase in hiring from non-traditional backgrounds, as organizations recognize the value of transferable skills. The 2024 ISC2 Cybersecurity Workforce Study [3] reports that 51% of hiring managers are actively adjusting their recruitment strategies to attract professionals from fields such as business, law, and finance. Furthermore, cybersecurity hiring managers are shifting focus toward transferable skills such as problem-solving, adaptability, and critical thinking over purely technical knowledge. These transferable skills can be gained through working in different disciplines and be adjusted to facilitate cybersecurity tasks. The 2024 ISACA report [2] highlights that companies prioritizing soft skills alongside technical expertise report faster onboarding times and improved team collaboration. To build a more proficient cybersecurity team, organizations are encouraged to actively seek individuals from diverse educational and professional backgrounds and broaden their recruitment strategies both internally and externally [5]. This shift aligns with government and industry efforts to create alternative pathways into cybersecurity, including apprenticeships, bootcamps, and cross-sector career transition programs [17].

Certain public sector organizations have opted to cultivate talent internally due to difficulties in recruiting senior cybersecurity professionals. These employers acknowledge that while there are limitations to this approach, investing in workforce development leads to long-term sustainability [16]. The UK government's cybersecurity skills strategy serves as an example of how public-private partnerships are addressing workforce shortages. The UK Cyber Security Council has introduced initiatives [20] aimed at creating structured career pathways, training programs, and mentorship opportunities to help professionals transition into cybersecurity.

Additionally, several private-sector organizations have expanded their focus beyond traditional education and certifications. Many now prioritize complementary soft skills such as communication, project management, business development, and client relations when assessing cybersecurity candidates. Attributes such as enthusiasm, curiosity, and adaptability are now considered essential traits for success in cybersecurity roles [16]. Research from the 2024 ISACA report [2] further highlights that organizations implementing structured mentorship and sponsorship programs report higher success rates in retaining cybersecurity talent. Programs that connect junior professionals with senior mentors help accelerate career development and increase workforce stability.

5 Discussion

5.1 The Importance of Attracting, Cultivating, and Retaining Talent from Diverse Backgrounds

The cybersecurity talent gap persists, and it seems that this trend will continue for the coming years. Whether this is a skills gap or a lack of available personnel, the fact remains; organizations are not adequately protected against a dynamic threat landscape that exploits the lack of human capacity to effectively defend and protect their assets. Addressing the talent gap from a multidisciplinary perspective is a potential solution to bridge supply and demand in cybersecurity [7]. In doing so, it is imperative that there is a clear understanding of the challenges and barriers that professionals from different disciplines might face when they want to pursue a career in cybersecurity and address them through innovative interventions.

Currently, the workforce predominantly is comprised of individuals from traditional backgrounds such as IT and cybersecurity, yet their numbers are insufficient to address the comprehensive needs of both public and private organizations on a global scale. Furthermore, the multidisciplinary nature of cybersecurity has become increasingly apparent, necessitating proactive measures to extend the pool of cybersecurity professionals. Utilizing domain-specific and transferable skills from various professional domains is crucial for effectively enriching the cybersecurity workforce.

An important factor to consider when investigating how to extend the pool of cybersecurity professionals is how people from the outside might perceive cybersecurity domain. This relates to how different employment aspects are presented, such as the limited opportunities for professional development, the high expectations over cybersecurity roles, not providing a clear view of learning pathways [21], and an aging workforce.

Enhancing diversity in cybersecurity pathways is essential to broaden the talent pool. Achieving this goal requires the development of strategies to attract and encourage diverse groups to pursue careers in cybersecurity. Expanding and diversifying the talent pool is critical for addressing skills shortages and promoting diversity within the field. Initiatives such as ENISA European Cybersecurity Skills Framework (ECSF) [19] and the UK Cyber Security Council's Careers Route Map [20] and play a significant role in supporting and guiding individuals with transferable skills to transition into cybersecurity roles.

5.2 The Way Forward

The critical analysis performed in this work confirmed that promoting diversity within the cybersecurity workforce is not only beneficial but also necessary for the industry's growth and resilience. By actively encouraging individuals from diverse backgrounds to pursue careers in cybersecurity, organizations can tap into a broader talent pool with varied perspectives and skill sets.

Professionals aiming to cultivate and enhance skill sets to address gaps and enhance their future work prospects must complement their education with practical, hands-on experience. As hiring managers often prioritize on-the-job experience over traditional cybersecurity education, individuals from diverse backgrounds, including those without prior cybersecurity experience, should seek to augment their education with technical, hands-on experience to enrich their resumes [5].

Organizations must take active measures to expand their hiring criteria, reduce barriers to entry, and create more inclusive career pathways that allow professionals from various backgrounds to transition into cybersecurity. Considering hiring based on transferable skills such as self-efficacy [22], problem-solving, risk management skills, and adaptability, rather than technical skills, can leverage expertise from a range of disciplines and actively contribute to increasing candidates. Investing in competency-based training and mentorship [23, 24] will have a pivotal role in considering recruiting multidisciplinary cybersecurity talent, as they can accelerate skills development of individuals originating from different disciplines and integrating them timely in the cybersecurity workforce.

Policy makers, higher institutions and vocational education training organizations, should focus on increasing visibility to the multidisciplinary nature of cybersecurity roles. By increasing awareness of the potential that the cybersecurity sector can have professionals from various disciplines, this can greatly contribute to the efforts to attract multidisciplinary talent in cybersecurity and bridge the skills gap.

6 Conclusions

Research indicates that cybersecurity is inherently multidisciplinary, yet systematic investigations into this aspect remain scarce. The field's multidisciplinary nature presents a significant opportunity to act as a catalyst for bridging the skills gap by fostering a diverse workforce. However, to fully leverage this potential, it is crucial to cultivate the conditions necessary for promoting multidisciplinary recruitment as a viable solution to effectively bridge the imbalance between skills' supply and demand in cybersecurity. This requires a comprehensive understanding of the challenges and barriers that could hinder such efforts, as well as an identification of promising trends and best practices that contribute to shaping a diverse cybersecurity workforce.

A crucial aspect to consider in future interventions is the career stage at which individuals originating from different disciplines are facing challenges. Current investigations indicate that professionals transitioning from other fields often encounter obstacles when entering cybersecurity, whether at entry-level stage or during mid-career changes. Depending on their career stage, they have different needs in terms of education and learning to effectively transition into a cybersecurity role. The absence of clear learning pathways to cybersecurity is another obstacle to attracting more diverse candidates, as it leaves professionals without a clear roadmap to enter the sector, develop the necessary skills and progress with their career within the industry. Addressing these challenges is crucial for accelerating skills development and contributing toward a more diverse and skilled workforce in cybersecurity.

Future work will explore various approaches to raise awareness about the multidisciplinary nature of cybersecurity and of the relevant entry points to attract, develop and retain talent from different disciplines, setting the fundamental element to increase the talent pipeline in cybersecurity.

References

1. World Economic Forum: The Cybersecurity Skills Gap is a Real Threat—Here's How to Address It, May 2023
2. ISACA: The State of Cybersecurity: Global Update on Workforce Efforts, Resources, and Cyberoperations (2024)
3. ISC2: Cybersecurity Workforce Study: Global Cybersecurity Workforce Prepares for an AI-Driven World (2024)
4. Goupil, F., Rubayyi, A., Meyer, U.: Towards understanding the skill gap in cybersecurity. In: Proceedings of the 27th ACM Conference on Innovation and Technology in Computer Science Education, vol. 1, pp. 477–483. ACM, Dublin (2022)
5. ISC2: Cybersecurity Workforce Study: How the Economy, Skills Gap, and Artificial Intelligence Are Challenging the Global Cybersecurity Workforce (2023)
6. Angafor, G.N., Yevseyeva, I., He, Y.: Bridging the cyber security skills gap: using tabletop exercises to solve the CSSG crisis. LNCS (LNISA, vol. 12434). Springer, 28 October 2020
7. Hulatt, D., Stavrou, E.: The development of a multidisciplinary cybersecurity workforce: an investigation. In: Furnell, S., Clarke, N. (eds.) Human Aspects of Information Security and Assurance. IFIP Advances in Information and Communication Technology. Springer, Cham, pp. 138–147 (2021)
8. Langner, G., Furnell, S., Quirchmayr, G., Skopik, F.: A comprehensive design framework for multidisciplinary cybersecurity education. In: Furnell, S., Clarke, N. (eds.) Human Aspects of Information Security and Assurance, pp. 105–115. Springer, Cham (2023)
9. U.S. Department of Homeland Security: The National Cyber Workforce & Education Strategy (NCWES) (2018). https://www.dhs.gov/publication/national-cyber-workforce-and-education-strategy. Accessed 14 Feb 2025
10. Blair, J.R.S., Hall, A.O., Sobiesk, E.: Educating future multidisciplinary cybersecurity teams. Computer **52**(3), 58–66 (2019)
11. Jacob, J., Peters, M., Yang, T.A.: Interdisciplinary cybersecurity: rethinking the approach and the process. In: Choo, K.-K.R., Morris, T.H., Peterson, G.L. (eds.) National Cyber Summit (NCS) Research Track, pp. 61–74. Springer, Cham (2020)
12. Chartered Institute of Information Security: The Security Profession Report (2022/2023)
13. World Economic Forum: Global Cybersecurity Outlook 2023: Insight Report, January 2023
14. ISACA: The State of Cybersecurity: Global Update on Workforce Efforts, Resources, and Cyberoperations (2023)
15. Chartered Institute of Information Security: The Security Profession Report (2023/2024)
16. Department for Science, Innovation & Technology: Cyber Security Skills in the UK Labour Market 2023 (2023)
17. Department for Science, Innovation & Technology: Cyber Security Skills in the UK Labour Market 2024 (2024)
18. World Economic Forum: Global Cybersecurity Outlook 2024: Insight Report, January 2024
19. European Union Agency for Cybersecurity (ENISA): European Cybersecurity Skills Framework (ECSF) Version 1.0 (2017). https://www.enisa.europa.eu/publications/european-cybersecurity-skills-framework. Accessed 14 Feb 2025
20. UK Cyber Security Council: Career Framework for Security Professionals in Government (2023). https://www.ukcybersecuritycouncil.org.uk/careers-and-learning/cyber-career-framework. Accessed 14 Feb 2025
21. Furnell, S., Stavrou, E.: Assessing the consistency of cybersecurity education. In: 2024 IEEE Global Engineering Education Conference (EDUCON), Kos Island, Greece (2024)
22. Stavrou, E., Piki, A.: Cultivating self-efficacy to empower professionals' re-up skilling in cybersecurity. Inf. Comput. Secur. **32**(4) (2024)

23. Kallonas, C., Piki, A., Stavrou, E.: Empowering professionals: a generative AI approach to personalized cybersecurity learning. In: 2024 IEEE Global Engineering Education Conference (EDUCON), pp. 1–10. IEEE, Kos Island (2024)
24. Koukou, C., Stavrou, E.: The potential of generative AI Chatbots as career advisors in cybersecurity: professionals' perspectives. In: WISE 2024. IFIP Advances in Information and Communication Technology, vol. 707. Springer, Cham (2024)

An Evaluation Process for Tools that Build or Evidence Competency in Cybersecurity: Development and Lessons Learned

Stephen Miller[1], Christopher Simpson[2], Eugene Vasserman[3], and Susanne Wetzel[4](✉)

[1] ENMU-Ruidoso, Ruidoso, NM, USA
stephen.miller@enmu.edu
[2] National University, San Diego, CA, USA
csimpson@nu.edu
[3] Kansas State University, Manhattan, KY, USA
eyv@ksu.edu
[4] Stevens Institute of Technology, Hoboken, NJ, USA
swetzel@stevens.edu

Abstract. There is a non-trivial gap in skills students possess upon graduation and what employers expect from graduates when they join the workforce. To address this problem, various efforts are underway to shift from the traditional knowledge-based model of educational programs to one that includes a competency-based approach. To foster the introduction and implementation of competency-based concepts to academic programs in a timely fashion, it is necessary to provide the faculty with as many resources as possible. In this context, this paper describes the development, testing, and use of an evaluation process for tools meant to build or evidence competency in Cybersecurity and reports on the lessons learned.

1 Introduction

Recent surveys show that the gap in skills students possess upon graduation and what employers expect from graduates when they join the workforce is widening [19]. Moreover, employers and graduates alike are increasingly dissatisfied with today's academic programs [21,25]. For example, 55% of the graduates state that their degree program did not prepare them for their job and 75% of HR leaders state that most graduates are not ready to "hit the ground running" [22]. Employers expect academic programs to better prepare the students as retraining graduates is costly and time-intensive.

In order to address this problem, various efforts (e.g., [24]) are underway to facilitate a shift from the traditional knowledge-based model of educational programs to also include a competency-based approach. This is particularly important for a field like Cybersecurity which sees new developments and challenges

Published by Springer Nature Switzerland AG 2026
L. Drevin et al. (Eds.): WISE 2025, IFIP AICT 742, pp. 31–45, 2026.
https://doi.org/10.1007/978-3-031-94924-1_3

on a daily basis. Two recent developments in this context include the addition of competency areas to the NICE Workforce Framework for Cybersecurity in 2020 [9,10] as well as the new requirements for (re-)designation as National Center of Academic Excellence in Cyber Defense (NCAE-CD) that include new competency elements such as identifying relevant work roles for the program of study as well as specifying and implementing competency statements that are associated with these work roles [16].

To foster the introduction and implementation of competency-based concepts to academic programs in a timely fashion, it is necessary to provide faculty with as many resources as possible. Recently, a handbook for educators at NCAE-C-designated institutions was published "focus[ing] upon building and sharing good practices in relation to developing the competencies of students within [these] institutions" [20]. A parallel effort was geared to identify and evaluate tools that can be used to build or evidence competency in Cybersecurity. This paper describes the development of the evaluation process and discusses the lessons learned.

The concept of evaluation that forms the core of this work is not new. In fact, there are processes and best practices in many contexts. Examples include evaluation processes for software [15] and comparative processes for purchases in general [17]. In the academic setting we are familiar with evaluation in the context of accrediting academic programs (e.g., ABET [1]) or even the process for obtaining the designation as NCAE-C [7]. Another line of potentially relevant work is that of using and building a governance structure to explore, establish, or provide common resources for a community of common interest (e.g., [23]). However, the constraints and setting under which we set out to develop an evaluation process differ from these prior efforts. First and foremost, the evaluation is not meant to drive any sort of committee decision that may result in a purchase or adoption of any one tool for everyone, i.e., *the evaluation is not focused on identifying the optimal tool based on a specific set of metrics.* Instead, the evaluation strives to ***establish key characteristics and approaches*** *to provide for an evaluation of identified tools in an objective manner based,* leaving it to members of the community to make a determination on their own whether one of the tools and if so which best meets their needs. Similarly, the effort is not about establishing a governance structure. Instead, the setting is that of a *community of volunteers for reviewing the tools on one side, and the tool "owners" (creators/maintainers) volunteering to engage in the review process* on the other. Together these define the constraints under which we set out to establish a process to evaluate tools to build and evidence competency as: community support, volunteer reviews, key characteristics, and balancing multiple goals such (1) capturing a detailed (e.g., as complete as possible) evaluation of the tool features (2) in a fair, consistent, objective, and impartial way with sufficient rigor independent reevaluation, and (3) without putting unsustainable burden on the tool owners or the reviewers.

Outline and Contributions: While our process was designed to uniquely fit our constraints, we nonetheless believe that describing the process, the rationale, and lessons learned will help interested readers to establish similar processes in other contexts. Section 2 describes the process that was developed to evaluate tools which build or evidence competency in Cybersecurity. We provide a rationale for our design decisions based on our unique set of multi-stakeholder requirements and constraints, discuss the lessons learned, and describe how the approach could be adapted to other contexts (Sect. 3). We then review some continuing efforts, and outline next steps in Sect. 4. Finally, we close the paper with some concluding remarks in Sect. 5.

2 Tool Evaluation Process

Before we can introduce the process developed to evaluate tools that build or evidence competency in Cybersecurity, we first need to review the context of this work in some more details. In particular, it is important to recall that there are many definitions of the term competency. This work is not meant to address these in a comprehensive fashion but instead is grounded in the NCAE-C definition of the term: "Competency is the ability for the student to complete a task in the context of a work role." [20]

> A competency is described through so-called competency statements which include five elements—referred to as ABCDE: "An actor (A) performs a behavior (B) within a context (C) to an acceptable degree (D) according to the normative expectations of an employer (E)." [20]

Consequently, the process to evaluate tools that build or evidence competency in Cybersecurity intended to be used institutions that hold an NCAE-C designation must reflect the definition and provide for a means to connect to the ABCDE concept that is at the core of the competency statements.

2.1 Established Process

We developed a six-step process to evaluate tools for building or evidencing competency in Cybersecurity. The process was designed to simultaneously inform the community about available options while not recommending (or even favoring) any tool; balancing the workload of everyone involved; and working under the assumption of honesty, integrity, and best effort.

The process combines elements of independent tool owner input, independent assessment by reviewers, and a joint review meeting—together geared to foster a collaborative and constructive environment.

Step 1. Nomination of Tools: Any and all members of the community are invited (via emails, fliers, community forum posts, etc.) to identify or nominate tools which they either already know are suitable to build or evidence competency, or those with which they have little to no experience with but would like to have them evaluated (further) in that context. This step is a short online questionnaire that asks for contact information for the nominator, some brief information about the tool itself, as well as the level of proficiency of the nominator with the tool.

Step 2. Initial Assessment: Following the nomination, an initial assessment is carried out by (a subset of) the reviewers to determine whether the nomination is suitable for further consideration. In particular, tools to be considered for evaluation need to exhibit some level of comprehensiveness. For instance, the focus is not on tools like a port scanner, but instead tools that may use a port scanner in a particular context or scenario in order to build and/or evidence competency in Cybersecurity.

Step 3. Input from the Tool Owner: For the nominations that have been determined to qualify as scenario-based tools, input from the tool "owner" is sought. An owner may be someone who is the lead developer, otherwise in charge, or someone who can speak to the tool itself, the development approach, and its functionality in regards to building or evidencing competency in Cybersecurity. The tool owner questionnaire includes three main parts (see Appendix A):

Part I is designed to obtain some general information about the tool such as when it was first released, how it is maintained or updated, the costs associated with the set-up, hosting, or running the tool, and actions needed to configure and support the operation of the tool.

Part II focuses on identifying the use cases for the tool, and what is needed of a student and/or institution in order to use it. Specifically, this part seeks to identify the level of student for whom the tool is intended (e.g., high school, four-year college/university, two-year college, etc.); in what contexts it can be best used; what system requirements are necessary for the setup and effective use of the tool; what prerequisite knowledge the student and/or instructor need in order to setup and use the tool; options for integration into a learning management system; whether the tool is geared for individual or group work and how contributions of individual group members can be differentiated; options for instructor intervention and variation of functionality; as well as supported assessment metrics.

Part III is geared to establish the relationship to competency in Cybersecurity and the NCAE-CD Knowledge Units (KUs) [18]. In particular, the purpose is to provide information on how the tool builds and/or evidences competency towards KUs in order to establish the tool's potential to build and/or evidence Cybersecurity competency for the CAE community. Tool owners are asked to explain the tool's approach to building and/or evidencing competency and identify the KUs towards which your tool best builds and/or evidences competency. For up to three of these identified KUs, the tool owners may then explain the tool's approach for building and/or evidencing competency described earlier is implemented for these KUs on an exemplary basis. (Note that not all evaluated tools were designed to integrate with KUs, and this did not prevent evaluation of the tools across other axes.)

Step 4: Review Tool Owner Input: The reviewers check the input from the tool owner for completeness and suitability w.r.t. building and evidencing competency in Cybersecurity. If need be, the tool owner may be contacted to provide further details and/or revise their input to the tool owner questionnaire.

Step 5: Demo of Tool: In an interactive teleconference, the tool owner demonstrates the most prevalent features of the tool in terms of evidencing and building competency in Cybersecurity to the group of reviewers. The real-time nature of these presentations allow reviewers to ask follow-up questions and request a deeper dive into certain parts of the tool.

Step 6: Documentation: The team of reviewers compiles documentation from all steps of the review process, including: (1) the input submitted by the tool owner as part of the owner questionnaire; (2) notes taken by each reviewer participating in the teleconference; (3) the individual summary write-ups each reviewer who participated in the tool owner demonstration teleconference; and (4) a single summary is prepared based on the synthesis of the questionnaire, individual reviewer notes, and post-teleconference thoughts. To achieve a level of uniformity across the reviews of different tools, both the individual reviewer notes as well as the overall summaries are structured into three main sections: (1) a description of the demonstration, i.e., an overview of what was demonstrated in the virtual meeting with the tool owner; (2) the tool's method of evaluation, i.e., how the tool evaluates a student's success at building and/or evidencing competency and the intervention required of an instructor in order to "grade" performance; and (3) the connection to competencies, i.e., how the tool relates to competency in Cybersecurity.

2.2 Infrastructure

In the previous section, the process was described without detailing the kind of a supporting infrastructure that is needed in order to implement the process. It is important to distinguish these two aspects: the pilot phase during which the process was first developed, and the necessary implementation of this process going forward.

Developing and Piloting the Process. As mentioned earlier, the effort to develop this process was carried out in the context of the NCAE-C, first as a working group and then as a task under the Career Preparation National Center (CPNC). Community members who expressed interest to develop the process and pilot the evaluation for an initial set of tools became the reviewers that supported and was involved in every step of the process as described above, evaluating an initial set of tools through this newly-established process. For some of the steps, this only required that reviewers made themselves available in case of questions (e.g., Steps 1 and 3) while other steps were entirely carried out or led by the group. While Steps 2 and 4 were typically done by the group at large, one member of the group was responsible for leading the meeting (Step 5) and compiling the summary documents (Step 6) based on the individual reviews of the others (the non-lead group members who actively participated in the meeting and wrote individual reviews).

Operational Use of the Process. In order to implement the process for operational use—so that tools can be suggested and evaluated on a continuing basis—it is necessary to (1) establish a group of people that will oversee and participate in the review process and (2) procure and maintain the supporting infrastructure to allow for the administration of the questionnaires, the compiling of the necessary documentation, supporting the proper record keeping, and teleconferencing.

Establishing a group to "own" the process can start with (some of) the core group that developed and piloted the process. Additional reviewers need to be recruited in order to allow for a smooth and timely review process without overloading individual group members. Recognizing the fact that the NCAE-C is thriving because faculty from designated institutions continuously participate in various efforts, volunteering their time for the benefit of the community at large, establishing this group is not expected to pose a major challenge. For example, the review processes for the (re-)designation of NCAE-C institutions is similarly organized. Depending on the number of tools that are proposed for review and the frequency with which members will leave the group and others may join, it may be necessary to implement more formal measures for onboarding and/or training to ensure operational continuity and consistency of the process.

The supporting infrastructure for operational use is expected to be facilitated through the CAE in Cybersecurity Community as part of their main functions which call for "provid[ing] technical and logistical support for CAE events, activities, and curriculum" and "provid[ing] a portal of CAE resources for the community, geographic regions, and the Nation as a whole" [2]. As discussed before, the support necessary is fairly standard and should not pose challenges beyond the ongoing support that is currently provided to the community.

3 Discussion of Process Design and Generalization

Aiming to provide some help and guide the establishing of similar processes in other contexts, we now discuss some of the challenges we encountered, the rationale behind some of the approaches taken and decisions made, as well as lessons learned.

3.1 Rationale and Lessons Learned

The two overarching goals of our work were (1) to develop a process that is not only fair, consistent, objective, and impartial, but also one that can be carried out without overburdening any of the parties involved, and (2) maintain a process which is sufficiently rigorous to establish the suitability and utility of the tools in the context of building and evidencing competency in Cybersecurity as defined above. We learned that these seemingly complementary goals required compromises in order to strike a practical balance of these constraints.

Process Development: As one might expect, the process as it stands today and is described above was not developed at once. Instead, we started with a skeleton of elements we felt were necessary and made iterative changes and refinements over time. In particular, we typically made some changes every time we evaluated another tool and worked with another tool owner. We believe that the tools we have evaluated to date are a representative sample of the landscape at large. Thus, we do not expect that major changes to the process will be necessary going forward while recognizing that minor adjustments and improvements will always be warranted.

Trust Model and Tool Selection: One of the first challenges we faced was how to ensure the correctness of the information solicited and compiled while making the process manageable for all involved. It became obvious that it was infeasible for a review group as envisioned to test a tool and the information provided in its entirety. Instead we made a deliberate decision *to develop a process and operate under the assumption of honesty, integrity, and best effort.* As a consequence, we focused on *tools that are freely available.*[1]

Notion of a Tool in the Context of Work Roles: The second challenge encountered was due to the notion of a tool. We quickly came to realize that there are many different notions of what a tool is—especially with regards to comprehensiveness, granularity, and scope. Oftentimes, we received nominations at the level of individual utilities, e.g., port scanners, password crackers, and network sniffers. While these are, of course, commonly referred to as tools, in the context of this work they do not fit the definition of competency for the NCAE-C, which calls for the completion of tasks in the context of a work role. The utilities above would be used as part of the tasks, but they do not themselves define the task. Consequently, the types of tool we seek would use, e.g., a port scanner in a scenario-based setting in order to enable the building or evidencing of competency as per the NCAE-C definition. We eventually elected to use the term "learning environment" instead of "tool" in order to stress the necessary level of comprehensiveness and grounding in a scenario-based setting.[2]

Comprehensiveness vs. Practicality: We encountered three main aspects of these competing constraints, working to strike a suitable balance:

- **Scoping of Tool Owner Questionnaire:** The next challenge was in correctly scoping the tool owner questionnaire. It is important to recognize that tools which are freely available are oftentimes supported, maintained, and further developed by (groups of) faculty and students at academic institutions. Typically, these tools were first developed in the context of a grant and frequently faced the challenge of sustainability once the grant funding has ended. Simply put, these groups do not have the time and resources to provide input to a questionnaire that takes a long time to complete. Even in cases where such constraints are not (yet) a factor, an excessively long questionnaire is a deterring factor. We were

[1] We do not claim that this assumption does not hold for commercial tools. However, it is clear that, in the context of commercial tools and for-profit entities, there are factors and forces that may pose a challenge to this assumption. As such, it will be necessary to re-evaluate the suitability of our process for commercial tools.

[2] For the purpose of this paper, we only use the term tool.

lucky to work with tool owners who helped us tailor the questionnaire to strike a balance between effort required to complete the questionnaire while still collecting enough detail to allows the tool owners to demonstrate the suitability of their tool for building and evidencing competency in Cybersecurity. Our questionnaire changed from asking for a comprehensive coverage of all elements of the tool's functionality to describing the overall approach and "philosophy" of the tool together with representative examples.

- **Grounding in Taxonomy and Framework:** Related to this is the challenge of anchoring the questionnaire in (a) some taxonomy that establishes the knowledge and skills requirements in Cybersecurity and (b) some workforce framework to enable the connecting to tasks and work roles as per the NCAE-C definition of competency. Given the context of this work, we opted to use the NCAE-CD Knowledge Units (KUs) [18] as taxonomy. However, it is important to note that the tool owner questionnaire is structured in a modular fashion such that it is possible to switch this out for another taxonomy as deemed necessary. In earlier versions of the tool owner questionnaire, we asked the tool owners to map their tool to the NICE Framework [10]. We quickly learned that of the four free tools we have reviewed by means of this process to date (NICE Challenge Project—now re-branded as XP Challenge [8], Labtainers [6], SEED Labs [11], and CHEESEHub [3]), only the NICE Challenge Project can provide such a mapping as it was specifically designed and developed in accordance with the NICE Framework. For the others, it would be a major effort (they cannot afford) to establish such a mapping. We adapted the questionnaire to deliberately exclude questions on mappings to workforce frameworks such as the NICE Framework or the DoD Cyber Workforce Framework (DCWF) [5]. Instead, we rely on a crosswalk, which establishes a connection between KUs and the NICE work roles [4]. (Note that the crosswalk we used is still highly specific to our situation and desired outcomes, but the modularity of the survey allows for different mappings to be employed.)
- **Virtual Review:** Linked to the previous challenge is how to facilitate a meaningful demonstration of the tool without getting caught up in details. So far, we have successfully addressed this challenge by allowing the tool owners to select and demonstrate those elements of the tool that they consider to be most representative of the tool's functionality in building or evidencing competency in Cybersecurity. As with the tool owner questionnaire, this focus shift was purposeful, but reduced the completeness of review in order to place less time burden on reviewers and tool owners.

Adaptability: Lastly, whatever the process is at a given point in time, there needs to be room for change and adaptation. Every tool we have evaluated so far has had some unique features that helped us to improve and generalize the process. Oftentimes, this has even led to achieving a better balance of competing factors.

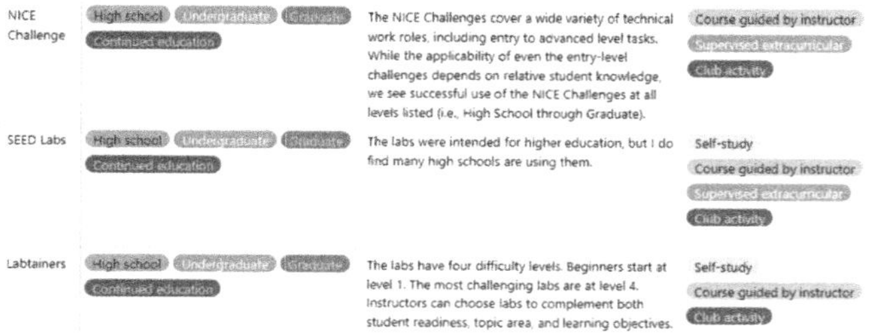

Fig. 1. Example Comparison of Tools using Airtable.

In addressing the challenges and adjusting the process even as we were prototyping, it was possible to improve the balance between the various competing constraints. However, we once again stress that the viability of the process as it stands today is contingent on the core assumption of honesty, integrity, and best effort of all parties involved.

3.2 Transferring Process to Other Contexts

The context in which this process was developed consists of three core factors: (1) The NCAE-C definition of competency (see Sect. 2) as well as (2) the NCAE-CD Knowledge Units as taxonomy, and (3) the NICE Framework as workforce framework (see above). Thus, in order to transfer the process described in this paper to other contexts, it will be necessary to first establish and define those three core elements of the respective contexts. Given the modular design of our overall process in general, and the tool owner questionnaire in particular, it then is sufficient to change or adapt the questions in Part III of the tool owner questionnaire (see Appendix). What and how much needs to be changed depends on how much this new context differs from the context for which we developed the process described above.

4 Current Efforts and Next Steps

We now describe directions and efforts (some already ongoing) that build on the core process and infrastructure described above. These are focused on further improving the balances and compromises discussed before in order to better achieve our overarching goal for the review process and provide for additional benefits to the various stakeholders. Furthermore, these efforts are designed to ensure that the information remains timely and can be adapted or augmented to keep pace with the fast-changing nature of the Cybersecurity field.

Use of Review Results: First and foremost is the continuing effort to make the results of the already-completed reviews available to the community. This requires selecting an information hosting platform as well as clarify requirements for an access control system (if needed) to prevent unauthorized access to the data. Our initial work uses Airtable [12] as the underlying platform for the data repository as it supports structured data storage and representation, grouping and comparing of tools, qualitative labels (with filtering), and displays results in a visually attractive fashion (see Fig. 1). A still-open challenge is to decide whether access restrictions needed, and, if so, how can they be implemented (i.e., in the context of the CAE community [2]), and who should be allowed to access this data.

Added Value: We envision, and have begun to pursue, a number of avenues to increase the value of this process, not only for the faculty making tool adoption decisions but also for the tool owners.

- We are working to link the reviews to curricular materials that provide specific examples of how the tools can be used in various instructional settings (e.g., integration with CLARK, currently one of the largest centralized collections of Cybersecurity education and evaluation materials [13]). This will allow better discoverability of tools by faculty members who are already browsing related material.
- We are planning to provide a means for connecting the tool reviews to specific competency statements (e.g., as submitted to a library such as the Competency Constructor [14]). This provides the tool owners with at least some initial connection towards a mapping to workforce frameworks, as the ABCDE framework for the competency statements includes a direct reference to such frameworks [20]. Additionally, this provides faculty a crucial starting point to competency-based assessment.
- As a next step, we envision that faculty members become contributors to the data set, further enriching it. As faculty use the tools, they may provide additional insights into the tools' "quirks", post helpful hints, describe interesting/unusual use cases, configuration/deployment examples, and contribute example KUs where the tools allows the building and/or evidencing of competencies. Similarly, such functionality may be leveraged by tool owners to submit updated information as their tools evolve. As an immediate next step, we plan to explore how such a functionality can be integrated and what—if any—kind of vetting process would be needed.

Beyond Free Tools: The process described above was developed for free tools based on the assumption of honesty, integrity, and best effort by all parties involved in the process. We have already begun to extend our efforts to "freemium" tools, i.e., tools that offer some functionality for free while an extended functionality set is available for purchase. In focusing on the free functionality, our experience so far suggests that the process developed for free tools can continue to operate under the same assumptions, without major changes.

5 Conclusion

In this paper we have described a tool evaluation process tailored to the specific needs of building or evidencing competency in Cybersecurity in the multi-stakeholder community of NCAE-C designated institutions. While the initial process focuses on free tools, ongoing efforts are geared to evaluate the freely available functionality of freemium tools. A major piece of future work is to explore whether, and if so how, a suitable process can be established for commercial tools.

Acknowledgements. The authors would like to thank Gianna Fazio and Justine Ho for their tremendous support of the project. The authors would also like to thank the anonymous reviewers for their thoughtful suggestions that allowed us to further improve the paper.

This work was supported by the 2020–2022 Evidencing Competency grant and the 2022 Careers Preparation National Center grant, awarded by the National Centers of Academic Excellence for Cybersecurity (managed by the National Security Agency). Any opinions, findings, and conclusions or recommendations expressed in this material are those of the author(s) and do not necessarily reflect the views of the funding entity.

A Tool Owner Questionnaire

Directions: This questionnaire is designed to gather information about your tool and its potential to build (teach) or evidence (require demonstration of) cybersecurity competency in students. Please provide as much detail as possible when answering the questions, as this will help reviewers to determine whether or not the tool will be effective at building and/or evidencing cybersecurity competencies. Failure to provide adequate, well thought-out explanations may result in a request for more information, or a failure to acknowledge the tool.

In the context of this questionnaire, we will use the following definitions - as established by the working group and/or the NICE framework: *Competency:* the ability for students to complete a task or tasks in the context of a work role. *Task:* An activity that is directed toward the achievement of organizational objectives. *Knowledge:* A retrievable set of concepts within memory. *Skill:* The capacity to perform an observable action.

Part I - Tool Description: The purpose of this section is to obtain general information about the tool.

1. Please provide the URL to the tool's official website.
2. What year was the tool first released? (YYYY)
3. Is the tool currently supported/being maintained? Yes/No
4. What year was the tool last revised/updated? (YYYY)
5. Please describe the kinds of revisions/updates the tool has undergone or regularly undergoes.
6. What kind of costs are associated with using the tool? Select all that apply. None/One-time purchase cost/Renewal costs/Maintenance costs/Upgrades/Other
7. Please describe the costs, and/or provide a link to the website that details the costs.

8. What action(s) must be taken to support the operation of the tool? Select all that apply. None/Regular updates (e.g., version updates, patches)/Reconfiguration/Account management/Initial configuration/Other
9. It is understood that the selections above can vary in scope, so please provide detailed explanations of the actions that are necessary to support the operation of the tool.

Part II - Use Cases and Requirements: The purpose of this section is to identify the best use cases for the tool, and what is needed of a student and/or institution in order to use it.

10. What level of students is this tool intended for? Select all that apply. K-8th grade students/High school students/Undergraduate students/Graduate students/Continuing education (e.g., certifications, career change)/Other
11. Please explain why the tool is suitable for the level(s) of students selected above.
12. In what context(s) can this tool be best used? Select all that apply. Self-study outside of a course (e.g., prep for certification)/Course offering under instructor/TA guidance (e.g., hands-on exercise, homework, project)/Supervised extracurricular activity (e.g., competition)/Club activity/Other
13. Please explain your answer(s) in terms of the most appropriate use case(s) of the tool, including descriptions of the courses and/or extracurricular activities this tool is most suited for, if applicable.
14. What prerequisite knowledge, if any, must a student have in order to ensure successful setup and use of this tool?
15. What system requirements are sufficient to use this tool effectively? None/Internet connectivity/Cloud computing capabilities/Basic laptop configuration (i.e., Intel core i3 or equivalent, 4GB memory, 80GB Hard Drive)/Moderate laptop configuration (i.e., Intel core i5 or equivalent, 8GB memory, 150GB Hard Drive)/Advanced laptop configuration (i.e., Intel core i7 or equivalent, 16GB memory, 250GB Hard Drive)/Other
16. Please provide further details, noting any specifications/ minimum requirements for components such as the OS, CPU, RAM, GPU, etc., where applicable.
17. Is the tool best suited for individual or group work amongst students? Individual/Group/Both
18. If used amongst a group, is there a way to differentiate an individual's contribution and/or performance from the group's? Yes / No / N/a
19. If Yes, how would you differentiate a student's contribution?
20. What kind of instructor intervention is needed for a student to use the tool? None (appropriate for self-study)/Minimal (e.g., initial setup is required by an instructor/supervisor, no further moderation required)/Moderate (e.g., initial setup is required by an instructor/supervisor, and minimal intervention by the instructor/assistant

required during use)/Extensive (e.g., instructor/supervisor intervention/monitoring is required for the duration of the tool's use)

21. Please explain your answer in terms of the degree of instructor involvement needed.
22. What kind of prerequisite knowledge must an instructor have to ensure successful setup and use of the tool? Why?
23. Does the tool integrate into an LMS such as Canvas, Blackboard, etc.? Yes/No
24. If so, which LMS?
25. Does the tool and/or its components lend themselves to variation (i.e., in content, difficulty, etc.), or are they fixed? Permits variation/Fixed
26. Please explain your answer, including who can modify/tailor the tool, what can be modified, and what is involved in doing so.
27. What kinds of metrics does the tool employ to assess the student(s)? Select all that apply. Time limit/Time tracking/Degrees of completion (i.e., allowance of partial completion)/Degrees of correctness (i.e., measure partial credit)/Other
28. Please provide further details as to what the tool uses to assess the students.

Part III - Relation to Competency and CAE-CD Knowledge Units: Providing detailed explanations as to how your tool builds and/or evidences competency towards specific cybersecurity areas (used here: the CAE-CD Knowledge Units) will help the reviewers to assess its potential to build and/or evidence cybersecurity competency for the CAE community.

29. The Evidencing Competency Working Group defines competency for the purpose of the National Centers of Academic Excellence in Cyber Defense Education as" The ability for a student to complete a task or tasks in the context of a work role." Please indicate whether your tool is most suitable for building (teaching) or evidencing (requiring demonstration of) competency in this context. Build/Evidence/Both/Neither
30. Please explain your tool's approach to building and/or evidencing competency. Should your tool have several approaches or types of content for building and/or evidencing competency, please provide separate responses for each.
31. Please identify the KUs towards which your tool best builds and/or evidences competency. Please note that the working group may request further information to support your claims as part of the review process (e.g., as a discussion and/or demonstration of the modules in the tool that support these areas).
    (a) Foundational KUs (all listed as per [16])
    (b) Technical Core KUs (all listed as per [16])
    (c) Non-technical Core KUs (all listed as per [16])
    (d) Optional KUs (all listed as per [16])
32. In question 30 you described your tool's approach(es) to building and/or evidencing competency. Pick no more than 3 KUs selected in questions

31(a–d) and explain how this (these) approach(es) is (are) implemented on an exemplary basis. In each case, provide or point to the content or sections of content within your tool where the respective KU is being built and/or evidenced.

References

1. ABET Accreditation. https://www.abet.org/accreditation/. Accessed 14 Feb 2025
2. CAE in Cybersecurity Community. https://www.caeommunity.org. Accessed 14 Feb 2025
3. CHEESEHub. https://www.hub.cheesehub.org/. Accessed 14 Feb 2025
4. NICE Framework and CAE Knowledge Units (KUs). https://www.ncyte.net/academia/faculty/faculty-resources/nice-framework-and-cae-knowledge-units-kus. Accessed 14 Feb 2025
5. DoD Cyber Workforce Framework (DCWF). https://dodcio.defense.gov/Cyber-Workforce/DCWF/. Accessed 14 Feb 2025
6. Labtainers. https://nps.edu/web/c3o/labtainers. Accessed 14 Feb 2025
7. National Centers of Academic Excellence in Cyber. https://public.cyber.mil/ncae-c/. Accessed 14 Feb 2025
8. NICE Challenge Project. https://nice-challenge.com/. Accessed 14 Feb 2025
9. NICE Framework Comopetencies: Preparing a Job-Ready Cybersecurity Workforce. https://csrc.nist.gov/News/2023/nice-framework-competencies-nist-ir-8355. Accessed 14 Feb 2025
10. NICE Workforce Framework for Cybersecurity (NICE Framework). https://niccs.cisa.gov/workforce-development/nice-framework. Accessed 14 Feb 2025
11. SEED Labs. https://seedsecuritylabs.org/. Accessed 14 Feb 2025
12. Airtable. https://www.airtable.com/. Accessed 14 Feb 2025
13. CLARK. https://clark.center/about. Accessed 14 Feb 2025
14. Competency Constructor. https://cybercompetencies.com/login. Accessed 14 Feb 2025
15. Ensuring Excellence: A Comprehensive Software Evaluation Checklist. https://www.avenga.com/magazine/comprehensive-software-evaluation-checklist/. Accessed 14 Feb 2025
16. Redesignation Competency Requirements, November 2023. https://caecommunity.org/sites/default/files/national_centers/Redesignation%20Competency%20slides_NOV%202023.pdf. Accessed 14 Feb 2025
17. Comparative Evaluation Process Before Purchasing, November 2023. https://cashflowinventory.com/blog/comparative-evaluation-process-before-purchasing/. Accessed 14 Feb 2025
18. National Centers of Academic Excellence in Cybersecurity NCAE-C 2024 Designation Requirements and Application Process For CAE-Cyber Defense (CAE-CD) (2024). https://dl.dod.cyber.mil/wp-content/uploads/cae/pdf/unclass-cae-cd_designation_requirements.pdf. Accessed 14 Feb 2025
19. ISE Development Survey 2024 (2024). https://ise.org.uk/page/ise-development-survey-24. Accessed 14 Feb 2025
20. Competency in Cybersecurity Education—A Handbook for Educators at NCAE-C Designation Institutions (Version 2, Updated March 2024), March 2024. https://www.caecommunity.org/sites/default/files/national_centers/CPNC_CYBER_EDU_Competency_Handbook_Mar%202024.pdf. Accessed 14 Feb 2025

21. Borgeaud, A.: Preparedness of Recent University Graduates in Cybersecurity for Work Challenges in 2024, December 2024. https://www.statista.com/statistics/1322394/cybersecurity-university-graduates-ready-worldwide/. Accessed 14 Feb 2025
22. Brown, E.: New Survey Reveals Traditional Undergraduate Education is Not Preparing Students for the Workforce (2025). https://www.hult.edu/blog/wi_skills_survey/. Accessed 14 Feb 2025
23. Hou, C.-Y., Mayernik, M.S., Worley, S.. Building Community Informed and Driven Data Services at the National Center for Atmospheric Research. In: Practice & Experience in Advanced Research Computing, PEARC '17, New York, NY, USA. Association for Computing Machinery (2017)
24. Kumar, A.N., et al.: Computer Science Curricula 2023. Association for Computing Machinery, New York, NY, USA (2024)
25. Perna, M.C.: New Data Reveals Just How Deep The College Crisis Goes, December 2025. https://www.forbes.com/sites/markcperna/2025/01/28/new-data-reveals-the-depth-of-college-crisis/. Accessed 14 Feb 2025

Curriculum and Research Development

A Transdisciplinary Approach to Embedding Cybersecurity Across the Curriculum of an Undergraduate Computing Degree Program in South Africa

Michael de Jager[1(✉)], Reolyn Heymann[2], and Japie Greeff[2,3,4]

[1] Unit for Data Science and Computing (UDSC) Research Unit, North-West University, Vanderbijlpark, South Africa
michael.dejager@nwu.ac.za
[2] Optentia Research Unit, North-West University, Vanderbijlpark, South Africa
reolyn.heymann@nwu.ac.za, greeff.j@belgiumcampus.ac.za
[3] Belgium Campus ITversity, Pretoria, South Africa
[4] National Institute for Theoretical and Computational Sciences (NITheCS), Stellenbosch, South Africa

Abstract. Industry 5.0, with its focus on human-centered, ethical, and sustainable technology, highlights an increased need for strong cybersecurity to protect interconnected systems. As digital infrastructures evolve to prioritize collaboration between humans and machines, ensuring cybersecurity becomes essential to safeguard both users and the technologies they interact with. As these systems become more integrated, the complexity of cyber threats grows, highlighting the need for cybersecurity education that prepares graduates to tackle these challenges. However, undergraduate computing programs in South Africa often don't provide enough focus on security topics, leaving many graduates unprepared for industry needs. This paper employs an Educational Design Research methodology to propose a conceptual transdisciplinary decision-making model for integrating cybersecurity education throughout a three-year BSc computing degree program at South Africa's North-West University (NWU). While this research focuses on NWU's undergraduate computing curriculum, the model is adaptable and can guide other institutions seeking to embed cybersecurity more broadly. Using the guidance of frameworks like the ACM Computing Curricula 2020 (CC2020), Cybersecurity Curricular Guidelines 2017 (CSEC2017), and Computer Science Curricula 2023 (CS2023), the model introduces key cybersecurity topics, such as cryptography, network security, and secure software development, across various modules from mathematics to programming. This approach ensures students build cybersecurity skills over time which aligns with Industry 5.0's focus on ethical, human-centered technology. Practical activities like security labs, hackathons, and interdisciplinary projects give students hands-on experience, promoting critical thinking and teamwork across different fields. By making cybersecurity a core part of NWU's computing curriculum, the decision-making

L. Drevin et al. (Eds.): WISE 2025, IFIP AICT 742, pp. 49–63, 2026.
https://doi.org/10.1007/978-3-031-94924-1_4

model aims to help address the cybersecurity skills gap in South Africa and produce graduates ready to contribute to a secure digital future.

Keywords: Cybersecurity Education · Cybersecurity Awareness · Transdisciplinary Curriculum · Industry 5.0 · BSc Computing Program

1 Introduction

The Fifth Industrial Revolution (5IR), or Industry 5.0, prioritizes human-centered, ethical, and sustainable technology, emphasizing collaboration between humans and machines rather than just automation [1]. As digital systems become more interconnected, cyber threats grow in complexity, making robust cybersecurity education essential. The increasing reliance on digital infrastructures for healthcare, finance, and communication has heightened the need for comprehensive cybersecurity training [2]. Addressing these challenges requires not just technical solutions but also a holistic approach to cybersecurity education. However, many undergraduate computing programs in South Africa lack sufficient cybersecurity emphasis, leaving graduates unprepared for high-stakes risks.

This shortage of cybersecurity training exacerbates the skills gap, with research indicating that limited investment and institutional support further hinder South Africa's ability to produce qualified cybersecurity professionals [3]. To bridge this gap, cybersecurity education must extend beyond computing disciplines, ensuring graduates have the expertise to secure critical infrastructure and sensitive data.

Updating curriculum structures to include cybersecurity is time-consuming and costly, often requiring years for design, approval, and accreditation [4]. This paper explores how cybersecurity can be effectively integrated without disrupting existing curricula.

To address this, a transdisciplinary decision-making model is proposed for embedding cybersecurity topics throughout a computing program. Using North-West University's (NWU) three-year computing degree as a case study, the model integrates cybersecurity seamlessly across modules. Unlike a multidisciplinary approach that keeps subjects separate, this model embeds cybersecurity within diverse courses, creating a cohesive learning experience. Core computing modules cover technical skills, while service modules introduce cybersecurity awareness in non-computing fields like business and accounting. This ensures students gain practical, adaptable cybersecurity knowledge applicable to real-world challenges.

Guided by ACM Computing Curricula 2020 (CC2020) [5], Cybersecurity Curricular Guidelines 2017 (CSEC2017) [6], and Computer Science Curricula 2023 (CS2023) [7], the model ensures alignment with global standards, enhancing graduates' employability and industry readiness. The Educational Design Research (EDR) methodology supports an iterative integration process, allowing for continuous refinement based on pilot implementations. This model aligns with Industry 5.0's focus on ethical, human-centered technology, ensuring graduates develop the critical skills needed to secure complex digital environments responsibly.

This paper is structured as follows: It begins by reviewing challenges in cybersecurity education, including limited undergraduate security exposure and the need for a transdisciplinary approach. It then examines the CC2020, CSEC2017, and CS2023 frameworks for integrating cybersecurity across computing programs. Followed by the discussion on the application of the EDR methodology, emphasizing iterative design and stakeholder feedback. The proposed model for NWU's curriculum is presented next, showing how to possibly embed cybersecurity in various modules. The paper concludes by discussing expected outcomes, such as improved graduate readiness and alignment with Industry 5.0, along with implications for South African cybersecurity education and future research.

2 Background

2.1 Current Challenges in Undergraduate Curricula

Globally, studies have also emphasized the importance of cybersecurity education and awareness in response to Industry 4.0 and 5.0 shifts [8], but local data suggests South African institutions have yet to fully respond [3]. An analysis of the top eight South African undergraduate computing programs, ranked by Times Higher Education (THE), found that only two universities offer dedicated cybersecurity courses [9,10]. North-West University provides a second-year module, *Information Security*, covering security principles, risk management, and basic cybersecurity techniques [11]. The University of Pretoria offers a third-year *Computer Security* module, where 50% of the content focuses on ethics, with outcomes emphasizing secure system design and ethical IT debates [12].

This limited integration of cybersecurity topics leaves graduates underprepared for industry demands, where security awareness and practical skills are essential. Without adequate training, they may struggle to identify vulnerabilities or apply effective security measures in an increasingly interconnected world [13,14]. The global demand for cybersecurity professionals is high, and South Africa faces similar shortages as its digital economy expands [3]. With cyber threats targeting key sectors like finance, healthcare, and energy, graduates need stronger cybersecurity skills to mitigate risks.

Addressing this shortfall requires integrating cybersecurity more effectively into curricula, ensuring progressive training throughout students' studies [4,15]. Without such changes, graduates may face career limitations, and industries could remain vulnerable due to a lack of skilled cybersecurity talent. Embedding security content within existing modules can help bridge this gap and better prepare graduates for industry expectations [16].

2.2 Importance of a Transdisciplinary Approach

Addressing the skills gap in cybersecurity education demands a transdisciplinary approach that integrates cybersecurity across a range of courses within undergraduate computer science programs. Unlike multidisciplinary methods, which address cybersecurity as a separate domain alongside other disciplines, a transdisciplinary approach fully integrates security concepts into various fields, creating a cohesive learning experience that fosters a deeper understanding of cybersecurity's role across multiple contexts. While the primary focus of this study is on embedding cybersecurity within the undergraduate computer science curriculum, this approach also offers potential for broader application. It can inform future adaptations in non-computing service modules such as those offered to business and social science students where foundational cybersecurity awareness is increasingly important for understanding digital risks and data privacy [17,18].

The transdisciplinary method aligns with Industry 5.0's focus on ethical, human-centered technology use, emphasizing the importance of developing technology with a broader social perspective. By embedding cybersecurity within courses such as mathematics, programming, and business, a transdisciplinary curriculum prepares students to think critically about security not just as a technical problem but as an ethical and societal issue. Embedding cybersecurity education across disciplines not only builds practical skills but also promotes a culture of digital responsibility among students, preparing them to navigate security issues across different fields.

2.3 ACM CC2020, CS2023 & CSEC2017 Guiding Frameworks

The ACM Computing Curricula 2020 (CC2020) [4], Cybersecurity Curricular Guidelines 2017 (CSEC2017) [5], and the Computer Science Curricula 2023 (CS2023) [6] provide essential frameworks for developing modern computing programs that address the evolving demands of the cybersecurity landscape. These guidelines are established by leading experts and reflect industry expectations, ensuring that computing curricula stay current with technological advancements and prepare graduates effectively. For example, CC2020 and CSEC2017 recommend teaching cybersecurity concepts as core subjects instead of optional ones, making security a fundamental part of computing. CS2023 offers updated guidance specifically for computer science programs, emphasizing computational thinking, security by design, and ethical considerations within computing.

CS2023 enhances CC2020 and CSEC2017 by updating computing standards to account for recent advances in areas such as AI, data science, and cybersecurity. It emphasizes the importance of embedding cybersecurity concepts from the earliest stages of students' computing education, recommending that these topics be introduced at foundational levels and revisited with increasing complexity. Aligning curricula with these frameworks ensures consistency across institutions and enhances employability, as industry increasingly prioritizes cybersecurity skills in candidates. For South African institutions aiming to develop cybersecurity-ready graduates, aligning curricula with these frameworks offers a pathway to ensure that students are prepared to meet both local and global industry standards.

2.4 Key Cybersecurity Knowledge Areas

The CC2020, CSEC2017, and CS2023 frameworks outline essential cybersecurity knowledge areas that form the foundation of a computing curriculum, including cryptography, network security, secure software development, and cybersecurity ethics. These areas each contribute uniquely to students' understanding of cybersecurity. For example, cryptography is critical for protecting sensitive data, especially in fields like finance and healthcare, where data security is crucial [19]. Network security addresses the practices and technologies used to protect digital networks from unauthorized access [20]. Secure software development ensures that security measures are embedded throughout the software lifecycle, reducing vulnerabilities that could lead to breaches [21]. Cybersecurity ethics encourages students to consider societal implications, fostering responsible practices and decision-making [22]. In addition to technical skills such as secure coding, cryptography, and network security, cybersecurity professionals must also develop soft skills such as communication, teamwork, and ethical decision-making. These skills are vital for effectively navigating interdisciplinary collaboration, understanding user needs, and addressing the human aspects of security challenges. By emphasizing these core areas, the frameworks promote a well-rounded skill set, preparing students for diverse cybersecurity challenges. CS2023 further highlights emerging fields, such as AI security and privacy-aware computing, to keep the curriculum aligned with the latest advancements and future roles.

2.5 Linking Frameworks to Curriculum Integration

Embedding core cybersecurity knowledge across multiple modules allows students to develop both theoretical understanding and practical skills progressively. For example, cryptography could be introduced in mathematics courses to establish foundational concepts, then applied practically in secure coding within software engineering. A transdisciplinary approach further encourages students to connect security concepts with other areas, such as secure data handling and privacy in data science, which reinforces the ethical aspects of cybersecurity. This layered approach enables students to move from foundational awareness to practical application, culminating in advanced topics and independent projects by their final year. Therefore, the model proposed in this paper could not only assist in addressing the cybersecurity skills gap but also ensure students understand the relevance of security within various professional and societal contexts. Aligning with the CC2020, CSEC2017, and CS2023 frameworks enables South African institutions to design a curriculum that meets international standards while preparing graduates for unique local and global challenges. However, while CC2020, CS2023, and CSEC2017 are primarily intended for computing and cybersecurity curricula, the guiding principles of these frameworks, such as scaffolded learning, ethical awareness, and secure thinking, can be adapted to non-computing modules in a contextual and appropriate manner. For example, in mathematics modules, foundational cryptographic concepts can be introduced to illustrate real-world relevance of number theory, while in business or statistics modules, awareness-level content on digital risk and data privacy aligns with CSEC2017's emphasis on ethical and societal considerations of cybersecurity. The frameworks help shape what level of depth and which content themes are appropriate, rather than prescribing full technical coverage in all modules. The following section outlines the proposed decision-making model for implementing a transdisciplinary cybersecurity approach within a BSc computer program degree, with a structured approach that progressively equips students with both theoretical and practical cybersecurity competencies.

3 Educational Design Research Methodology

Educational Design Research (EDR) is a methodological approach that facilitates the systematic design, implementation, and refinement of educational interventions. Van den Akker, Plomp, and Nieveen [23] defines EDR as developing programs, teaching strategies, and curricula to solve educational problems while advancing knowledge about their design. EDR follows an iterative process conducted in multiple cycles across distinct phases. Adopting the *development study approach*, this study aims aiming to design an integrated cybersecurity curriculum model rather than validate an existing theory. The flow of this specific study is described in Fig. 1 and the conceptual model is proposed in the following section.

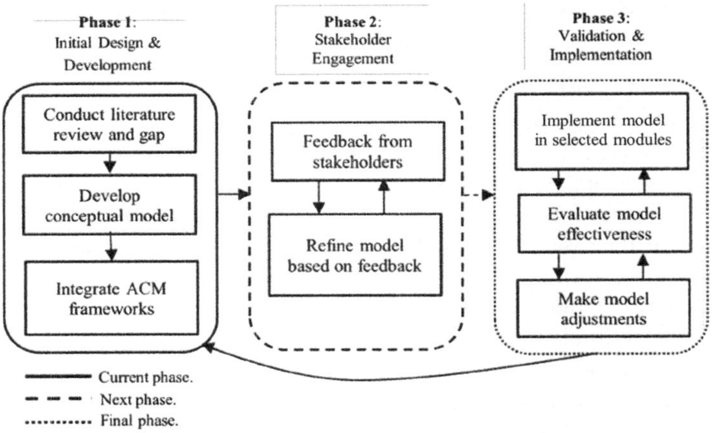

Fig. 1. EDR process for the cybersecurity curriculum integration.

The study follows a three-phase process: *Phase 1: Initial Design & Development*, which involves conducting a literature review, identifying gaps in cybersecurity education, and developing a conceptual decision-making model informed by ACM frameworks; *Phase 2: Stakeholder Engagement*, where feedback from stakeholders will be gathered and used to refine the model; and *Phase 3: Validation & Implementation*, which will involve piloting the model in selected modules, evaluating its effectiveness, and making final adjustments to ensure its readiness for full-scale implementation.

This paper presents only the first phase of the research cycle, focusing on completing the literature review and the development of the conceptual model for embedding cybersecurity into undergraduate computing curricula. The decision-making model proposed in this study is informed by established frameworks such as ACM CC2020, CSEC2017, and CS2023, ensuring alignment with international standards. While this iteration does not include stakeholder engagement or empirical validation, these steps are planned for future studies, where the model will be tested in pilot implementations and refined based on real-world feedback.

4 Integrating Cybersecurity Into a BSc Computing Degree Program: A Conceptual Decision-Making Model

4.1 Introduction to Credit Allocation and Integration

In alignment with the ACM CC2020, CS2023, and CSEC2017 frameworks, it is recommended that a 10–15% allocation of program credits be dedicated to cybersecurity over a three-year undergraduate program. The model aims to structure and distribute cybersecurity credits across core and service modules within a BSc computing degree program to ensure consistent, practical, and integration of security concepts.

4.2 Total Security Credits Calculation

NWU's BSc computing degree program consists of 392 total credits. To maximize security education, a 15% credit allocation was selected. Given the program's total credits of 392, this 15% credit allocation results in approximately 59 credits dedicated to cybersecurity. In order to ensure a balanced and progressive learning experience, these 59 credits should be strategically distributed across core and service modules within the three-year program. By adhering to this 15% guideline, the program ensures that students receive a comprehensive cybersecurity education in line with international standards. This distribution aligns with the ACM's emphasis on integrating essential security concepts across undergraduate curricula, preparing students with the foundational and advanced skills needed to address the evolving cybersecurity landscape. In core modules, students engage with technical cybersecurity concepts including core information security domains such as secure coding, cryptography, and network security. Service modules, in contrast, focus on building cybersecurity awareness, providing foundational understanding relevant to non-computing disciplines. For example, students in fields like mathematics or statistics may not need to implement technical cybersecurity skills directly but will benefit from awareness of data privacy, digital risk, and safe practices, which are increasingly relevant across fields. This distribution equips students with the skills and knowledge necessary to address modern security challenges within both specialized and interdisciplinary contexts.

4.3 Distribution of Cybersecurity Credits Across Program Levels

The distribution of cybersecurity credits aims to balance foundational learning with increasing depth as students progress. In the first year, allocating around 30% of credits introduces essential security awareness and basic competencies without overloading new students adjusting to the university setting. The second and third years receive around 35% each, supporting a gradual intensification of technical skills and applied knowledge. This consistent allocation across the final two years encourages a balanced progression, allowing students to build on foundational concepts and refine advanced skills, ultimately culminating in a robust understanding of cybersecurity principles and practices.

Practically, 59 credits are allocated for cybersecurity, and are distributed across the three program years as follows: 18 credits for the first year, 20 for the second and 21 for the third.

Note: NWU's BSc computing program already includes a dedicated Information Security module in the second year, covering foundational topics such as cloud security, basic cryptography, and access control. As this module has dedicated credits allocated to cybersecurity it was not restructured in the integration model. Instead, the proposed model complements this existing offering by distributing additional security concepts across other modules to create a more holistic and transdisciplinary learning experience

4.4 Decision-Making Model for Cybersecurity Integration

The decision-making model offers a systematic framework for integrating cybersecurity education within undergraduate computing programs. This generalized model consists of five steps designed to ensure that cybersecurity content aligns with educational standards, addresses diverse learning needs, and remains feasible across varied academic backgrounds.

The five steps of the decision-making model are outlined in Fig. 1 and are as follows:

1) **Determine Modules:** Identify core and service modules suitable for embedding cybersecurity content. This includes selecting modules that can benefit from cybersecurity topics without overwhelming the existing curriculum.
2) **Allocate Credits:** Distribute cybersecurity credits across the selected modules, ensuring a balanced credit load while providing meaningful cybersecurity exposure within the program.
3) **Align with Bloom's Taxonomy:** Map cybersecurity learning objectives to Bloom's Taxonomy to ensure that knowledge, skills, and competencies are appropriately developed at each stage of learning.

4) **Adjust Module Content:** Refine and adjust module content to integrate cybersecurity topics effectively, maintaining alignment with existing module objectives and outcomes.
5) **Embed Practical Application:** Include hands-on activities or cross-disciplinary projects to enhance student engagement and provide real-world cybersecurity experience

This generalized framework serves as a foundation that can be adapted to various institutions and program structures. At NWU, the existing BSc computing degree program is organized into core and service modules, each serving a distinct purpose within the curriculum.

The decision-making model is applied to NWU as follows:

Step 1: Determining Core and Service Modules The existing BSc program is organized into core and service modules, each serving a distinct purpose within the curriculum. The proposed approach for embedding cybersecurity concepts across these module types is as follows:

- **Core Modules**: Cybersecurity credits are integrated into essential computing modules, focusing on practical, hands-on skills such as secure coding, encryption, and network security.
- **Service Modules**: Cybersecurity credit integration should emphasize awareness, helping students understand the importance of security in their respective fields without requiring technical skills. Topics may include data privacy in statistics or digital risk in business management, with pathways to entry-level certifications for those interested in further learning.

Step 2: Aligning with Notional Hours and Credit Load To balance cybersecurity learning with existing program requirements, credits are allocated according to notional hours. Each credit represents **10 notional hours**, leading to a total of **590 h** over the three-years:

- **1st Year**: Basic awareness (180 h) integrated into introductory modules.
- **2nd Year**: Intermediate practical skills (200 h) in core modules.
- **3rd Year**: Advanced applications (210 h) with hands-on learning.

Step 3: Bloom's Taxonomy Alignment Aligning content with Bloom's Taxonomy ensures a structured development of skills:

1. **1st Year (Understanding & Awareness)**: Focus on basic concepts like data privacy, secure communication, and threat awareness integrated into core modules. Service modules introduce security concepts without requiring technical applications.
2. **2nd Year (Application & Analysis)**: Expansion on practical skills development within core modules, such as data encryption and secure software practices, to enhance analytical and technical abilities. Service modules continue to reinforce cybersecurity awareness, focusing on analysing basic security principles relevant to non-technical fields.

3. **3rd Year (Analysis, Evaluation & Creation)**: Advanced topics (e.g., system security, ethical hacking) with hands-on labs and projects in core modules.

Step 4: Adjusting Existing Modules Integrating cybersecurity into existing modules requires careful adjustments to enhance learning without overloading students. A structured decision-making process ensures seamless integration while maintaining program objectives:

- **Module Content Audit:** Assess each module's content to identify overlaps and areas where cybersecurity concepts can replace less critical topics, ensuring relevance without redundancy.
- **Prioritizing Cybersecurity Relevance**: Align cybersecurity topics with module objectives; core modules focus on technical skills like secure coding, while service modules emphasize cybersecurity awareness.
- **Bloom's Taxonomy Alignment**: Structure content progression using Bloom's Taxonomy, starting with foundational knowledge in the first year and advancing to critical thinking and application in later years.
- **Industry Relevance and Employability**: Replace less industry-relevant content with cybersecurity topics that reflect current demands, such as adding secure network practices to networking modules.
- **Transdisciplinary Relevance for Service Modules**: Integrate cybersecurity awareness within discipline-specific contexts, such as digital risk in business or data privacy in healthcare, making it accessible for non-computing students.
- **Aligning Credit Load and Notional Hours**: Ensure content adjustments fit within designated credit hours, preventing increased student workload while maintaining academic balance.
- **Feedback and Iteration**: Pilot the changes, gather feedback from instructors and students, and refine content iteratively to optimize learning outcomes.

  This decision-making model ensures that the integration of cybersecurity content is both purposeful and balanced, providing students with relevant skills and knowledge across their entire program without detracting from the program's foundational learning objectives.

Step 5: Practical and Transdisciplinary Application To fully embrace a transdisciplinary approach, practical applications should be embedded throughout the program, fostering collaboration and hands-on learning that extends beyond computing-specific fields. This approach exposes students from various disciplines to cybersecurity concepts, encouraging cross-disciplinary understanding and engagement with security challenges. Key components could include:

1. **Hackathons and Workshops**: Organize interdisciplinary cybersecurity workshops and hackathons involving students and faculty from various fields

(e.g., business, engineering, social sciences). These events simulate real-world security challenges, fostering cross-disciplinary teamwork and problem-solving. Collaboration with industry partners enhances practical exposure through internships and real-world experiences. Through these "horizontal pathways," participants experience cybersecurity's relevance across fields, fostering cross-disciplinary teamwork, innovation, and secure problem-solving.
2. **Project-Based Learning (PBL) with Real-World Scenarios**: Integrate real-world cybersecurity projects within core and service modules. Business students may develop data protection strategies, while psychology students explore secure handling of sensitive information. This approach reinforces cybersecurity awareness and practical application in diverse fields.
3. **Pathways to Certification and Further Study**: Encourage students, particularly those in service modules, to pursue entry-level cybersecurity certifications like ECH or ISC2 CC. This provides a structured path for further specialization, enhancing career prospects and digital risk management skills.
4. **Transdisciplinary Research and Capstone Projects**: Offer senior students transdisciplinary capstone projects integrating cybersecurity with other fields, such as ethical AI, data privacy in public health, or financial risk analysis. These projects mirror the interdisciplinary nature of cybersecurity in the real world.

4.5 Example of Decision-Making Applied

To demonstrate the decision-making model in action, this section provides examples of how the decision-making model integrates cybersecurity into specific modules within NWU's BSc computer program degree. Following each model step ensures that cybersecurity content enhances both technical and awareness-oriented learning objectives, balancing cybersecurity with existing curricula.

Core Module Example: CMPG111 (Introduction to Computing and Programming Python)

- **Step 1: Module Content Audit**
  - *Current Module Focus*: CMPG111 is a foundational 12-credit module focusing on programming skills using Python and introductory computing concepts.
  - *Identified Areas for Cybersecurity Integration*: Basic secure coding and data privacy.
- **Step 2: Credit Allocation** *Allocation*: Dedicate 4 of the 12 credits to cybersecurity topics. This allows students to engage with secure coding practices and data privacy early in their studies.
- **Step 3: Bloom's Taxonomy Alignment** *Objective Level*: At the 'Understanding' level, students will learn secure input handling, basic encryption, and introductory data protection techniques, aligning with Bloom's 'Awareness' and 'Application' stages.

- **Step 4: Adjusting Module Content** *Notional Hours Distribution*: Allocate 40 out of 120 h for cybersecurity topics, integrating lab exercises on secure coding and discussions on data privacy while maintaining sufficient time for programming fundamentals.

This approach introduces cybersecurity concepts in a way that complements the module's primary focus on programming, laying a foundation for secure coding as students advance.

Service Module Example: STTN111 (Descriptive Statistics)

- **Step 1: Module Content Audit**
  - *Current Module Focus*: STTN111, a 12-credit service module, introduces students to statistical methods and data analysis. Most students are from non-computing disciplines.
  - *Identified Areas for Cybersecurity Integration*: Basic cybersecurity awareness in statistical contexts, particularly data privacy and anomaly detection.
- **Step 2: Credit Allocation** *Allocation*: Allocate 2 out of 12 credits to cybersecurity awareness, covering data privacy and the use of statistical methods for detecting anomalies.
- **Step 3: Bloom's Taxonomy Alignment** *Objective Level*: Target 'Understanding' and 'Awareness' levels, enabling students to appreciate how cybersecurity principles relate to data privacy in statistical analysis without requiring technical expertise.
- **Step 4: Adjusting Module Content** *Notional Hours Distribution*: Approximately 20 of the 120 h are dedicated to cybersecurity topics. Activities could include case studies on data privacy and discussions on ethical data handling, allowing students to see the role of cybersecurity in their field.

In this example, cybersecurity awareness is embedded in a non-technical module, helping students recognize the importance of security in data handling and statistical analysis.

5 Expected Impact and Outcomes

NWU's integrated approach to embedding cybersecurity into its BSc computing degree program is anticipated to produce graduates with a good, well-rounded cybersecurity skill set, aligning them with the demands of Industry 5.0, which emphasizes human-centered, ethical technology use and resilience. By strategically allocating 59 credits to cybersecurity concepts across core and service modules, students gain essential technical skills, including secure coding, cryptography, and network security, along with cybersecurity awareness in non-technical fields without having to make changes to the structure of the curriculum. This balanced approach equips graduates to handle cybersecurity issues from multiple perspectives, fostering both practical expertise and an understanding of digital risks across disciplines.

A further establishment of a cybersecurity honours program could further position NWU as a pioneer in transdisciplinary cybersecurity education within South Africa. This program would distinguish the university as a forward-thinking leader in cybersecurity, appealing to students and professionals alike who are seeking specialized, industry-relevant skills. Moreover, by introducing cybersecurity awareness into service modules, NWU cultivates a culture of digital security across various fields of study, such as business and healthcare, promoting cybersecurity literacy and best practices among future professionals in non-technical sectors.

This approach could play a critical role in addressing the cybersecurity skills gap in South Africa. Graduates with a broad-based understanding of cybersecurity will contribute to enhancing the country's digital resilience, better equipping organizations to manage evolving security threats. Furthermore, the decision-making model developed at NWU could offer a scalable framework that other institutions can adopt. This model provides a structured, adaptable approach to introducing cybersecurity education in a way that aligns with diverse academic disciplines, thereby supporting the broader goal of creating a secure digital environment through widespread educational initiatives.

6 Conclusion

This study presents a decision-making model for integrating cybersecurity concepts into NWU's BSc computing program, allocating 59 credits to security-focused content across core and service modules. While this study targets the integration of cybersecurity into a computing degree at NWU, the proposed model is designed to be scalable and adaptable for other undergraduate programs and institutions, especially those seeking to align curricula with Industry 5.0 and national digital resilience goals. By embedding both technical and awareness-based cybersecurity topics, students gain essential skills like secure coding and network security, while non-computing fields benefit from broader cybersecurity awareness. This balanced approach ensures graduates are industry-ready while fostering a culture of digital security advocacy across sectors.

Following the Educational Design Research (EDR) methodology, this paper represents the first cycle, focusing on a literature review and conceptual model development. The model provides a scalable framework for integrating security content into curricula without disrupting core learning outcomes, addressing the growing demand for cybersecurity skills in South Africa.

Future research of this work could include a comparative review of international curriculum integration strategies to benchmark global practice and strengthen the proposed model. Further research will refine and validate the model through real-world testing and stakeholder feedback. A subsequent study will detail how specific modules will integrate cybersecurity topics while addressing emerging concerns like data ethics, AI safety, and quantum security, ensuring continued alignment with industry and academic needs. Additionally, investigating staff skill set and upskill for a transdisciplinary approach.

References

1. Adel, A.: Future of Industry 5.0 in society: human-centric solutions, challenges, and prospective research areas. J. Cloud Comput. **11**(1) (2022). https://doi.org/10.1186/s13677-022-00314-5
2. Goni, A., Jahangir, U., Chowdhury, R.: A study on cybersecurity: analyzing current threats, navigating complexities, and implementing prevention strategies. Int. J. Res. Sci. Innov. **X**(XII), 507–522 (2024). https://doi.org/10.51244/ijrsi.2023.1012039
3. de Jager, M., Futcher, L., Thomson, K.L.: An investigation into the cybersecurity skills gap in South Africa. In: IFIP Advances in Information and Communication Technology, pp. 237–248. Springer. (2023). https://doi.org/10.1007/978-3-031-38530-8_19
4. Cooper, T.: Curriculum renewal: barriers to successful curriculum change and suggestions for improvement. J. Educ. Train. Stud. **5**(11), 115–128 (2017)
5. ACM: Computing Curricula 2020 (2020). https://doi.org/10.1145/3467967
6. ACM: Cybersecurity Curricula 2017 (2018). https://doi.org/10.1145/3184594
7. ACM: Computer science curricula 2023 (CS2023). In: Proceedings of the 54th ACM Technical Symposium on Computer Science Education, vol. 2 (2023). https://doi.org/10.1145/3545947.3569591
8. Ahamed, B., Polas, M., Kabir, A., Shohel-Uz-Zaman, A.: Empowering students for cybersecurity awareness management in the emerging digital era: the role of cybersecurity attitude in the 4.0 Industrial Revolution Era. Sage Open **14**(1) (2024). https://doi.org/10.1177/21582440241228920
9. Times Higher Education: World University Rankings 2024 (2024). https://www.timeshighereducation.com/world-university-rankings/2024/world-ranking
10. Times Higher Education. World University Rankings 2025 (2025). https://www.timeshighereducation.com/world-university-rankings/latest/world-ranking
11. North-West University: 2024 Yearbook: Faculty of Natural and Agricultural Sciences Undergraduate (2024). https://studies.nwu.ac.za/sites/studies.nwu.ac.za/files/files/yearbooks/2024/FNAS-UG-2024-v1.pdf
12. University of Pretoria: University of Pretoria Yearbook 2023. B.Sc. (Computer Science) (12134001) (2023). https://www.up.ac.za/yearbooks/2023/pdf/programme/12134001 (2023)
13. Hong, W.C., et al.: The influence of social education level on cybersecurity awareness and behavior: a comparative study of university students and working graduates. Educ. Inf. Technol. **28**(1), 439–470 (2022). https://doi.org/10.1007/s10639-022-11121-5
14. Van Slyke, C., et al.: Employer preferences for cybersecurity skills among information systems graduates. In: Proceedings of the 2019 Computers and People Research Conference, pp. 131–134 (2019). https://doi.org/10.1145/3322385.3322418
15. Zivanovic, M., Lendak, I., Popovic, R.: Dynamic cybersecurity curriculum optimization method (DYCSCOM). In: Proceedings of the 18th International Conference on Availability, Reliability and Security, pp. 1–9. (2023). https://doi.org/10.1145/3600160.3605008
16. OCED: Building a skilled cyber security workforce in five countries: insights from Australia, Canada, New Zealand, United Kingdom, and United States. OECD Publishing (2023). https://doi.org/10.1787/5fd44e6c-en

17. Ferdousi, B.: The importance of defining cybersecurity from a transdisciplinary approach. J. Syst. Cybern. Inf. **22**(1), 150–164 (2024). https://doi.org/10.54808/jsci.22.01.150
18. Schaeffer, D.M., Olson, P.C., Eck, C.K.: An interdisciplinary approach to cybersecurity curriculum. J. High. Educ. Theor. Pract. **17**(9) (2017). https://doi.org/10.33423/jhetp.v17i9.1419
19. Patel, P.: The crucial role of cryptography in cybersecurity. eInfochips (n.d.). https://www.einfochips.com/blog/the-crucial-role-of-cryptography-in-cybersecurity
20. Kizza, J.M.: Computer network security protocols. In: A Guide to Computer Network Security, pp. 365–395 (n.d.). https://doi.org/10.1007/978-1-84800-917-2_17
21. Odera, D., Otieno, M., Ekume Ounza, J.: Security risks in the software development lifecycle: a review. World J. Adv. Eng. Technol. Sci. **8**(2), 230–253 (2023). https://doi.org/10.30574/wjaets.2023.8.2.0101
22. Sadeghi, B., et al.: Experiential learning or direct training: fostering ethical cybersecurity decision-making via serious games. In: LNCS, pp. 262–272 (2024). https://doi.org/10.1007/978-3-031-58226-4_20
23. van den Akker, J.J.H., Plomp, T., Nieveen, N.M.: Educational Design Research. SLO (2013)

Using Attack Trees for Security Education and Training: Simplifying Threat Analysis

Damas Gruska[1(✉)], Aliyu Tanko Ali[2], and Martin Leucker[2]

[1] Department of Applied Informatics, Comenius University in Bratislava, Mlynská dolina, 842 48 Bratislava, Slovakia
gruska@fmph.uniba.sk

[2] Institute for Software Engineering and Programming Languages, University of Lübeck, Ratzeburger Allee 160, Lübeck, Germany
{aliyu.ali,leucker}@isp.uni-luebeck.de

Abstract. Modern cybersecurity education must prepare learners to understand how security threats can be realized and to diagnose and respond to attacks, under real-world constraints—such as incomplete or ambiguous information. This paper introduces two educational approaches. First, we adapt *attack trees*, a threat-modeling technique, into an intuitive framework for teaching security reasoning to non-experts, including children. By breaking down attacks into visual, step-by-step scenarios, learners systematically identify risks and countermeasures, fostering critical thinking and collaboration. Second, we propose a method to quantify the *diagnosability* of attacks, measuring how much information is needed to identify an attacker's actions (which are unseen). This approach helps educators design realistic training exercises where learners prioritize evidence and act decisively under uncertainty. Finally, we discuss how this framework could be translated into a security tool accessible to a wide range of users.

Keywords: Attack Trees · Diagnosability · Security · Human and Societal Aspects of Security · Cybersecurity Education

1 Introduction

The increasing complexity of modern systems has made them vulnerable to sophisticated cyberattacks, posing significant challenges not only to technical defenses but also to security education. Defenders tasked with protecting critical infrastructure must not only respond to attacks but also learn how to reason

Work by Damas Gruska founded by the EU NextGenerationEU through the Recovery and Resilience Plan for Slovakia under the project No. 09I03-03-V04-00095. Others by the KiMeKo project/Federal Ministry of Education and Research of Germany grant number 01IS24056A.

Published by Springer Nature Switzerland AG 2026
L. Drevin et al. (Eds.): WISE 2025, IFIP AICT 742, pp. 64–79, 2026.
https://doi.org/10.1007/978-3-031-94924-1_5

systematically under uncertainty—a skill rarely emphasized in traditional cybersecurity curricula. In educational contexts, learners often struggle to grasp the diagnosis of attacks due to incomplete information, mirroring real-world scenarios where defenders face ambiguity in identifying an attacker's actions or location. This gap highlights a critical need for pedagogical tools that simplify threat analysis and teach learners to quantify uncertainty, prioritize evidence, and make informed decisions—a cornerstone of fostering a cybersecurity mindset in both professionals and citizens.

Attack trees (AT) have emerged as a powerful graphical technique for modeling and analyzing the various ways an asset can be compromised. Introduced by [21], AT decompose complex attack scenarios into smaller, manageable components, enabling a systematic exploration of potential attack paths. This hierarchical representation not only facilitates the identification of vulnerabilities within a system but also provides a structured framework for analyzing the interactions between attackers and defenders. Extensions of AT, such as Attack-Defense Trees (ADTrees) [16] and Attack Countermeasure Trees (ACT) [19], have further enriched this framework by incorporating defensive actions and countermeasures.

Quantitative approaches to security, such as information entropy [22] and AT [21], have gained traction in research for modeling threats and measuring uncertainty [3]. However, their potential as educational tools remains underexplored. For instance, AT, originally designed for technical risk analysis, can be repurposed to teach security reasoning by decomposing threats into intuitive, hierarchical components. This aligns with emerging trends in serious games and gamification [15], where visual and structured representations help learners—including non-experts like children—grasp complex attack paths and countermeasures. Similarly, entropy-based metrics, which are widely used in vulnerability assessments under uncertainty [23], have the potential to empower learners by allowing them to quantify the effort needed to diagnose attacks. This approach can bridge the gap between theoretical concepts and practical cyber defense training.

Recent work has advanced quantitative analysis of AT using techniques such as Markov decision processes [18], fuzzy logic [13], priced timed automata [17], and efficient algorithms [9]. Additionally, methodologies for evaluating attributes on attack trees with incomplete information [2,3,10] and combining qualitative/quantitative analysis of weighted AT [8] have been proposed. While these approaches provide valuable tools for analyzing attack scenarios, they primarily focus on risk assessment, prevention, or mitigation. In contrast, our work addresses the problem of *diagnosability*—quantifying the information needed to diagnose an attack. We provide a framework for assessing the diagnosability of attack scenarios that can be used to teach security reasoning.

Recent work on AT has focused on making them more powerful by adding quantitative elements, like time and cost [1,5] or even more parameters for attack-defense trees [14]. These enhancements help analysts better understand how long an attack might take or how much effort it would require. In addition, researchers have used techniques such as Markov decision processes and fuzzy logic to improve risk assessment and mitigation strategies [13,18]. However, these advanced methods are often aimed at technical experts and do not always consider how they could be used in education. While traditional AT can be easily understood (even by non-experts), using them to model dynamic threat environment [2] or analyzing partial information about an attack is difficult [3,10]. Meanwhile, existing security education programs often prioritize prevention over diagnosis, leaving learners unprepared to address ongoing threats [11]. This misalignment highlights the necessity for an easy-to-grasp security analysis model tailored for non-experts, which can later be expanded with more advanced concepts like attack diagnosability. Unlike the work of [7], in this paper we do not focus primarily on the consistency of the attack tree with the analyzed system. In this paper we present:

- *Attack Trees as a Pedagogical Tool:* We demonstrate how AT can simplify threat modeling for non-expert audiences, including children and professionals outside cybersecurity. By breaking down real-world attacks into logical components, learners gain a structured framework to analyze risks, and evaluate attack paths.
- *Security Quantification:* We introduce the concept of security quantification to measure the amount of actionable information available to defenders during an ongoing attack. By quantifying this information, learners would have a clearer understanding of the attack's nature, scope, and potential impact.

The long-term goal of this work is to bridge the gap between technical cybersecurity research and security education. We aim to provide tools that cultivate a cybersecurity mindset for non-experts and offer advanced quantification techniques for experts. These tools would enable users to reason about security threats and diagnose ongoing attacks. In this paper, the focus is to introduce the basic formal model for our implementation (based on an AT variant). This model includes methods for quantifying the attacks, which can ultimately lead to improved diagnosis of an attack.

2 Using Attack Trees for Security Education: Simplifying Threat Analysis

In this section, we will very briefly present the motivation for the considered formal model on the example from the field of physical security, but its use is universal and can also be used for cybersecurity. Depending on the complexity of the system and its formalization, it can later be used for educational purposes for pupils and students of various age categories, but mainly for regular testing of security staff. Limited space does not allow us to go into detail, but we believe that it will allow the reader to better understand the model introduced in the following section.

An attack tree is a diagram that maps out how an attacker might compromise a target (e.g., a building). The root of the tree represents the attacker's ultimate goal (e.g., "Gain entry to the building"), while branches show possible methods to achieve it, such as:

- **Physical methods:** Picking a lock, breaking a window.
- **Social engineering:** Tricking a guard into granting access.
- **Technical exploits:** Hacking an electronic keypad.

Each method can be further broken down into sub-tasks (e.g., "Pick a lock" requires tools, skill, and time). This hierarchical structure mirrors how learners naturally solve problems by breaking them down into smaller steps. Consider, as an example, an attack description of how the security of a secured building could be breached. The exercise proceeds in three stages:

- **Define the Goal:**
  - *Root node:* "Steal valuables from the building."
- **Decompose the Attack:**
  - *Branches:*
    - *Method 1:* Enter through the front door (requires picking a lock).
    - *Method 2:* Climb through a window (needs a ladder and avoiding guards).
    - *Method 3:* Pretend to be a maintenance worker (social engineering).
- **Evaluate Countermeasures:**
  - For each attack path, learners are tasked with proposing defenses. For instance:
    - Front door: Install a reinforced lock.
    - Window: Add window burglar bars.
    - Social engineering: Train staff to verify identities.

These steps demonstrate how AT describes how to compromise a secure building and proposes protections [4] or defenses [16] against the attack. In AT terminology, the **Goal** defined would be referred to as the *root node* or *attack target*, the **Branches** are referred to as *sub-goals*. A branch that cannot be **decomposed** is referred to as a *leaf node*. The fashion in which the attacker is required to execute the attack depends on the gate refinements (OR, AND, SAND) on the (non-leaf) nodes (see Fig. 1, ignore the numbers for now). The OR gate indicates disjunction of actions, the AND gate conjunction, and the SAND gate sequential execution of actions.

While this approach can be used to introduce a security thinking mindset to children and non-experts, intermediate and professional learners might want to analyze more complex real-world scenarios where constraints such as resources (e.g., cost, time) could be applied. In the next section, we describe this in a basic formal way. The ultimate goal is to develop a graphical tool that can be used to educate and train students or employees. Our tool will allow us to describe security threads using AT and can also be used to explain and train situations that may occur in practice.

3 Basic Formal Model

In the previous section, we showed how AT can be used to guide learners (children/non-experts) in reasoning about security. Now, to model and analyze more complex scenarios (for professionals), we use the AT variant with time and cost [1,5] as a basis.

3.1 Attack Trees with Time and Cost

We would like to refer the reader back to Fig. 1. We associate the nodes with a set of attributes, namely time and cost. The time represents an interval during which the node is vulnerable to compromise, while the cost represents the resources required by the attacker to compromise the node. For example, we previously defined the attack goal as *Steal valuables from the building*. The time interval could be when no one is at home, for instance, between 1 and 7, and it could take an attacker 2 units of time to carry out the attack. For every branch, there is also a time interval during which an attacker must compromise it. The cost, on the other hand, represents the amount of resources the attacker expends, i.e., in Fig. 1 see node n_r $[1,7],2,5$. The formal definition of attack trees with time and cost is as follows.

Definition 1 (Attack Tree with Time and Cost). *An attack tree with time and cost is a tuple* $T_{rct} = (\mathbb{N}, \mathbb{E}, g, c)$, *where* $(\mathbb{N}, \mathbb{E})$ *is a tree with root* n_r *and leaves* $\mathbb{N}_l$. *The function* $g : \mathbb{N} \setminus \mathbb{N}_l \rightarrow \{OR, AND, SAND(s)\} \times I \times \mathbb{R}^+$ *and* $g : \mathbb{N}_l \rightarrow I \times \mathbb{R}^+$ *maps each non-leaf node to a gate type, and to each node a time interval* $I = [q, q']$ *(with* $q, q' \in \mathbb{Q}^+, q \leq q'$*), and a non-negative real value from* $\mathbb{R}^+$ *representing the time to compromise the node. The function* $c : \mathbb{N} \rightarrow \mathbb{R}^+$ *assigns a non-negative real cost to compromise each node.* s *in* $SAND(s)$ *represents a sequence specifying the order of child nodes for SAND gates.*

Generally, an attack on the tree starts from the leaf nodes, which represents atomic actions that initiate an attack. As such, an attack $\mathbb{A}$ on T_{rct} is defined as a subset of leaf nodes, each associated with the time at which it is compromised. We define an attack as follows:

Definition 2 (Attack). *Given* T_{rct}, *an attack is a subset* $\mathbb{A} \subset \mathbb{N}_l \times \mathbb{R}^+$. $\mathbb{N}_l$ *is the set of leaf nodes and* $\mathbb{R}^+$ *represents the set of positive real numbers, indicating when a leaf node is attempting to be compromised, and each leaf nodes appears in* $\mathbb{A}$ *at most once. By* $\mathbb{A}_{\mathbb{N}}$ *we denote the set of attacked leaf nodes by* $\mathbb{A}$.

Let $\mathbb{A} = \{(n_1, t_1), \ldots, (n_k, t_k)\}$, which denotes an attempt to compromise the leaf node n_i at time t_i. Note that $\mathbb{A}_{\mathbb{N}} = \{n_1, \ldots, n_k\}$. A leaf node n_i is compromised only if $t_i \in I$, where $g(n_i) = (I, c)$, where c is a cost. The attack $\mathbb{A}$ propagates further according to the following rules. For the **OR gate**, the parent node is compromised as soon as the first child is compromised within its valid time interval, plus the additional time r representing its duration. For the **AND gate**, the parent node is compromised after all children are compromised, with its compromise time determined by the latest child's completion time plus r. In the case of a **SAND gate**, the parent node is compromised sequentially following the order of the sequence s, with its compromise time determined by the last child in the sequence plus r (see Fig. 2). The total cost to compromise a node n, denoted as $C(n)$, is derived from the mapping c and the costs of compromising its child nodes (see Fig. 3). These rules are formalized below.

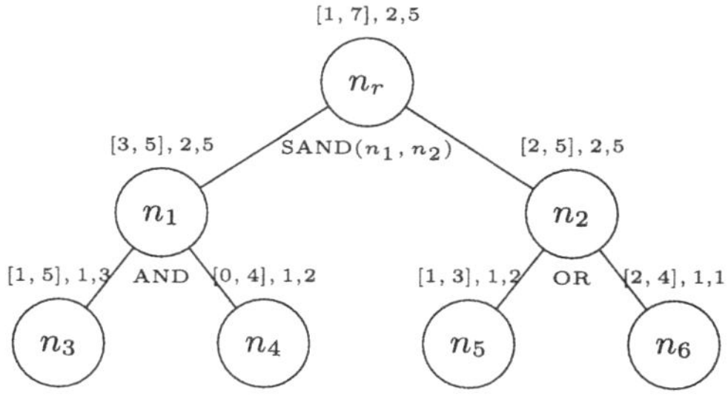

Fig. 1. Attack trees with time and costs.

Definition 3 (Attack Propagation). *Let $T_{rct} = (\mathbb{N}, \mathbb{E}, g, c)$ be an attack tree with time and cost. Let $\mathbb{A} = \{(n_1, t_1), \ldots, (n_k, t_k)\}$ be the attack. The leaf node $n_i, 1 \leq i \leq k$, $g(n_i) = (I, c)$, is compromised if the attack time is valid i.e. $t_i \in I$ and it is compromised at time $t_i + r$ with the cost $C(n_i) = c(n_i)$ Let n be a non-leaf node with children $n_1, \ldots, n_k$.*

- *let $g(n) = (OR, [q_1, q_2], r)$ then n is compromised if at least one of its children is compromised in time from $[q_1, q_2]$, and it is compromised at the time given by $t_{\mathbb{A}}(n_i) + r$ where n_i is the child of n compromised as the first at time $t_{\mathbb{A}}(n_i), t_{\mathbb{A}}(n_i) \in [q_1, q_2]$. The cost to compromises n is given as $C(n) = c(n) + \sum c(n_i)$ for all compromised children n_i.*
- *let $g(n) = (AND, [q_1, q_2], r)$ then n is compromised if all of its children are compromised at a time within $[q_1, q_2]$, and it is compromised at the time given by $t_{\mathbb{A}}(n_i) + r$ where n_i is the child of n compromised as the last one. The cost to compromises n is given as $C(n) = c(n) + \sum c(n_i)$ for all children n_i.*
- *let $g(n) = (SAND(s), [q_1, q_2], r)$ and s is a sequence of children $n_1, \ldots, n_k$ of n then n is compromised if all of its children are compromised at a time within $[q_1, q_2]$ in an order given by s i.e. $t_{\mathbb{A}}(n_i) \leq t_{\mathbb{A}}(n_j)$ if n_i is before n_j in s, and it is compromised at the time given by $t(n_k) + r$. The cost to compromises n is given as $C(n) = c(n) + \sum c(n_i)$ for all children n_i.*

Note that the cost of compromising an OR node n is given by the expression $c(n)$ and the cost for each of its compromised children, regardless of when it happened. Not all attacks can be propagated further, hence we define meaningful ones.

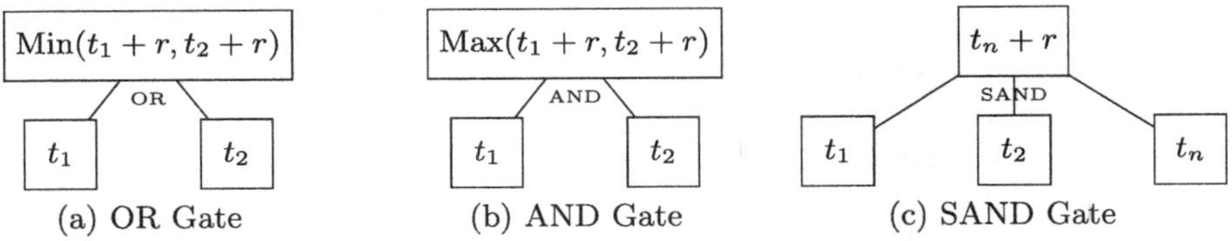

Fig. 2. Time propagation rule for AND, OR, and SAND Gates.

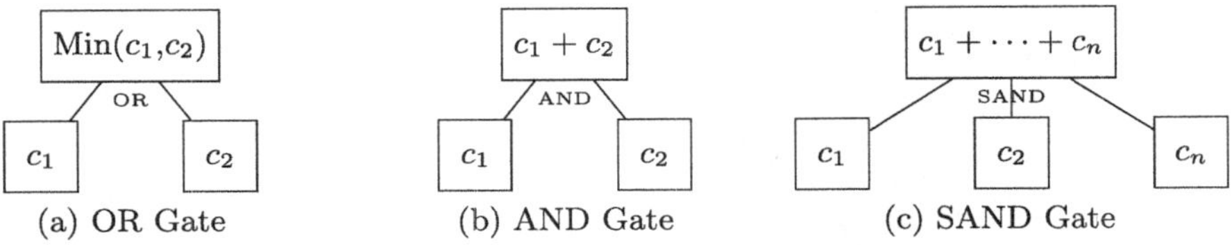

Fig. 3. Cost propagation rule for AND, OR, and SAND Gates.

Definition 4. *Let* $T_{rct} = (\mathbb{N}, \mathbb{E}, g, c)$ *be an attack tree with time and cost. An attack* $\mathbb{A} = \{(n_1, t_1), \ldots, (n_k, t_k)\}$ *is meaningful if it can compromise at least one node.*

Example 1. Let us refer back to Fig. 1. We will demonstrate an example for an attack targeting n_1 as the attack path. Notice that this node requires the compromise of n_3 and n_4. Now, since compromising n_3 requires an attack in time within the range of $[1, 5]$, but since it takes one time unit it can start only in the interval $[1, 4]$. Similarly, for n_4 it is also in time interval $[1, 4]$. Both nodes can be compromised in time interval $[2, 5]$. But since n_1 can start to be compromised within time interval $[3, 5]$ we see that actually an attacker who wants to compromise n_1 has to compromise both n_3 and n_4 within time interval $[2, 4]$. The cost to compromise n_1 is given as $3 + 2 + 5$.

From now on we will assume that an attack is always meaningful. Note that there are infinitely many attacks as well as infinitely many meaningful attacks due to real values of timings. Without loss of generality, we can assume that time intervals have borders natural numbers since they are rational we can multiply them by the least common multiple. Moreover, if the time needed to compromise is a natural number for each node, then we can use similar techniques of regions as it was used in the case of *Timed Automata* and their transformation to region automatons (see [6]). But we can compute compromised nodes by an attack as well as solve other problems more effectively.

4 Quantification

Let us assume that we have a system whose security risks are expressed by an attack tree with time and cost. Next, let's assume a defender, for example, a system administrator, security staff, night guard, etc., has partial information about the ongoing possible attack, i.e. knows that some leaf nodes (for example sensors) were compromised and also some non-leaf nodes are already compromised. From this partial information, the defender tries to determine which attack led to this situation.

For example, the defender knows that no windows are broken, but the intruder was captured on a security camera in the hallway. Depending on the time, the defender may conclude that the intruder was able to mechanically break the side door or knows the lock code. In the latter case, the defender can expect that the intruder will know other codes depending on the security organization and will have to adapt his further actions accordingly. However, the defender's decision-making becomes more complex as more options open up. In the first part of this section, we will quantify these options. We will show how they differ depending on what the defender can monitor (already compromised nodes, or time and cost). This allows us to identify security vulnerabilities in the entire system, since the defender is expected to react immediately, and too much uncertainty about an ongoing attack reduces his ability to react correctly. The planned software system will not only allow visualization of possible threats depending on the situation observed by the defender, which will be used during regular training of security workers. In addition, it will also allow identifying vulnerabilities in the entire security system. These can be eliminated, for example, by additional installation of sensors, cameras or other detection devices.

In this section, we formalize this concept, moreover we show how it relates to a security property called opacity, and explore how to change the system to make it more secure because the defender has a better chance of preventing successful attacks. In the following, we will assume that if the defenders do not see all nodes of the AT, it is either due to the absence of the relevant sensors or they are broken.

4.1 Quantified Diagnosability

Now let's assume that we have threats to the system described using attack trees with time and cost $T_{rct} = (\mathbb{N}, \mathbb{E}, g, c)$ and we have a defender who has partial information about the ongoing security threat. The defender can have partial information about the attack, that is, (s)he can observe some nodes and see whether they are compromised or not. Moreover, the defender might have information about the time and cost of an ongoing attack. From this information, (s)he wants to make an accurate picture (to diagnose it) of what is happening, namely which attacks have led to that. This should serve her(him) both for effective defense, but also for system changes to the system, which will fall to his monitoring (installation of additional sensors, cameras, etc.).

Example 2. Let us consider the attack tree with time and cost from Fig. 1 and suppose that a defender knows that node n_1 has been compromised. Then it is clear that an attack which leads to this result should contain both n_3 and n_4. If node n_2 has been compromised then an attack which leads to this result should contain both n_5 or n_6. But if it is known that cost of this is equal to 6, than it was n_6 which was attacked, if it is known that n_2 is compromised at time 4 then it has to be n_5 which was attacked.

Suppose that we have a set of observable nodes $\mathbb{N}_o \subseteq \mathbb{N}$. Now we will formalize quantification as a property which enables determine a set of attacks that leads to a given result, under an assumption that not all its compromised nodes are observable. First, we define attack states as a set of all compromised nodes by a given attack.

Definition 5 (Attack State). *Let $T_{rct} = (\mathbb{N}, \mathbb{E}, g, c)$ be an attack tree with time and cost. Given an attack $\mathbb{A} = \{(n_1, t_1), \ldots, (n_k, t_k)\}$ and time $t, t \in \mathbb{R}^+$, attack state s of this attack is the triple $s_{(\mathbb{A},t)} = (\mathbb{N}_{(\mathbb{A},t)}, t_{(\mathbb{A},t)}, c_{(\mathbb{A},t)})$ where $\mathbb{N}_{(\mathbb{A},t)} \subseteq \mathbb{N}$ is the set of nodes which are compromised by $\mathbb{A}$ due to attack propagation at time t. The time of the attack state (denoted as $t_{(\mathbb{A},t)}$) is defined as $\max\{t_{\mathbb{A}}(n) | n \in \mathbb{N}_{(\mathbb{A},t)}\}$ clearly $t_{(\mathbb{A},t)} \leq t$. The cost of the attack result $c_{\mathbb{A}}$ is given by $\sum_{n \in \mathbb{N}_u} c(n)$ where $\mathbb{N}_u$ are those nodes from $\mathbb{N}$ for which parent node does not belong to $\mathbb{N}$.*

Assume that we have partial information about the state of the attack. It could be that we don't see all attacked nodes, we don't have time or cost information. We now define the set of possible attacks that would lead to this attack state. Note that there might be many different attacks leading to it.

Definition 6 (Attack State Observations). *Let $T_{rct} = (\mathbb{N}, \mathbb{E}, g, c)$ be an attack tree with time and cost and let $\mathbb{N}_o \subseteq \mathbb{N}$. Any $n_n \subseteq \mathbb{N}_o$ will be called node observation, any $o_t = (O_n, t)$ will be called node and time observation and $O_c = (O_n, t, c)$ will be called node, time and cost observation.*

Definition 7 (Sets of Possible Attacks). *Let $T_{rct} = (\mathbb{N}, \mathbb{E}, g, c)$ be an attack tree with time and cost, and o_n, o_t, o_c will be node, time and cost observations, respectively.*

- *By D_n we will denote a set of attacks such that for resulting state of attack $s_{(\mathbb{A},t)} = (\mathbb{N}_{(\mathbb{A},t)}, t_{(\mathbb{A},t)}, c_{(\mathbb{A},t)})$ we have $o_n \subseteq \mathbb{N}_{(\mathbb{A},t)}$ at time $t \geq 0$*
- *By $D_{n,t}$ we will denote a set of attacks such that for resulting state of attack $s_{(\mathbb{A},t)} = (\mathbb{N}_{(\mathbb{A},t)}, t_{(\mathbb{A},t)}, c_{(\mathbb{A},t)})$ at time t we have $o_n \subseteq \mathbb{N}_{(\mathbb{A},t)}$ and $t_{(\mathbb{A},t)} \leq t$*
- *By $D_{n,t,c}$ we will denote a set of attacks such that for resulting state of attack $s_{(\mathbb{A},t)} = (\mathbb{N}_{(\mathbb{A},t)}, t_{(\mathbb{A},t)}, c_{(\mathbb{A},t)})$ at time t we have $o_n \subseteq \mathbb{N}_{(\mathbb{A},t)}$, $t_{(\mathbb{A},t)} \leq t$ and $c_{(\mathbb{A},t)}) = c$*

To calculate all possible attacks for a given observable state, we propose an Algorithm 1 based on the propagation rules defined for attack trees with time and cost (Sect. 3.1). The algorithm starts by identifying all leaf nodes in the attack tree that match the observed compromised nodes $\mathbb{N}_o \subseteq \mathbb{N}$, ensuring their compromise times fall within valid intervals as per the attack tree's constraints. For each non-leaf node, the algorithm propagates compromises upward using the gate types (OR, AND, SAND) to determine whether their children satisfy

Algorithm 1: CalculatePossibleAttacks($T_{rct}, \mathbb{N}_o, t, c$)

Input: $T_{rct} = (\mathbb{N}, \mathbb{E}, g, c)$, $\mathbb{N}_o \subseteq \mathbb{N}$, t, and c.
Output: A set of possible attacks $D_{n,t,c}$.
Function `CalculatePossibleAttacks`($T_{rct}, \mathbb{N}_o, t, c$):
  Initialize $D_{n,t,c} \leftarrow \emptyset$;
  for *each leaf node* $n_i \in \mathbb{N}_l$ **do**
    if $n_i \in \mathbb{N}_o$ *and* $g(n_i) = (I, x)$ **then**
      Compute the valid compromise time $t_i \in I : t_i + x \leq t$;
      Add (n_i, t_i) to the set of potential compromises P;
  while *there exists a non-leaf node* $n_j \in \mathbb{N} \setminus \mathbb{N}_l$ *not yet processed* **do**
    Let $C(n_j)$ be the children of n_j;
    switch $g(n_j)$ **do**
      case $(OR, [q_1, q_2], r)$ **do**
        Find the earliest child $n_k \in C(n_j)$ that satisfies $t_{\mathbb{A}}(n_k) + r \leq t$;
        If such a child exists, add n_j to the set of potential compromises P;
      case $(AND, [q_1, q_2], r)$ **do**
        Check if all children $n_k \in C(n_j)$ satisfy $t_{\mathbb{A}}(n_k) + r \leq t$;
        If true, add n_j to the set of potential compromises P;
      case $(SAND(s), [q_1, q_2], r)$ **do**
        Verify that all children $n_k \in C(n_j)$ are compromised sequentially according to s within $[q_1, q_2]$;
        If true, add n_j to the set of potential compromises P;
  Construct all possible attacks $\mathbb{A} = \{(n_1, t_1), \ldots, (n_k, t_k)\}$ using the set P;
  Filter $\mathbb{A}$ to include only those attacks where $t_{\mathbb{A}} \leq t$ and $c_{\mathbb{A}} = c$;
  Return $D_{n,t,c} \leftarrow \mathbb{A}$;

the conditions for compromise. This process continues until all possible combinations of compromised nodes are identified, resulting in sets D_n, $D_{n,t}$,$D_{n,t,c}$, which represent attacks inferred from node observations, node and time observations, and node, time, and cost observations, respectively. Given the exponential complexity of the algorithm, its application is very limited for very large systems, but it still allows for obtaining local information for selected subtrees.

Note that not all (possible attack) observations are meaningful in the sense that there is no attack that could lead to such an observation. We now formally define this term.

Definition 8 (Meaningful Observations). *Observations o_n, o_t, o_c are meaningful observations if corresponding sets $D_n, D_{n,t}, D_{n,t,c}$, respectively, are nonempty.*

Example 3. Let us return to example from Fig. 1. $D_n = \{n_1, n_3\}$ Suppose that $\mathbb{N}_o = \{n_1, n_2, n_3, n_4\}$. Then neither $D_n = \{n_1, n_3\}$ nor $D_{n,t} = \{n_2, 1\}$ are meaningful.

From now on we will well assume only meaningful observations.

Definition 9 (Quantification of Diagnosability of Observation). *Let* $T_{rct} = (\mathbb{N}, \mathbb{E}, g, c)$ *be an attack tree with time and cost, and* o_n, o_t, o_c *its observations. We define their quantifications as* $Q_{o_n} = \frac{1}{|D_n|}, Q_{o_t} = \frac{1}{|D_{n,t}|}, Q_{o_c} = \frac{1}{|D_{n,t,c}|}$.

Definition 10 (Quantification of Diagnosability). *Let* $T_{rct} = (\mathbb{N}, \mathbb{E}, g, c)$ *be an attack tree with time and cost, and* O_n, O_t, O_c *are sets of its corresponding meaningful observations.* $QD_n^{T_{rct}} = \min_{o_n \in O_n} Q_{o_n}, QD_t^{T_{rct}} = \min_{o_t \in O_t} Q_{o_t}$, $QD_c^{T_{rct}} = \min_{o_c \in O_c} Q_{o_c}$

Example 4. Let us consider the attack tree with time and cost from Fig. 1 and suppose that $\mathbb{N}_o = \{n_1, n_2\}$. If a defender sees that n_2 is compromised and n_1 is not compromised at time 5 then there are two possible corresponding attack states.

Lemma 1. *Let* $T_{rct} = (\mathbb{N}, \mathbb{E}, g, c)$ *be an attack tree with time and cost, and* O_n, O_t, O_c *are sets of its corresponding meaningful observations. Then it holds* $Q_{o_c} \leq Q_{o_t} \leq Q_{o_n}$.

Proof. Clearly, we have $D_c \subseteq D_t \subseteq D_n$ and hence the Lemma holds.

Corollary. Let $T_{rct} = (\mathbb{N}, \mathbb{E}, g, c)$ be an attack tree with time and cost. Then it holds $QD_c^{T_{rct}} \leq QD_t^{T_{rct}} \leq QD_n^{T_{rct}}$.

We say that an attack is not x-diagnosable if $QD_x^{T_{rct}} < 1$ where x $\in \{n, t, c\}$. We say just diagnosable if the corresponding parameter is clear from a contest or is not important. The quantification of diagnosabilities are rather general and allows us to model different situations depending on the set $\mathbb{N}_o$. If this set contains all but leaf nodes, a defender cannot see the starting of an attack if the attack tree is not diagnosable. If $\mathbb{N}_o$ contains only some top nodes then the defender can recognize only very last phase of the attack but if it is diagnosable, it can learn how and where the attack has started. If the defender can see only the root node the corresponding attack tree is fully diagnosable if it contains only AND and SAND nodes. If a defender can see all leaf nodes the system is trivially diagnosable. Now we will show a relationship between diagnosability and a security property initial-state opacity.

4.2 Opacity and Quantified Diagnosability

In this subsection, we examine when it is possible to diagnose an attacker's action when the attack is observed incompletely. We show the connection between diagnosability and a security property called initial-state opacity (see [20]). In general, this property expresses that from observing public events of the system's behavior we cannot determine from which state it started. To define an initial-state opacity we need some preliminaries.

Let Σ be an alphabet and denote by Σ^* the set of all finite- length strings of elements of Σ, including the empty string ϵ. A language $L \subseteq \Sigma^*$ is a subset of finite-length strings from strings in Σ^*. A discrete-event system (DES) of interest is modeled as a non-deterministic finite automata (NFA) $G = (X, \Sigma, \delta, X_0)$, where X is the finite set of states, Σ is the finite set of events, X_0 is the set of initial states, $\delta : X \times \Sigma \rightarrow 2^X$ is the transition function, which can be extended to $\delta : X \times \Sigma^* \rightarrow 2^X$ in the usual manner. We use $L(G, x)$ to denote the language generated by from state x , i.e. $L(G, x) = \{s \in \Sigma^*, \delta(x, s) \neq \emptyset\}$ and the language generated by G we denote as $L(G)$ is defined as $L(G) = \bigcup_{x_o \in X_o} L(G, x_0)$.

Suppose that Σ is divided into two disjoint subsets of observable Σ_o and unobservable events Σ_{uo} such that $\Sigma = \Sigma_o \cup \Sigma_{uo}$ and $\Sigma_o \cap \Sigma_{uo} = \emptyset$. Let as define projection $P : \Sigma^* \rightarrow \Sigma_o^*$ which removes unobservable events from a string, i.e. $P(s.x) = P(s)$ if $x \in \Sigma_{uo}$ and $P(s.x) = P(s).x$ if $x \in \Sigma_o$. Suppose that we have a subset S of initial states of a given DES which are considered to be secrete. Initial-state opacity requires that for any sequence of actions starting from a state belonging to S, there exists another sequence of actions starting from a state that does not belong to S, such that the two sequences cannot be distinguished by observation (expressed by the projection P).

Definition 11 *(Initial-State Opacity). Given a non-deterministic finite-state automaton $G = (X, \Sigma, \delta, X_0)$, a projection P with respect to the set of observable events Σ_o, and a set of secret initial states $S \subset X_0$, automaton G is initial-state opaque with respect to S and P if for all $x \in S$ and for all $s \in L(G, x)$ there exists $x' \in X_0 \setminus S$ and $s' \in L(G, x')$ such that $P(s) = P(s')$.*

As regards decidability, initial-state opacity is decidable for finite state automata and it is PSPACE-complete (see [20]). Now we will first show how to translate an attack tree to non-deterministic finite automaton and then we demonstrate a relation between initial-state opacity and diagnosability. We start with some simplifications and later we will show how to do this transformation for a more general settings. Let $T_{rct} = (\mathbb{N}, \mathbb{E}, g, c)$ be an attack tree with time and cost. Without loss of generality we can assume that all time constraints and durations are represented by natural numbers, costs are equal to zero and all leaf nodes are attacked at time given by a natural numbers. For T_{rct} we construct NFA which simulates its behavior.

Suppose that a time constraint associated with a node n is given by time interval $[q, q']$ and time needed to compromise this node is equal to k. This means that the node can be compromised in time t_n from the set $\{l_n, l_n + 1, l_n + 2, \ldots, h_n\}$ where $l_n = q + k, h_n = q' + k$ that is earliest time to compromise the node is given as $q + k$ and the latest as $q' + k$. We can encode this information as a pair (n, t_n) indicating that node n is compromised at time t_n.

Now we construct NFA which would correspond to given attack tree with time and cost $T_{rct} = (\mathbb{N}, \mathbb{E}, g, c)$. Let $\mathbb{N}^T = \{(n, t_n) | n \in \mathbb{N}, t_n \in \{l_n, l_n + 1, l_n + 2, \ldots, h_n\}\}$, and $\mathbb{N}_l^T = \{(n, t_n) | n \in \mathbb{N}_l, t_n \in \{l_n, l_n + 1, l_n + 2, \ldots, h_n\}\}$, then we have set of states of NFA as $X \subset 2^{\mathbb{N}^T}$ such that for every $x \in X$ every node appears in n appears at most once in x. With initial states corresponding to all possible sets of leaf nodes of T_{rct} as $X_0 \subset X$ such that for every $x \in X_O$ it contains only leaf nodes. As a set of events, we chose a pair of node and time when it is compromised. Hence $\Sigma = \{(n, t) | n \in \mathbb{N}, t \in \{l_n, l_n + 1, l_n + 2, \ldots, h_n\}\}$.

As regards a transition function, this simulates the propagation of an attack i.e. $\delta(x,(n,t)) = x'$ iff x is the set of already compromised nodes, n is a new node compromised by x at time t, and x' is a news set of compromised nodes which include x and node n.

Example 5. Let us consider the attack tree with time and cost from Fig. 1. For simplicity we explain this construction on a subtree consisting of nodes n_1, n_3, n_4. First we construct meaningful attack tree to this tree which has time constraints for n_3, n_4 changed from $[1,5]$ and $[0,4]$ to $[2,4]$ and $[2,4]$, respectively. Nodes n_3, n_4 can be compromised at time from interval $[3,5]$ hence corresponding initial states are $\{(n_3,3)\}, \{(n_3,4)\}, \{(n_3,5)\}, \{(n_4,3)\}, \{(n_4,4)\}, \{(n_4,5)\}$, $\{(n_3,3),(n_4,3)\}$, $\{(n_3,4),(n_4,3)\}, \{(n_3,3), (n_4,4)\}$, $\{(n_3,4),(n_4,4)\}$, $\{(n_3,3),(n_4,5)\}$, $\{(n_3,5),(n_4,3)\}$, $\{(n_3,4),(n_4,5)\}$, $\{(n_3,5), (n_4,4)\}, \{(n_3,5), (n_4,5)\}$. From these states only the following states are reachable by events $\{(n_1,t)\}$ which indicates that also node n_1 is compromised at time t: $\{(n_3,3),(n_4,3),(n_1,5)\}$, $\{(n_3,4),(n_4,3),(n_1,6)\}$, $\{(n_3,3),(n_4,4),(n_1,6)\}$, $\{(n_3,4),(n_4,4),(n_1,6)\}$, $\{(n_3,3),(n_4,5),(n_1,7)\}$, $\{(n_3,5),(n_4,3),(n_1,7)\}$, $\{(n_3,4),(n_4,5),(n_1,7)\}$, $\{(n_3,5),(n_4,4),(n_1,7)\}$, $\{(n_3,5),(n_4,5),(n_1,7)\}$.

Theorem 1. *Let $T_{rct} = (\mathbb{N}, \mathbb{E}, g, c)$ be an attack tree with time and cost and $G = (X, \Sigma, \delta, X_0)$ be a corresponding NFA as defined above. Then for every attack $\mathbb{A} = \{(n_1,t_1),\ldots,(n_k,t_k)\}$ there exist a corresponding initial state of G and moreover for every newly compromised non-leaf node there exist a transition of G which simulates this compromising.*

Proof. The proof is straightforward from the construction of NFA G for a given attack tree with time and cost. The resulting construction does not need necessarily lead to an effective attack tree but thanks to Lemma 1 we can transform it to the meaningful one.

Now we can formulate the relationship between quantified diagnosability and opacity for an observer who sees time passing.

Theorem 2. *Let $T_{rct} = (\mathbb{N}, \mathbb{E}, g, c)$ be an attack tree with time and cost and and let $G = (X, \Sigma, \delta, X_0)$ be its corresponding NFA as defined above. Then $QD_t^{T_{rct}} = 1$ with respect to $\mathbb{N}_o$ iff G is not initial-state opaque with respect to observable labels $\Sigma_o = \{(n,t)\} | n \in \mathbb{N}_o, t \in [l_n, h_n]\}$.*

Proof. The main idea. It is clear from the construction of NFA G for a given attack tree with time and cost that it simulates the propagations of attacks. Observable node n corresponds to observable action (n,t). Opacity guarantees that from the set of observable events we cannot deduce an initial state and hence we cannot deduce an attack, which means the attack tree is not diagnosable.

Note that due to Corollary of Lemma 1 we have $QD_t^{T_{rct}} = 1$ implies $QD_n^{T_{rct}} = 1$. For simplicity, we have assumed that the cost to compromise a node is always zero. But allowing arbitrary values causes no problem and can be handled similarly to the time needed to compromise nodes. But in this case, for example automata from Example 5, could become unreadable for a reader. In fact, other parameters than time and cost can be added. For example, the cost itself can be divided into several items such as energy, human labor, maintenance, etc. The presented method allows this, but we think that for the explanation of the principle it was enough to consider only one parameter.

In the preceding sections, we explored diagnosability, opacity, and the interplay between them within the context of attack trees. Diagnosability aids defenders in tracing the origins of an attack, while opacity preserves security by ensuring that an intruder cannot deduce the system's initial state merely by observing its behavior. This brings us to an intriguing paradox: while diagnosability provides comprehensive insight for defenders, it inherently compromises initial-state opacity.

4.3 Connecting Educational Tools with Quantitative Analysis

The pedagogical approach introduced in Sect. 2 provides an intuitive framework for teaching security reasoning to non-experts by breaking down complex threats into manageable components using attack trees. While this approach simplifies threat analysis for learners, the formal model presented in Sect. 3 extends its applicability to professional contexts by incorporating time and cost attributes. Section 4 builds upon this foundation by introducing quantified diagnosability, enabling defenders to reason about ongoing attacks under uncertainty. By combining these methods and accompanying with a software tool, educators can design training exercises that progressively introduce complexity, starting with basic attack decomposition and culminating in advanced scenarios requiring quantitative analysis. For instance, learners could begin by analyzing simple attack paths (as shown in Sect. 2) and then add complexity to it. This transition fosters critical thinking and prepares learners for real-world challenges where incomplete information is common.

In addition to its educational value, this framework lays the groundwork for developing practical tools that can assist both novice learners and experienced professionals. There are several tools to support work with Attack Trees (open source as ADTool, AT-AT, Deciduous, Ent, SeaMonster or commercial as AttackTree+ from Isograph, SecurITree from Amenaza Technologies, RiskTree from 2T Security, RiskyTrees from RiskyTrees). Moreover we have some experience with transforming presented attack trees to TAPAAL formalism [12]. But for education purposes we might need something slightly different. Imagine a software system where users—whether they're students or seasoned cybersecurity analysts—can input observed data about an ongoing attack, such as compromised nodes or timestamps, and receive insights into potential attack paths. Such a tool would not only visualize possible threats but also help users prioritize their responses by highlighting the most likely scenarios. For example, if a defender knows that a certain node has been compromised at a specific time, the tool could be used to calculate the set of possible attacks and their likelihoods (probabilities). This kind of functionality bridges the gap between theoretical knowledge and hands-on practice, making it easier for people at all levels to engage with cybersecurity concepts.

5 Conclusion and Future Work

In this paper, we introduced two complementary approaches for leveraging attack trees in cybersecurity education and professional analysis. First, we demonstrated how attack trees can be adapted into an intuitive framework for teaching security reasoning to non-experts, including children and professionals outside cybersecurity. By decomposing attacks into visual, step-by-step scenarios, learners gain hands-on experience in identifying risks and devising countermeasures. Second, we formalized the concept of quantified diagnosability, providing a method to measure the amount of actionable information available during an ongoing attack. Furthermore, we established connections between diagnosability and opacity, showing how these properties interact within the context of attack trees. Through the proposed algorithm, we provided a practical mechanism for calculating all possible attacks given a set of observable states. Our work bridges the divide between technical cybersecurity research and security education, offering tools that cater to diverse audiences—from beginners learning basic threat modeling to experts analyzing sophisticated attack scenarios.

In the future, we plan to consider cases where the attacker uses various distraction techniques and various diversionary actions, but we have not yet implemented this into our formalism. We have also focused mainly on passive monitoring of the attack and have not considered the possibility of active defense, which we will also leave for further work in the future. We realize that adding a non-trivial example of well-known cybersecurity incidents would better demonstrate the practical applicability of our approach, but due to space limitations, we used a simple example to demonstrate the basic features of the model. As for the quantification itself, a universal interpretation is not entirely possible, it depends on the specific modeled system, but we believe that our approach serves well as a starting point.

Future work includes also developing a graphical interface for the proposed model, allowing users to interactively explore attack trees and simulate various attack propagation rules. Additionally, extending the framework to incorporate probabilistic models could enhance its predictive capabilities, enabling defenders to anticipate attacker behavior more effectively.

References

1. Ali, A.T.: Simplified timed attack trees. In: International Conference on Research Challenges in Information Science, pp. 653–660. Springer (2021)
2. Ali, A.T., Gruska, D.: Dynamic attack trees methodology. In: 2022 Interdisciplinary Research in Technology and Management (IRTM), pp. 1–9. IEEE (2022)
3. Ali, A.T., Gruska, D.: States of attack under incomplete information. In: 2022 IEEE 12th Annual Computing and Communication Workshop and Conference (CCWC), pp. 0801–0807. IEEE (2022)
4. Ali, A.T., Gruska, D.P.: Attack protection tree. In: CS&P (2019)
5. Aliyu Tanko, A., Damas, G., Karam, K., Martin, L.: Analysis of attack time and costs in attack trees via SMT resolution. In: Proceedings of the 8th International Conference on Future Networks and Distributed Systems (2024)

6. Alur, R., Dill, D.L.: A theory of timed automata. Theoret. Comput. Sci. **126**(2), 183–235 (1994)
7. Audinot, M., Pinchinat, S., Kordy, B.: Is my attack tree correct? In: Foley, S.N., Gollmann, D., Snekkenes, E. (eds.) ESORICS 2017. LNCS, vol. 10492, pp. 83–102. Springer, Cham (2017). https://doi.org/10.1007/978-3-319-66402-6_7
8. Bobbio, A., Egidi, L., Terruggia, R.: A methodology for qualitative/quantitative analysis of weighted attack trees. IFAC Proc. Vol. **46**(22), 133–138 (2013)
9. Budde, C.E., Stoelinga, M.: Efficient algorithms for quantitative attack tree analysis. In: 2021 IEEE 34th Computer Security Foundations Symposium (CSF), pp. 1–15. IEEE (2021)
10. Buldas, A., Gadyatskaya, O., Lenin, A., Mauw, S., Trujillo-Rasua, R.: Attribute evaluation on attack trees with incomplete information. Comput. Secur. **88**, 101630 (2020)
11. Burley, D.L., Bishop, M., Buckalew, L., Joint task force on cybersecurity education: cybersecurity curricula 2017: curriculum guidelines for post-secondary degree programs in cybersecurity. Technical report, ACM, IEEE-CS, AIS, and IFIP, New York, NY, USA, December 2017. https://doi.org/10.1145/3184594
12. Byg, J., Jørgensen, K.Y., Srba, J.: TAPAAL: editor, simulator and verifier of timed-arc petri nets. In: Liu, Z., Ravn, A.P. (eds.) Automated Technology for Verification and Analysis, pp. 84–89. Springer, Heidelberg (2009)
13. Dang, T.K.N., Lopuhaä-Zwakenberg, M., Stoelinga, M.: Fuzzy quantitative attack tree analysis. In: International Conference on Fundamental Approaches to Software Engineering, pp. 210–231. Springer, Cham (2024)
14. Fila, B., Wideł, W.: Efficient attack-defense tree analysis using pareto attribute domains. In: 2019 IEEE 32nd Computer Security Foundations Symposium (CSF), pp. 200–20015 (2019). https://doi.org/10.1109/CSF.2019.00021
15. Kapery, G., Snyman, D.: A framework for integrating gamification in information security awareness programmes for higher education students. In: IFIP World Conference on Information Security Education, pp. 50–64. Springer (2024)
16. Kordy, B., Mauw, S., Radomirović, S., Schweitzer, P.: Attack-defense trees. J. Log. Comput. **24**(1), 55–87 (2014)
17. Kumar, R., Ruijters, E., Stoelinga, M.: Quantitative attack tree analysis via priced timed automata. In: Sankaranarayanan, S., Vicario, E. (eds.) FORMATS 2015. LNCS, vol. 9268, pp. 156–171. Springer, Cham (2015). https://doi.org/10.1007/978-3-319-22975-1_11
18. Lopuhaä-Zwakenberg, M.: Quantitative analysis of attack-fault trees via Markov decision processes. arXiv preprint arXiv:2408.06914 (2024)
19. Roy, A., Kim, D.S., Trivedi, K.S.: Attack countermeasure trees (ACT): towards unifying the constructs of attack and defense trees. Secur. Commun. Netw. **5**(8), 929–943 (2012)
20. Saboori, A., Hadjicostis, C.N.: Verification of initial-state opacity in security applications of des. In: 2008 9th International Workshop on Discrete Event Systems, pp. 328–333 (2008). https://doi.org/10.1109/WODES.2008.4605967
21. Schneier, B.: Attack trees. Dr. Dobb's J. **24**(12), 21–29 (1999)
22. Shannon, C.E.: A mathematical theory of communication. Bell Syst. Tech. J. **27**(3), 379–423 (1948)
23. Wang, L., Jajodia, S., Singhal, A., Noel, S.: k-Zero day safety: a network security metric for measuring the risk of unknown vulnerabilities. IEEE Trans. Dependable Secure Comput. **11**(1), 30–44 (2014)

Regulatory Challenges in Cybersecurity – A Critical Analysis of the EU AI Act

Féderic Tronnier(✉), Sascha Löbner, Marie-Hermance Lacombe, and Kai Rannenberg

Goethe University Frankfurt am Main, Frankfurt, Germany
frederic.tronnier@m-chair.de

Abstract. The recently enacted European regulation on Artificial Intelligence (AI), the AI Act, seeks to mitigate risks associated with AI systems and to protect fundamental rights while promoting innovation within the European Union (EU). For cybersecurity educators and professionals, Article 4 of the AI Act promotes the tremendous challenge of obliging organizations that use AI systems to educate their employees on the subject, in order to promote AI literacy. This article therefore provides a systematic literature review on the AI Act and its criticisms, with the intention of fostering an understanding of the challenges ahead, by providing an educational overview on the subject of AI regulation. We find research on the AI Act from a cybersecurity perspective to be scarce. The results of our review demonstrate that the Act has faced significant criticism for its lack of clarity and the challenges of concrete application, stemming from the complexity of algorithms and the diverse range of sectors it encompasses. The complexity of implementation of the regulation hinders compliance and, overall, innovation, leaving several opportunities for regulatory improvement and academic research.

Keywords: AI Act · Security · Cybersecurity Regulation · Artificial Intelligence Regulation

1 Introduction

Artificial Intelligence (AI) is seen as the driver of the next worldwide revolution, affecting researchers, information and computer science professionals as well as experts on cybersecurity and cybersecurity education. AI, Large Language Models (LLMs) and machine learning (ML) are seemingly mixed, offering possibilities hitherto unimagined, yet it is up to regulators to provide order and structure where previously chaos ruled. In less than a decade, AI has undergone rapid advancements and has emerged as a critical force shaping our societies at an accelerating pace. Consequently, this acceleration culminated in a surge of public and private interest. Indeed, as AI continues to disrupt industries, governments recognize its potential to revolutionize areas like healthcare, education, or finance, while also acknowledging risks to privacy and cybersecurity. The reliance

Published by Springer Nature Switzerland AG 2026
L. Drevin et al. (Eds.): WISE 2025, IFIP AICT 742, pp. 80–93, 2026.
https://doi.org/10.1007/978-3-031-94924-1_6

of ML systems on vast data sets presents a variety of ethical and legal challenges, e.g. through a lack of accountability, fairness and transparency, highlighting the need for clear guidelines.

Aware of the scale of these concerns and with the ambition of ensuring excellence in the field, the European Union (EU) has adopted a strategic approach, aiming to position itself as a pioneer in the regulation of AI. This ambition involves establishing standardized norms and rules to govern the behavior of the many actors, in order to safeguard individual privacy and security and ensure that AI systems align with societal values. The European Commission (EC) implemented legislative initiatives such as the General Data Protection Regulation (GDPR) in 2018, which aims to protect the confidentiality of personal data and guarantee the privacy of EU citizens. It introduced transparency and information requirements, which were later complemented and formalized in the specific field of AI by the AI Act, which came into force in August 2024. The Act seeks to mitigate risks associated with AI technologies and to ensure its secure and ethical use across various sectors. It aims to regulate AI as a whole, ensuring trust, in order to foster innovation among the EU while protecting fundamental rights. However, the implementation of these regulations is complicated by the complexity of ongoing technical innovation and the diversity of applicable sectors. Considering the recency of the regulation, the objective of this work is therefore to provide a comprehensive overview of the existing literature on the scope and the limitation of EU AI Act. A specific focus is put on the field of cybersecurity. The results aim to provide guidance and orientation for the continuous improvement of AI regulation, and depict the status quo of research on the AI Act for cybersecurity professionals that will be affected by the implementation of the Act. Thus, this work addresses the following research question:

RQ: *What limitations, challenges and gaps have been observed in the AI Act?*

In the following, the second section provides background information on the AI Act and its link to cybersecurity education. Section three introduces the methodology, a systematic literature review following [3]. The results are then presented in Sect. 4. This work concludes with a summary of the identified challenges, while outlining limitations as well as areas for future research.

2 The AI Act and Its Link to Cybersecurity Education

The European Commission's definition of AI in the AI Act (Art. 3 AI Act) emphasizes the autonomy of systems. Concretely, the AI Act mainly targets AI applications that rely heavily on algorithms using ML. As ML systems become increasingly integrated into various aspects of society, their socio-technical implications are becoming more apparent. The use of ML systems has raised significant concerns [33], e.g. surrounding data usage [11]. Consequently, the widespread adoption of AI and ML across sectors can lead to harmful consequences if ethical concerns are not addressed [34]. To address such concerns, the

EU AI Act, proposed in 2021 and in force since August 2024, establishes a risk-based regulatory framework to mitigate potential harm arising from the use of AI systems. Unlike the GDPR, which applies to all automated decisions affecting individuals, the AI Act focuses exclusively on AI systems, categorizing them based on their potential detrimental impacts on health, safety, and fundamental rights. These legal regimes cover four clusters of AI systems with (i) unacceptable (severe), (ii) high, (iii) limited, and (iv) minimal risks. This classification ensures tailored regulatory approaches to manage the risks associated with different AI uses effectively. The AI Act integrates ethical considerations aimed at promoting AI development while safeguarding human rights and values. It contains a closed list of prohibited AI practices associated with AI systems which are rated with Unacceptable-Risk (Art. 5 AI Act). These are AI systems that pose clear threats to human safety, dignity or rights. Limited-risk AI systems need to comply with transparency obligations defined in the regulation. AI systems whose risk is deemed minimal can follow a voluntary code of conduct defined in the Act. The AI Act primarily focuses on high-risk systems, which pose a greater potential threat to society, categorizing them in two types (Art. 6 AI Act): (i) AI intended to be used as a product covered by specific EU legislation, such as civil aviation, and (ii) AI systems listed in Annex III of the AI Act, such as systems for law enforcement and education and vocational training. Providers of high-risk AI systems must meet strict requirements to ensure that their AI systems are trustworthy, transparent and accountable (Chap. III AI Act). Particularly important for cybersecurity professionals are the obligations introduced in the Act. They must conduct risk assessments (Art. 9 AI Act), use high-quality data (Art. 10 AI Act), document their technical and ethical choices (Art. 11), keep records of their system's performance (Art. 12 AI Act), inform users about the nature and purpose of their systems (Art. 13 AI Act), enable human oversight and intervention, and ensure accuracy, robustness, and cybersecurity (Art. 14 AI Act). They must also test their systems for conformity with the rules before placing them on the market or putting them into service, but they also have to establish a post-market monitoring system (Art. 72 AI Act). As transparency in AI systems is a major point of the act, accountabilities are shifted at all stages along the value chain imposing strict obligations not only on the 'provider' of a high-risk AI system, but also on the 'importer', 'distributor' and 'deployer' of such systems (Chap. III-Section 3 and Chap. 4 Art. 50 AI Act).

Several comments and opinions were published throughout the development process of the AI Act. De Cooman [7] argues the AI Act's deficiency in addressing the full range of risks associated with AI systems by referring to the potential harms of non-high-risk AI, i.e. AI systems with limited or minimal risk. The author also highlights the importance of culture and social tolerance in determining harmful applications of AI. Gyevnar et al. [15] argue that there is a lack of concrete mechanisms to ensure real explainability of AI systems. The transparency requirements defined by the Act are likely to remain superficial without clear criteria for explainability and robust audit measures. Scantamburlo et al. [31] evaluated the challenges of determination of risk level in AI systems. Their report includes a critical evaluation of legal requirements, and urgent recommendations to help providers achieve compliance.

In the context of cybersecurity education, the AI Act needs to be addressed from two main perspectives. Firstly, AI systems and solutions are increasingly being used for cybersecurity purposes, as well as for cybersecurity education. For instance, the authors of [1] use Generative Pre-Trained Transformers (GPT) to create tailored and dynamic cybersecurity training material. The results indicate the solution's applicability in enhancing cybersecurity awareness. As another area of application, [20] study the applicability of AI chatbots for career counselling for cybersecurity professionals. Such work thereby corresponds to Recital 56 of the AI Act which aims to foster the use of AI for educational purposes by stating that *"the deployment of AI systems in education is important to promote high-quality digital education and training and to allow all learners and teachers to acquire and share the necessary digital skills and competences, including media literacy, and critical thinking, to take an active part in the economy, society, and in democratic processes. [...] When improperly designed and used, such systems may be particularly intrusive and may violate the right to education and training as well as the right not to be discriminated against and perpetuate historical patterns of discrimination [...] " (Recital 56 AI Act).* As observed, the Recital highlights the need for caution when introducing AI for educational purposes, which further emphasizes the need for more research on both, AI systems and the AI Act in ensuring security. This serves as a motivation for this work. Secondly, cybersecurity researchers and practitioners need to work on mitigating threats and risks of AI applications, while being aware of the requirements set forth by the corresponding regulation: *"Providers and deployers of AI systems shall take measures to ensure, to their best extent, a sufficient level of AI literacy of their staff and other persons dealing with the operation and use of AI systems on their behalf, taking into account their technical knowledge, experience, education and training and the context the AI systems are to be used in, and considering the persons or groups of persons on whom the AI systems are to be used." (Art.4 AI Act).* Thus, cybersecurity education is seen as an incremental task when working with AI systems. Therefore, we investigate the AI Act in more detail, aiming to find whether and how cybersecurity research is currently addressing the AI Act.

3 Methodology

Our research fills the identified gap in academic research by conduction a systematic literature review on the scope, limitations and issues with respect to the implementation of the AI Act, following its introduction. The aim of this work is to provide a comprehensive overview of on the topic at hand. Thus, the recency of our articles found was set as a priority. To conduct a systematic literature review, we followed the guidelines and best practices provided by Brocke et al. [3]. In accordance with the taxonomy of Cooper [6], the goal is to structure existing criticism towards the AI Act as well as to define central issues with and of the regulation. In doing so, we focus on research outcomes

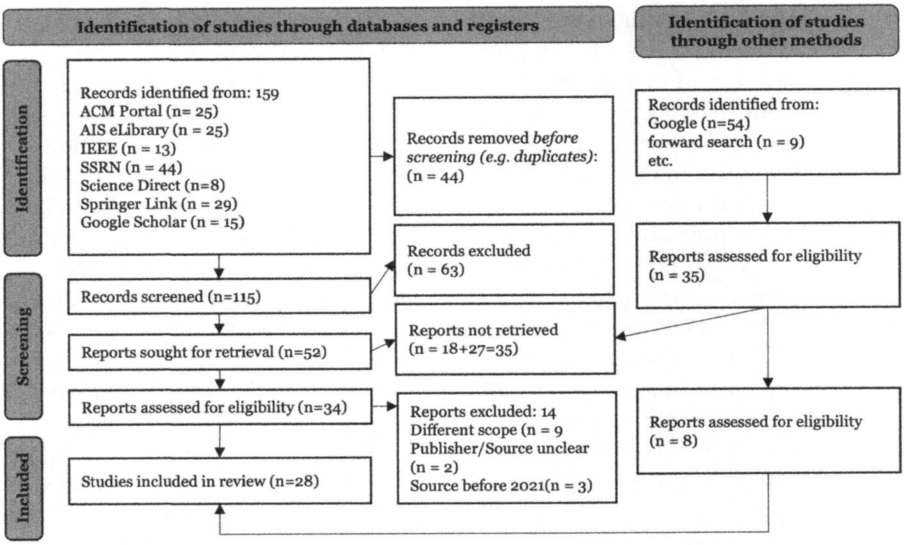

Fig. 1. PRISMA literature review process, following Page et al. [26].

rather than research theories. The coverage is to be seen as representative, while the perspective is espousal of position. The target audience are general scholars and practitioners, interested in the application and limitations of the AI Act, in the context of cybersecurity. We utilized the PRISMA 2020 checklist [26] as a framework to report our literature identification process. The focus on the AI Act and its relation to cybersecurity education guided the research process. However, too few articles met these initial criteria. Therefore, the scope was broadened towards cybersecurity and the AI Act in general, by also including few additional information sources from academic and legal blogs and websites. The database used to analyse the official regulatory texts from the European Commission was EUR-Lex, as well as the official sites of the DGPR and the AI Act. The scientific databases consulted to identify relevant academic studies were ACM Portal, Google Scholar, IEEE Xplore Digital Library, Science Direct, AiS Library, Science Direct, Springer Link and the SSRN platform. The term "AI Act" was included in all search queries. Key additional search inputs included the following keywords: "AI Act analysis", "AI Act regulation" and "AI Act AND cybersecurity". 28 final hits emerged that were selected for our analysis in the results section. The most relevant studies were chosen based on a critical analysis of the AI Act applied to general cases, ensuring a representative sample of the respective domains. The detailed PRISMA flowchart illustrating the selection process is provided in Fig. 1. We used the concept-centric approach by Webster and Watson [37] to analyse trends and key concepts highlighted in each of the selected articles.

4 Results

Table 1 provides an overview of the occurrence of different observations and identified limitations of the AI Act across the relevant literature. The results depict the identified domain of research in which the obtained articles were conducted. Individual articles were often located at the interface between two or more research domains, for example in cybersecurity law journals, which represent the intersection between legal and information technology research. In addition, the presumed addressee of the article is indicated by the perspective of the article. It can be seen that many articles are aimed at regulators or policymakers, while only a few articles are addressed to academics or companies, or consider their perspective on the AI Act. The common thread running through all articles is a dedicated analysis of the AI Act and its regulatory challenges. Trends and notions mentioned in the reviews were recurrently noted, enabling them to be classified into generalized categories. If a paper focuses or discusses one of the aggregated categories, we indicate it with an "✔" in Table 1. In the following, the main identified research themes are discussed.

4.1 Ambiguity of Definitions and Scope

The first category of findings in Table 1 refers to the lack of clarity in the definition of terms and requirements outlined by the AI Act and was the topic identified most frequently in the reviewed literature. The current regulation is criticized by multiple identified articles for creating ambiguity and uncertainty due to overly broad definitions of legal status that necessitate clarification. Gyevnar et al. [15] refer to the mismatch of views as "the transparency gap" which argues that the definitions, scope and purpose of transparency in regulations are not in agreement with how technological approaches understand them. Policymakers view transparency as a mean that supports wider values such as accountability, human rights, and sustainable innovation. In contrast, explainable AI (XAI) views transparency narrowly as an end in itself, focusing on explaining complex algorithmic properties without considering the socio-technical context. This difference leads to challenges in aligning technical applications with regulatory requirements. Musch et al. [24] underline the lack of direct translation of the instructions described in the regulations into concrete process. Consequently, this unclarity can leave room for interpretation, weakening its implementation across stakeholders of the value chain of systems but also across member states [8]. Moreover, according to the scenarios, the question of legal responsibility between developers, providers, and users is not fully resolved by the AI Act. Yet, they are necessary to prevent damage caused by AI systems if too many liberties are taken, to avoid undermining stakeholder trust, and prevent negative impacts on innovation [38]. Clarifying accountability is crucial, particularly when it comes to opaque ML algorithms like black boxes, where the risk of error is inherent. The question of responsibility for the results arises further when it comes to unintelligible probabilistic models [22]. Ruschemeier [30] provides an exemplary work on the challenge of regulating AI. The authors discuss how AI

Table 1. Classification of literature by research domain, perspective and identified issues with the AI Act.

Literature	Lack of clarity	Risk assessment challenges	Conflicts/ gaps in standards	Competitive disadvantages	Technical challenges	Organizational challenges	Self-governance challenges	Research domain	Perspective
[2]						✓		Legal	Policymaker
[4]	✓		✓		✓	✓		Non-scientific	Policymaker
[5]			✓					Legal	Policymaker
[8]	✓			✓		✓	✓	Business	Organizational
[9]	✓				✓	✓		Non-scientific	Policymaker
[10]	✓	✓		✓	✓		✓	Legal	Policymaker
[12]	✓			✓		✓		Non-scientific	Policymaker
[13]						✓	✓	Information Systems	Organizational
[14]	✓		✓					Informatics	Societal / Research
[15]	✓	✓			✓		✓	Informatics	Academic Research
[16]		✓		✓	✓			Non-scientific	Policymaker
[17]	✓	✓	✓			✓		Information Systems	Organizational
[19]						✓		Information Systems	Organizational
[18]		✓	✓			✓		Legal	Organizational
[21]		✓			✓		✓	Politics	Societal
[22]	✓	✓			✓	✓		Information Systems	Organizational
[23]	✓							Legal	Policymaker
[24]	✓	✓			✓	✓		Ethics	Societal
[25]	✓	✓				✓	✓	Legal	Policymaker
[27]	✓		✓			✓		Legal	Policymaker
[28]					✓		✓	Informatics	Policymaker
[29]		✓	✓		✓	✓		Non-scientific	Organizational
[30]	✓							Legal	Policymaker
[31]	✓		✓		✓	✓		Informatics	Organizational
[32]	✓	✓		✓				Legal	Policymaker
[35]	✓	✓			✓		✓	Legal	Policymaker
[36]	✓	✓	✓	✓		✓	✓	Legal	Organizational
[38]	✓	✓	✓	✓				Non-scientific	Societal
$\sum$	19	14	10	7	12	16	9		

can be regulated, given the constantly evolving topic and a plethora of differing definitions of AI. A solution mentioned by White [38], although purely theoretical, is then to start attributing legal personality to AI. Therefore, the author is optimistic about the AI Liability Directive (AILD), a proposal introduced by the European Commission in 2022 that aims to clarify the legal responsibilities of parties involved in AI systems.

4.2 Risks and Risk Classification

The second category of identified findings criticizes the risk classification of the AI Act, which is deemed to be too static, causing the omission of certain AI systems, particularly those deemed "low-risk", yet still capable of generating significant social, ethical, or psychological consequences [36]. Therefore, the AI Act does not capture the full scope of consequences, neglecting intangible impacts such as systemic discrimination particularly linked with algorithmic bias of ML models. According to the author, one danger of the Act is that it creates "grey areas" in the regulation, leaving many harmful applications outside the regulatory scope. As Ebers et al. [10] point out: "The Commission should avoid what this article humorously labels as the Humpty Dumpty fallacy. Just because the Proposal dichotomizes high-risk and non-high-risk AI systems does not mean the latter are not worthy of discussion." Even the categorization of "high-risk" AI systems is considered "unduly blunt and simplistic" [32]. Indeed, high-risk AI systems may still be deployed even if they interfere with fundamental rights, if those deploying them adhere to the requirements set out under Chapter III. The protection afforded by the Act hence entirely depends on whether the closed 'high-risk list' provided in Annex III, is sufficiently comprehensive and up to date. But, according to the authors, this demand may be hard to meet, especially given the technology's evolving nature. In addition to the complexity of preemptively assessing the risks, another major challenge lies in concretely applying the risk-based approach. The Act does not cover all algorithmic methods encompassed by ML. As a matter of fact, it overlooks a crucial technological aspect, particularly in Article 10, by limiting the scope of requirements to training, validation, and testing data. While datasets are undeniably critical for data-driven AI systems, such as reinforcement learning, methods like planning and reinforcement learning do not rely on the same techniques as supervised learning, from which these terms originate. It remains unclear what requirements should be met for systems that rely on the input data of such methods to generate their explanations [15]. For more complex types of ML algorithms, compliance with these requirements becomes even more challenging, particularly in monitoring system quality and managing bias and discrimination due to their complexity and opacity. Scantamburlo et al. [31] point out that applied to even more general- purpose AI systems, the compliance process becomes rather complicated due to their potential for diverse purposes. Delegating the responsibility of defining permissible uses to providers, along with the corresponding obligations for compliance of potentially harmful systems, raises legitimate concerns. Therefore, the establishment of more precise criteria is deemed necessary to define which requirements a system is subject to and what constitutes the validity of the different requirements. To address the multiple and changing high-risk classifications and the unknown land of AI risks, Golpayegani et al. [14] developed an open resource vocabulary for AI risks (VAIR) to represent and assist with AI risk assessments of systems that respect Annex III conditions and help with documentation. VAIR is intended to facilitate the Ai acts applicability by providing a common vocabulary that facilitates knowledge sharing and connectivity between stakeholders in the AI value chain. A set of guiding principles for cybersecurity requirements for high-risk AI systems is provided by [18] of the Joint Research Centre (JCR) as a service by the European Commission. It aims to address some of the challenges and limitations in this work by providing a high-level assessment of the AI Act.

4.3 Missing Coordination of Standards and Regulation

To ensure the AI Act's effectiveness in achieving harmonization, legal challenges arise from the coordination with existing standards. This issue falls under the third category of Table 1. Indeed, current standards, such as industry-specific standards, need to be adapted. Heidemann et al. [17] illustrate this point using existing road-vehicle safety standards that align well with Article 9 of the EU AI Act but provide weaker coverage than the act of certain requirements for human oversight and transparency. Quintais [27] provide a legal analysis with respect to copyright issues when dealing with Generative AI and the interaction between the AI Act and EU copyright law such as the Digital Single Market Directive (CDSMD). Similarly, the first challenge highlighted by Scantamburlo et al. [31] in their analysis of the AI Act, is the conflicts arising from potential coordination issues with existing legal frameworks, such as competition law and consumer law. Assessment requirements can lead to challenges involving more extensive considerations, such as intersections with other legal obligations (e.g., GDPR, Copyright Law). The transparency mandated by the GDPR and further reinforced by the AI Act also necessitates the disclosure of specific system techniques. The article of Fernhout and Duquin [12] takes the example machine learning algorithms used for credit scoring, classified as high-risk system. The economic model and competitive advantage of these systems rely on the precise weightings and parameters, which are protected as trade secrets. Under the transparency requirement, there is a risk of infringing proprietary rights by requiring the disclosure of motivations and design decisions. This could reveal detailed information about the algorithms and data used, thereby affecting intellectual property, trade secrets, and competitive advantage. Casarosa [5] follows this conclusion by stating that the missing alignment between the AI Act and another regulation, the Cybersecurity Act, is to be seen as a missed opportunity, as "different approaches adopted in the two acts may undermine the goal of certification mechanisms as trust-enhancing and transparency instruments". In the cybersecurity domain, the missing coordination between different regulations is also discussed through the discussion of the Network and Information Security System Directive reform (NIS 2), whereby Biasin and Kamenjašević

[2] reach the same conclusion as [5]. At the time of writing, no specific standard was introduced for the certification of AI systems. And some of the already available standards, technical specifications, and technical reports proposed by the ISO are insufficient and are often criticized for failing to meet the requirements of the AI Act. For example, there is a divergence in approach between the requirements of the AI Act and the ISO/IEC 23894 standard, titled "Artificial Intelligence—Guidance on Risk Management," which aims to guide organizations in managing AI system risks. This standard primarily focuses on internal risks to the organization developing AI. However, the AI Act, as outlined in Article 9, takes a broader view of risk management, considering external risks such as health, safety, and the fundamental rights of individuals affected by AI systems. In [14], the authors map the standardization activities undertaken by the committee ISO/IEC JTC 1/SC 42 to the high-risk AI requirements. The conclusions highlight that: (i) there is a lack of standards for technical documentation (Art. 11 AI Act), user instructions (Art. 13 AI Act), and record-keeping management (Art. 12 AI Act); (ii) there is a shortage of certifiable organizational standards. Most standards are primarily designed to provide guidelines b, but not yet offer precise and measurable criteria for official certification. Without certifiable standards, proving that AI systems comply with legal requirements will be challenging, even if those standards are followed; (iii) access to current ISO standards is costly, which creates a barrier that disadvantages smaller organizations (startups, SMEs, research institutions). Requests for standardization are expected to be issued by the European Commission (Art. 40 AI Act). Other organizations like the AI Watch have started to propose a preliminary roadmap of international standards in support of the requirements set out by the AI Act. [31] propose the adaptation of existing standards, such as ISO/IEC TR 24368:2022 for describing technical specifications for the assessment of machine learning classification performance.

4.4 Challenges Relating to the Implementation of the AI Act

The compliance process is hindered by the complexity of the organizational implementation of the AI Act requirements. By trying to comply, AI providers could face shortages in human resources, technical expertise, as well as financial resources, especially when adhering to paid standards. For instance, it is foreseen that deployers of high-risk AI systems must implement human oversight, monitoring, and report serious incidents and malfunctions, adding to operational costs [8]. These requisites may carry a premium, potentially leading to higher prices for consumers. Moreover, meeting EU AI Act requirements may increase administrative burdens, delaying and discouraging the launch of new AI products or updated versions. Gengler and Schmalenbach [13,19] assess the AI Act from an organisational point-of-view. By observing the response behaviour of 400 organizations, [19] derive four distinct response strategies, circumvent, comply, compromise, and control, as well as multiple response practices towards AI regulation. Similarly, Ramos and Ellul [28] provides one of the few works on the AI Act from a cybersecurity perspective. The authors argue that the utilization of blockchain technology may aid in complying with some of the AI Act requirements on data governance, transparency and record keeping. Furthermore, several authors argue that time-consuming and costly processes could favour large companies at the expense of smaller ones, because of their greater resources and advanced expertise, creating a competitive disadvantage [25]. But, the EU AI Act could also discourage the development of AI solutions by affecting international competition with regions that are not subject to such regulations [8]. An interdisciplinary collaboration mechanism between the public and private sectors has been proposed to promote a holistic approach to allow a better application of the overly rigid framework to different AI use cases [31]. However, this collaboration is often seen as lobbying, facilitating the self-governance process of large technology companies. Accused of "secret negotiations" by Metikos [23], it is claimed that policymakers allowed and favour the influence of Big Tech lobbyists during the legislative process of the AI Act. It cites the French company Mistral, which opposed the regulation of generative AI to defend its own interests. This illustrates the need for balanced cooperation between legislators and the private sector, to avoid excessive lobbying and compelling self-governance.

5 Discussion

The main challenges and issues raised by researchers with the AI Act may be grouped into three categories: (i) First, the lack of clarity in the definitions of used terms, the lack of precision in the risk-classification of AI systems, the unclear definition of the necessary requirements, and the lack of clear legal responsibilities assigned to the various stakeholders. (ii) The gap and partly overlap between existing regulations and the absence of certifiable standards. (iii) The technical and organizational difficulties in applying the regulation, which may slow down its implementation and act as a competitive disadvantage for organisations. By providing an overview of ongoing trends in critiques of the AI Act, these results confirm the concerns raised regarding existing regulations. For instance, the financial and organizational resources required could risk stifling innovation by favouring large, influential companies capable of mobilizing such resources to shape the legal framework to serve their own interests. As a result, this could distort competition and discourage overall AI innovation. Thus, this analysis highlights the need to adapt future regulations to ensure their applicability to the entire market and alignment with the complexity of AI systems. A first step in addressing particularly the identified lack of clarity (i), could be the Code of Practice, for which the EC will start its drafting process in Mai 2025.

Naturally, this work is not without limitations. The literature review process did only identify a representative set of findings, more work might be found in other domains, e.g. in legal or ethics databases. The potential presence of reporting bias need to be acknowledged, as does the lack of further analysis of the identified authors and their geographic and institutional perspectives that may explain their criticism. Nonetheless, for cybersecurity researchers, the lack of findings specifically tailored towards cybersecurity education, demonstrate the need for future research in this domain. Not only does AI regulation need to keep track with the rapid evolution of AI, but researchers need to keep track as well. Cybersecurity educators need to be aware of the regulation to identify strategies to educate AI system deployers as well as AI system users on the subject. As of now, research is found to focus strongly on a legal interpretation of the Act, by providing research from the perspective of a policymaker. Future work should therefore assess how exactly cybersecurity educators can comply with the AI Acts requirements on AI literacy, for instance by developing quality standards for AI education in different organisational and societal domains.

6 Conclusion

This work provides a systematic literature review on the recent AI Act, which aids cybersecurity professionals in understanding the current challenges and limitations of a regulation that might severely impact their daily work. In the context of cybersecurity, this work highlights current shortcomings with respect to the scope and applicability of the regulation, as well as challenges in the identification and classification of risks. According to the discussed research, the AI Act does not to adequately address the challenges posed by AI and ML systems. For cybersecurity educators, the AI Act will be another regulation to be considered, as the AI Act clearly emphasizes the importance of educating personnel on AI applications, systems and it's functioning. Therefore, future work should study not only study how cybersecurity education can be facilitated through AI [1,20], but how cybersecurity education on AI itself can be fostered, and AI compliance be achieved in a multi-perspective environment.

Acknowledgments. This article was co-funded through the FIIPS-at-Home project, funded by the German Federal Ministry of Education and Research under (funding code 16KISA068K) and CyberSecPro (Project Agreement no. 101083594), co-funded by the European Union. Responsibility for the contents lies with the authors.

Disclosure of Interests. The authors have no competing interests to declare that are relevant to the content of this article.

References

1. Al-Dhamari, N., Clarke, N.: GPT-enabled cybersecurity training: a tailored approach for effective awareness. In: IFIP World Conference on Information Security Education, pp. 3–20. Springer (2024)
2. Biasin, E., Kamenjašević, E.: Cybersecurity of medical devices: new challenges arising from the AI ACT and NIS 2 directive proposals. Int. Cybersecur. Law Rev. **3**(1), 163–180 (2022)
3. vom Brocke, J., et al.: Reconstructing the giant: On the importance of rigour in documenting the literature search process (2009)

4. Caroli, L.: Will the EU AI Act work? Lessons learned from past legislative initiatives, future challenges. International Association of Privacy Professionals (2024)
5. Casarosa, F.: Cybersecurity certification of artificial intelligence: a missed opportunity to coordinate between the artificial intelligence act and the cybersecurity act. Int. Cybersecur. Law Rev. **3**(1) (2022)
6. Cooper, H.M.: Organizing knowledge syntheses: a taxonomy of literature reviews. Knowl. Soc. **1**(1), 104 (1988)
7. De Cooman, J.: Humpty dumpty and high-risk AI systems: the ratione materiae dimension of the proposal for an EU artificial intelligence act. Mark. Competition Law Rev. **6**, 49 (2022)
8. Ditsche, J., Mikhaylenko, M.: European AI Act: Opportunities and challenges, May 2024. rolandberger.com
9. Djeffal, C.: The EU AI Act at a crossroads: generative AI as a challenge for regulation. European Law Blog (2023)
10. Ebers, M., Hoch, V.R., Rosenkranz, F., Ruschemeier, H., Steinrötter, B.: The European Commission's proposal for an Artificial Intelligence Act—a critical assessment by members of the Robotics and AI Law Society (RAILS). J. **4**(4), 589–603 (2021)
11. El Mestari, S.Z., Lenzini, G., Demirci, H.: Preserving data privacy in machine learning systems. Comput. Secur. **137**, 103605 (2024)
12. Fernhout, F., Duquin, T.: The EU Artificial Intelligence Act: Our 16 Key Takeaways, February 2024. stibbe.com
13. Gengler, E., Schmalenbach, K.: Exploring organizational ai governance maturity: a case study with six multinational companies. In: Proceedings of the International Conference on Information Systems (ICIS). AiS (2024)
14. Golpayegani, D., Pandit, H.J., Lewis, D.: To be high-risk, or not to be—semantic specifications and implications of the AI act's high-risk AI applications and Harmonised standards. In: Proceedings of the 2023 ACM Conference on Fairness, Accountability, and Transparency (2023)
15. Gyevnar, B., Ferguson, N., Schafer, B.: Bridging the transparency gap: what can explainable AI learn from the AI act? In: ECAI 2023, pp. 964–971. IOS Press (2023)
16. Hacker, P.: What's Missing from the EU AI Act. On Matters Constitutional, Verfassungsblog (2023)
17. Heidemann, L., et al.: The European Artificial Intelligence Act (2024)
18. Junklewitz, H., et al.: Cybersecurity of artificial intelligence in the AI act. Publications Office Europe Union (2023)
19. Kahdan, M., Hartwich, N.J., Salge, O., Cichy, P.: Navigating uncertain waters: how organizations respond to institutional pressure in times of the looming EU AI Act. In: Proceedings of the International Conference on Information Systems (ICIS). AiS (2023)
20. Koukou, C., Stavrou, E.: The potential of generative AI Chatbots as career advisors in cybersecurity: professionals' perspectives. In: IFIP World Conference on Information Security Education, pp. 191–206. Springer (2024)
21. MacCarthy, M., Propp, K.: Machines learn that Brussels writes the rules: the EU's new AI regulation. Brookings, 4 May 2021 (2021)
22. Maxwell, W., Caulier, S.: "AI Act", comment l'Europe veut réguler les machines. Polytechnique Insights, December 2021
23. Metikos, L.: The AI act: weak, weaker, weakest. Ljubiša Metikoš, Mediaforum **3**, 73–74 (2024)
24. Musch, S., Borrelli, M., Kerrigan, C.: The EU AI Act: a comprehensive regulatory framework for ethical AI development. SSRN 4549248 (2023)

25. Outeda, C.C.: The EU's AI act: a framework for collaborative governance. Internet of Things, p. 101291 (2024)
26. Page, M.J., et al.: The PRISMA 2020 statement: an updated guideline for reporting systematic reviews. bmj **372** (2021)
27. Quintais, J.P.: Generative AI, copyright and the AI act. Comput. Law Secur. Rev. **56**, 106107 (2025)
28. Ramos, S., Ellul, J.: Blockchain for artificial intelligence (AI): enhancing compliance with the EU AI act through distributed ledger technology. a cybersecurity perspective. Int. Cybersecur. Law Rev. **5**(1), 1–20 (2024)
29. Renieris, E.M., Kiron, D., Mills, S.: Organizations face challenges in timely compliance with the EU AI Act: a panel of experts weighs in on whether organizations are positioned to meet the requirements of the EU AI Act. MIT Sloan Manage. Rev. (2024)
30. Ruschemeier, H.: AI as a challenge for legal regulation–the scope of application of the artificial intelligence act proposal. In: Era Forum, vol. 23, pp. 361–376. Springer (2023)
31. Scantamburlo, T., et al.: Software systems compliance with the AI Act: lessons learned from an international challenge. In: Proceedings of the 2nd International Workshop on Responsible AI Engineering, pp. 44–51 (2024)
32. Smuha, N.A., et al.: How the EU can achieve legally trustworthy AI: a response to the European Commission's proposal for an Artificial Intelligence Act. SSRN 3899991 (2021)
33. Tan, S., Taeihagh, A., Baxter, K.: The risks of machine learning systems. arXiv preprint arXiv:2204.09852 (2022)
34. Terrier, F.: No trust without regulation! arXiv preprint arXiv:2311.06263 (2023)
35. Veale, M., Zuiderveen Borgesius, F.: Demystifying the draft EU artificial intelligence act-analysing the good, the bad, and the unclear elements of the proposed approach. Comput. Law Rev. Int. **22**(4), 97–112 (2021)
36. Wachter, S.: Limitations and loopholes in the EU AI Act and AI liability directives: what this means for the European Union, the United States, and beyond. Yale J. Law Technol. **26**(3) (2024)
37. Webster, J., Watson, R.T.: Analyzing the past to prepare for the future: writing a literature review. MIS Q., xiii–xxiii (2002)
38. White, J.: Understanding the EU AI Act's Impact and Ripple Effects in the US, October 2024. https://www.informationweek.com/machine-learning-ai/understanding-the-eu-ai-act-s-impact-and-ripple-effects-in-the-us

CSEC Foundations Guidelines

Melissa Dark[1](✉), Philip Huff[2], Jun Dai[3], and Matt Bishop[4]

[1] Dark Enterprises, West Lafayette, IN, USA
melissa.dark@darkenterprisesinc.com
[2] University of Arkansas at Little Rock, Little Rock, AR, USA
pdhuff@ualr.edu
[3] Worcester Polytechnic Institute, Worcester, MA, USA
jdai@wpi.edu
[4] University of California Davis, Davis, CA, USA
mabishop@ucdavis.edu

Abstract. This paper discusses a companion to the Computer Security Curriculum Guidelines 2017 (CSEC 2017). CSEC 2017 serves both introductory and advanced courses in a post-secondary program. The CSEC Foundations Guidelines focus specifically on the foundations of cybersecurity for introductory courses at the secondary and post-secondary school levels. This paper describes the methodology used to select the foundations, what those foundations are, and how the document is organized. It presents six knowledge areas based on those of CSEC 2017 (specifically, data security, network security, system security, software security, organizational security, and societal security) and makes recommendations about the sequencing and pacing of the material. Then, it provides examples of the learning outcomes for cryptography, access control, and data security topics in the Data Security knowledge area and instructional guidance for their use. The paper concludes with a discussion of the CSEC Foundations Guidelines used by the National Cybersecurity Teaching Academy and Coalition, which offers graduate certificates to US secondary school teachers to prepare them to teach cybersecurity. As a supplement to CSEC 2017, the resulting CSEC Foundations Guidelines were approved by the ACM in Jan 2025.

Keywords: cybersecurity foundations · CSEC 2017 · introductory course secondary school education

1 Introduction

In 2017, a task force formed from the ACM, the IEEE Computer Society, the AIS SIGSAC, and the International Federation of Information Processing Societies Working Group 11.8, Computer Security Education and developed a set of Computer Security Curriculum Guidelines (CSEC 2017) [3]. These guidelines recommended a set of learning outcomes basic to various areas of computer security, and identified several as "essential meaning that regardless of the area of

Published by Springer Nature Switzerland AG 2026
L. Drevin et al. (Eds.): WISE 2025, IFIP AICT 742, pp. 94–106, 2026.
https://doi.org/10.1007/978-3-031-94924-1_7

cybersecurity being studied, students should have a basic understanding of the material covered for those learning objectives.

As CSEC 2017 was a set of guidelines for post-secondary education, it did not focus on introductory courses in particular; rather, it serves a broad variety of both introductory and advanced courses. A class in cybersecurity in secondary school, and an introductory course in post-secondary education, should focus on the foundations of cybersecurity to provide a practical basis on which learners can build knowledge.

To this end, another task force was formed to extract the foundational learning objectives from the learning essentials identified in CSEC 2017. Foundational knowledge "includes content that can be taught in an introductory course sequence without requiring prior cybersecurity knowledge" [2, p. 5]. Specifically, this task force had three objectives:

- To provide guidance to institutions setting up introductory courses in cybersecurity that focus on foundations;
- To provide foundational content based on CSEC 2017 and, where necessary, update it; and
- To provide foundational cybersecurity courses that cover common material sufficiently to allow articulation agreements among educational institutions.

The contribution of this paper is to present the methodology used to select these foundational topics, describe the knowledge domain framework used to inform course packing, and offer examples of corresponding learning outcomes.

2 Background

The cybersecurity workforce shortfall is widely known. The U.S. has several national efforts aimed at addressing the cybersecurity workforce shortfall that serve as the impetus for initial development of CSEC 2017 in and this expansion. The post-secondary CAE program in Information Security (now called "CAE in Cyber Defense" or "CAE-CD") launched in 1997 with recognition to 7 U.S. universities for producing cybersecurity graduates. Today there are nearly 500 CAE-CD colleges and universities. These schools are developing and offering a variety of academic programs in cybersecurity. A recent study found 803 certificates, associates, minors and bachelor degrees at NCAE-C institutions as of Spring 2024 as shown in Table 1 [5, p. 27].

Table 1. Number and types of degrees awarded from universities and community (2-year) colleges in the US.

	Bachelor's Degrees	Associate's Degrees	Minor/Tracks	Certif-icate	Total
University ($n = 289$)	180	19	178	68	445
Community College ($n = 157$)	12	125	46	175	358
Total ($n = 446$)	192	144	224	243	893

Another study found approximately 385 universities and 384 community colleges with a cybersecurity Classification for Instructional Programs (CIP) code for bachelor's degrees and associate's degrees [12]. This sample included non NCAE-C schools as well. The growth in institutions and programs leads to growth in graduates. Ten-year growth in graduates from a Computer and Information Systems Security/Auditing/Information Assurance (CIP[1] Code 11.1003) is shown in Fig. 1(a). Figure 1(b) displays 2024 graduates by degree types.

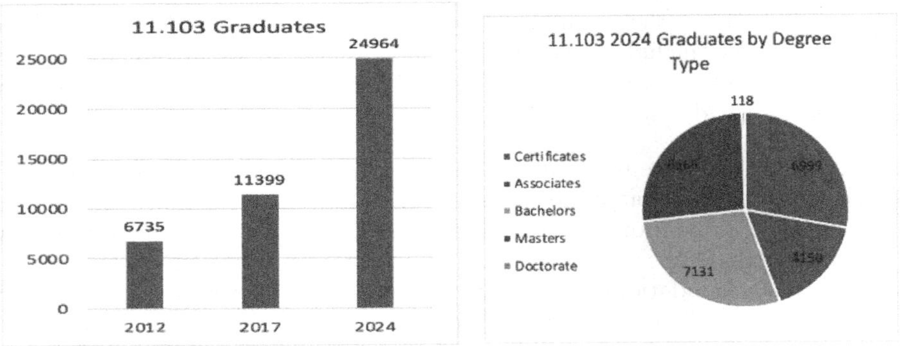

Fig. 1. (a) This shows the ten-year growth in CIP code 11.1003 (Computer and Information Systems Security/Auditing/Information Assurance) Grads. (b) shows the post-secondary graduates by degree types.

The CSEC2017 Joint Task Force on Cybersecurity Education (JTF) was officially launched in September 2015 in an effort to help standardize post-secondary cybersecurity education. The CSEC JTF published the curricular volume in 2017. The development process involved a broad global audience of stakeholders through continuous community engagement with the goals of aligning academic programs with industry needs in cybersecurity and developing curricular guidance that is comprehensive enough to support a wide range of program types. The resulting guideline rests on three cornerstones, namely knowledge areas, cross-cutting concepts, and disciplinary lens, to describes a vision of proficiency in cybersecurity. It defines a structure for the cybersecurity discipline by developing a thought model that defines the boundaries of the discipline and outlines key dimensions of the curricular structure. And it is grounded in fundamental principles that provide stability, yet is structured to provide flexibility to support evolving program needs. A recent search finds 49 ABET accredited programs using the search term "cybersecurity."

Since CSEC 2017 was published, the number of cybersecurity courses and pathways have started growing in U.S. secondary schools, spurred by pioneering programs such as GenCyber and Cyber Patriot, which are out-of-school-time

[1] The Classification of Instructional Programs (CIP) is the taxonomic coding scheme used for instructional programs in higher education in the United States.

curricular programs initiated between 2012–2014. When these programs were started, U.S. high schools were developing computer science courses and programs, but few to none had cybersecurity courses. A 2022 study found that 15% of the 23,882 public high schools in the United States offer a cybersecurity course [6]. The growth is notable.

The growth in secondary cybersecurity education presented a need to update CSEC 2017 to express foundational knowledge. This update serves as a benchmark for what students are expected to know and be able to do with respect to the foundations of cybersecurity. The purposes for the update are to guide instruction, assessment, and curriculum development to ensure consistent and appropriate learning outcomes across different schools and districts. The update can support both scalable high school to college and college to college articulation pathways nationwide whereas state standards are usually delimited to supporting local transfer.

3 Methodology

3.1 Deriving Foundational Topics from CSEC 2017

This work began by examining the essential topics identified in CSEC 2017, which are the knowledge areas and corresponding topics introduced early in a cybersecurity program regardless of specialization. Although these essentials offered a starting point, not all essential topics aligned with the goal of establishing foundational knowledge, which here means content that does not require prerequisite cybersecurity expertise. Consequently, the CSEC 2017 essential topics were mapped to those that could be introduced in a typical entry-level cybersecurity course.

Several CSEC 2017 knowledge areas were then merged to refine the foundational scope. Component Security was incorporated into System Security, based on the idea that systems comprise multiple components, and Human Security was similarly placed under Societal Security with the connection between individuals and society. A full review of CSEC 2017 also identified additional topics not officially labeled as essential but still appropriate for foundational instruction, including cross-border cyber law, ethics, and network hardware architecture. In contrast, topics such as data erasure were omitted upon determining that they were too advanced for entry-level instruction or no longer represented a widely required skill.

Many decisions regarding which topics to retain or revise were influenced by evolving industry trends and societal shifts, including the widespread adoption of social media, increasing privacy concerns, and the expanding global reach of supply chains, as evidenced by the new security control families introduced in NIST Special Publication 800-53 Revision 5 [10]. Moreover, technological advances since the release of CSEC 2017 have been substantial, with global cloud computing growing at an annual rate of 20% [8] and AI expanding by 27% [10]. Although AI was recognized as an increasingly important theme, its coverage was kept minimal in the current curriculum due to the concurrent development of dedicated AI curricular standards.

3.2 Structuring and Aligning Learning Outcomes

The guidelines build on the knowledge areas and topics outlined in CSEC 2017 but diverge by organizing these topics into structured units designed for course packaging. Unlike CSEC 2017, which includes the entire body of knowledge in cybersecurity, this supplement emphasizes the foundational learning outcomes for course packaging. A second topical level was added under the knowledge area to better group common topics that span multiple knowledge areas. For example, the topic of *Attacks* spans Network Security, Software Security, and Societal Security knowledge areas.

The update retains the cross-cutting concepts from CSEC 2017, including Confidentiality, Integrity, Availability, Risk, Adversarial Thinking, and Systems Thinking, while introducing the additional principle of Defense in Depth. These concepts are explicitly mapped to each learning outcome to reinforce core principles and foster a cohesive understanding of the security mindset throughout the curriculum. To define the appropriate cognitive level for each outcome, Bloom's Taxonomy, as adapted for computing [1], is employed to ensure the outcomes align with the depth of knowledge expected in an introductory cybersecurity course. Figure 2 shows these relationships pictorially.

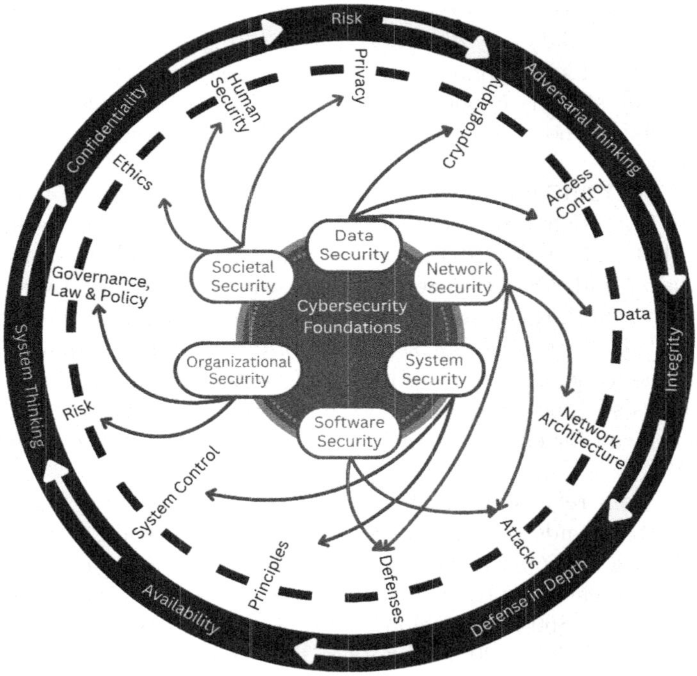

Fig. 2. Relationship among foundational concepts and knowledge areas.

3.3 Review and Feedback Process

Two formal review periods were conducted to gather public feedback on the learning outcomes across the domains of Data Security, Network Security, System Security, Organizational Security, and Societal Security. Reviewers raised several key issues:

- **Clarity and Specificity:** Feedback indicated that learning outcomes in areas such as cryptography, networking protocols, and system hardening were overly general and ambiguous.
- **Content Gaps and Level:** Respondents noted missing topics—such as key management and public key infrastructure (PKI)—and observed that many outcomes were set at too low a level of detail for foundational instruction.

In response, the drafting team revised the learning outcome language to emphasize higher-order abilities. They improved clarity by combining overlapping outcomes, filling content gaps with new outcomes, and updating instructional guidance, references, and course sequencing.

During the second comment period, additional feedback encouraged a broader treatment of emerging concerns and the integration of hands-on activities. Overall, reviewers were favorable of the changes in response to the first round of comments, but requested more detailed coverage of AI security, mobile and cloud security, digital forensics, and case studies of actual breaches.

Consequently, the instructional guide was further expanded to incorporate more lab-based exercises, recommendations to cover most of the emerging technologies requested, and the inclusion of case studies on data breaches to illustrate ethical and societal implications. However, while suggestions to include advanced topics like digital forensics and hybrid cloud configurations were considered, these were ultimately judged to fall outside the intended scope of foundational instruction.

4 The Document

4.1 Document Structure and Features

This CSEC 2017 supplement, approved by the ACM in January 2025, organizes the guidelines into knowledge areas. Each area is divided into topics. For every topic, there is a concise learning outcome summary that can help instructors or curriculum planners shape course objectives or module outlines. Each learning outcome is assigned a unique identifier to facilitate cross referencing throughout the curriculum.

The tables of learning outcomes also include references to the cross-cutting concepts. This approach highlights the shared principles that connect the knowledge areas. Many learning outcomes include a link to more detailed instructional guidance. Since the guidelines are intended for secondary schools, colleges, universities, and professional training, these additional materials clarify definitions, provide background information, and offer illustrative examples. Users of the guidelines can navigate through links between the concise outcomes and the more detailed supplementary guidance.

4.2 Knowledge Areas and Topics

The guidelines draw on CSEC 2017 but refine or merge topics where appropriate to maintain a foundational focus.

1. Data Security is divided into Access Control and Cryptography, followed by a broader view of data protection. Access Control and Cryptography covers authorization and encryption methods. Data Security is also a topic area focusing on protecting data in different states, such as at rest, in transit, or in use.
2. Network Security is organized into Network Architecture, Attacks, and Defense. Network Architecture introduces essential networking concepts, including the five-layer Internet model[2], routing, and standard protocols. Attacks examines the methods used to compromise networks, and Defense explores countermeasures and how they address the identified threats. A similar structure appears in Software Security and Societal Security when discussing attacks and defenses, so instructors can reinforce connections across these topics.
3. System Security includes Security Principles and System Controls and Lifecycle. Security Principles covers confidentiality, integrity, availability, trust, and defense in depth. System Controls and Lifecycle addresses how to design, build, and maintain systems with security as a central consideration. Access control also reappears here, but at a system level rather than a data level.
4. Software Security addresses fundamental ideas in secure software that focus on the software development lifecycle, common vulnerabilities, and defensive strategies. Attacks and defenses in software are introduced at a level appropriate for learners without programming experience. Topics include the nature of software weaknesses and awareness of frequent exploits, along with the basics of secure design practices.
5. Organizational Security concentrates on risk management and policy. This area explains how organizations address and mitigate security risks through formal processes and frameworks. A related topic is Governance, Law, and Policy, which overlaps with Societal Security but is approached here in terms of organizational structures, internal regulations, and practical enforcement.
6. Societal Security covers a broad set of fundamentals that frame cybersecurity in everyday life. Attacks in this context emphasize how adversaries affect people and institutions at a societal level. Ethics introduces principles of right and wrong behavior in cybersecurity, while Governance, Law, and Policy looks at major legal, regulatory, and policy considerations. Human Security, originally its own area in CSEC2017, is now part of Societal Security to underscore its close links with social and legal questions. Privacy is also highlighted, given the prominence of regulations such as the General Data Protection Regulation and recent updates to NIST guidelines.

[2] This is the same as the four layer model, with a physical layer added.

4.3 Sequencing and Pacing

Because the foundational topics are extensive, the guidelines recommend splitting them into a two course sequence called Cybersecurity I and Cybersecurity II. Cybersecurity I should begin with security principles and ethics, followed by technical foundations in topics like cryptography and access control. This prepares learners for deeper exploration of topics for attacks and defenses.

Cybersecurity II, as proposed in the guideline, focuses on conceptual foundations and covers topics such as attacks, defenses, data security, and risk management. It then transitions into broader societal themes, including law, policy, and ethics. The course sequence is designed to respect dependencies between foundational topics. For instance, understanding data security builds on knowledge of cryptography and network security, while all topics rely on core security principles such as confidentiality, integrity, and availability. This structured progression ensures that learners develop a strong technical foundation in Cybersecurity I, enabling them to apply that knowledge effectively to more complex and abstract topics in Cybersecurity II.

The guidelines propose weekly segment recommendations for both secondary and post-secondary institutions using a credit hour system in which one unit of credit represents approximately three hours of academic work per week over a 15-week semester [11]. Consequently, a three-credit-hour course translates to about nine hours of combined in-class and out-of-class instruction each week. The guidelines also include a breakdown of these weekly instructional hours by topic and estimates the number of hours based on the quantity and complexity of specific learning outcomes. For instance, the security principles topic comprises seven learning outcomes and is projected to require about three weeks of instruction in the credit hour system, compared to six weeks at the secondary level. In general, the estimated instructional hours are doubled for secondary schools to compensate for the additional holidays, attendance mandates, and testing requirements that reduce total classroom time. In fact, one study suggests that only around half of the available time in secondary schools is used for direct in-class instruction [7]. Altogether, the guidelines recommend approximately 28 instructional hours over a 15-week semester in the credit hour system. When exam periods are factored in, this aligns with the full 30-week duration of two three-credit-hour courses commonly offered at post-secondary institutions.

Finally, while these courses do not require prerequisites, secondary schools may have the opportunity to develop preparatory pathways leading to dual-credit or concurrent-credit cybersecurity courses. Likewise, the guidelines map topic areas to the Computer Science Curricula 2023 knowledge areas [9]. For instance, cryptography benefits from foundational knowledge in mathematics and statistics, such as sets, relations, and modular arithmetic. Although these are not required prerequisites, students with prior exposure to these topics are likely to benefit significantly.

5 Examples

The foundational learning outcomes are organized by knowledge areas, aligned with the CSEC 2017 structure, and then by topics to facilitate curriculum development. Topics have a summary learning outcome, suitable for course syllabi, while the core instructional focus is detailed through component learning outcomes, each labeled with unique IDs for easy reference. Most component learning outcomes link to corresponding guidance statements in the Instructional Guidance section, with the electronic version enabling seamless navigation between guidance and outcomes. These guidelines support educators and curriculum developers by ensuring consistent terminology, increasing awareness of reference materials, and highlighting cross-cutting concepts that connect themes across knowledge and topic areas.

The following uses Data Security as an example to illustrate the structure of the knowledge area and its corresponding instructional guidance. Similarly, other knowledge areas—such as Network Security, System Security, Software Security, Organizational Security, and Societal Security—are outlined in the same manner.
Data Security (*Knowledge Area*) Cryptography (*Topic*)
Learning Outcome Summary: Understand and apply the fundamental principles of cryptography to ensure the confidentiality, integrity, availability, and non-repudiation of data, while recognizing and utilizing cryptographic methods and secure protocols in practical scenarios. (*Summary Learning Outcome*)

ID	Component Learning Outcomes	Cross-Cutting Concepts
DS1	Explain cryptography including its relationship to confidentiality, integrity, and availability of data. [Guidance]	CIA
DS2	Encrypt a small data set using a simple encryption algorithm. [Guidance]	CIA
DS3	Describe basic cryptography terms, including ciphers, cryptographic keys, encrypt, decrypt, cryptanalysis, cryptographic hashing, non-repudiation, and cryptology. [Guidance]	CIA
DS4	Use symmetric ciphers with a shared secret key to transform plaintext to ciphertext. [Guidance]	CIA
DS5	Use asymmetric ciphers with a public key to transform plaintext to ciphertext. [Guidance]	CIA
DS6	Use cryptographic hash functions to create one-way transformations that convert data of arbitrary length into fixed-length hash values. [Guidance]	CIA
DS7	Recognize secure protocols, like HTTPS and SSH, which use cryptography to protect communication. [Guidance]	CIA, Systems thinking, Adversarial thinking
DS8	Recognize the critical role of key management and public key infrastructure (PKI) for ensuring the secure generation, distribution, and storage of cryptographic keys. [Guidance]	CIA, Systems thinking

Access Control (*Topic*)
Learning Outcome Summary: Understand and differentiate key access control models and terminologies, and explain how identification, authentication, and authorization work together to enforce effective access control mechanisms in various organizational contexts. (*Example Summary Learning Outcome*)

ID	Component Learning Outcomes	Cross-Cutting Concepts
DS9	Differentiate between identification, authentication, and access authorization of people and devices. [Guidance]	CIA, Systems thinking, Adversarial thinking
DS10	Articulate the basic differences between the following forms of access control: Discretionary Access Control (DAC), Mandatory Access Control (MAC), and Role-Based Access Control (RBAC). [Guidance]	CIA, Systems thinking

ID	Component Learning Outcomes	Cross-Cutting Concepts
DS11	Summarize the different states of data (data-at-rest, data-in-motion, and data-in-use) and the mechanisms used to secure each. [Guidance]	Systems thinking

Data Security (*Topic*)

Example Instructional Guidance for Data Security

Unless otherwise specified, all definitions come from the NICCS Glossary of Common Cybersecurity Words and Phrases [4].

LO	Guidance
DS1	Please see SS1 for definitions of confidentiality, integrity, and availability. The McCumber Cube and CIA Triad could be used to facilitate the explanation. The E-MATE 2.0 has an interactive lesson about "The McCumber Cube and CIA Triad" here: https://www.ncyte.net/faculty/cybersecurity-curriculum/college-curriculum/interactive-lessons/the-mccumber-cube-and-cia-triad To provide additional context, the MITRE ATT&CK framework[a] enumerates specific threats and impacts to data security within the Impact tactic. These include threats such as data destruction, manipulation, theft, and corruption. Each of these threats directly aligns with potential losses in confidentiality, integrity, or availability, which reinforces the need for cryptography as countermeasures to these threats. Add hands-on exercise: encrypting a word or message using a very simple encryption algorithm. Similarly, students can decrypt a small encrypted data set.
DS2	The E-MATE 2.0 has an interactive lesson about "Cryptography" here, which can be helpful: https://www.ncyte.net/faculty/cybersecurity-curriculum/college-curriculum/interactive-lessons/cryptography
DS3	Add hands-on applications to help learners with this challenging concept. **Cipher** refers to cryptographic algorithm, a well-defined computational procedure that takes variable inputs, including a cryptographic key, and produces an output. Cryptographic keys include symmetric key, public key, private key. **Encrypt** refers to the process of transforming plaintext into ciphertext. **Decrypt** refers to the process of transforming ciphertext into its original plaintext. **Cryptanalysis** refers to the operations performed in defeating or circumventing cryptographic protection of information by applying mathematical techniques and without an initial knowledge of the key employed in providing the protection. **Cryptographic hashing** refers to a process of applying a mathematical algorithm against a set of data to produce a numeric value (a hash value) that represents the data. **Non-repudiation** refers to a property achieved through cryptographic methods to protect against an individual or entity falsely denying having performed a particular action related to data. **Cryptology** refers to the mathematical science that deals with cryptanalysis and cryptography.
DS4	Add hands-on exercise: encrypting a word or message using a symmetric encryption algorithm, such as a DES or AES algorithm.

continued

LO	Guidance
DS5	Add hands-on exercise: encrypting a word or message using an asymmetric encryption algorithm, such as an RSA algorithm. The exercise includes the generation of an RSA key pair (i.e., public key and private key), followed by RSA encryption and decryption based on them. A recommended resource for further understanding is the NIST Hash Functions Project[b], which provides guidance on secure algorithms robust enough for use in modern systems. While detailed knowledge of specific algorithms is not required at this foundational level, understanding the concept of secure hashing is essential. To reinforce learning, students can experiment with Python scripts to generate cryptographic hash values and explore real-world examples, such as hashing in blockchain or cryptocurrencies.
DS7	Explain that HTTPS and SSH use cryptography to protect communications. Add hands on exercise: use wireshark to observe encrypted vs. unencrypted traffic.
DS8	Present a case study on the DigiNotar PKI failure, illustrating how poor key management led to a major security breach. Have students engage in a role-play exercise to simulate setting up a PKI, where they act as a Certificate Authority (CA), generate keys, and issue certificates, reinforcing the key components of secure key management.
DS9	**Identities** refer to who or what is requesting access. Credentials refer to the information used to prove identity. **Authentication** refers to the process of verifying the identity or other attributes of an entity (user, process, or device). **Authorization** refers to a process of determining, by evaluating applicable access control information, whether a subject is allowed to have the specified types of access to a particular resource. Controls for these can be physical as well. Examples: physical ID validation, visitor control, door locks, warning signs.
DS10	Cover the existence of DAC and MAC access control models. Describe **Discretionary Access Control (DAC)** as a form of access control where the owner of the resource determines access. Include instructional guidance on applying access control methodologies. Describe **Mandatory Access Control (MAC)** as a form of access control where access is governed by a centralized authority based on predefined rules. Describe **Role-Based Access Control (RBAC)** as a form of access control that restricts access based on the roles and responsibilities within an organization.
	The states of data include the following: – Data-at-rest refers to data stored on devices or systems that are not actively accessed or transferred, such as information on hard drives, databases, or flash drives. Example mechanisms used to secure data-at-rest: encryption, access control. Data-in-motion refers to data traveling between devices or networks, including information sent via web browsing, file transfer, email communication, or instant messaging. Example mechanisms used to secure data-in-motion: HTTPS, VPN. – Data-in-use refers to data that is actively accessed, processed, or read by a user or software, such as data retrieved and processed during a SQL query. Example mechanisms used to secure data-in-use: memory encryption, sandboxing, access control, and masking. Anonymization techniques enhance confidentiality and privacy across all states of data by removing or obscuring personally identifiable information (PII) and sensitive attributes. These techniques ensure that even if data is accessed, it cannot be attributed to specific individuals or entities.

[a] https://attack.mitre.org

[b] https://csrc.nist.rip/projects/hash-functions

6 Implementation

The CSEC 2017 update is already being used in the U.S. by an initiative called NCTAC (National Cybersecurity Teaching Academy and Coalition). NCTA was launched in 2021 with funding from NSA/NCAE-C to DePaul University, the University of Arkansas Little Rock (UALR), the University of Louisville, and DARK Enterprises. California State University-Sacramento joined in 2022 with additional NSA/NCAE-C support. These four universities developed and offer a graduate certificate to high school teachers that prepares them for teaching cybersecurity courses. The NCTA goals are:

1. increase teachers' cybersecurity content knowledge (teachers cannot teach what they do not know);

2. expand national capacity for dual credit in cybersecurity; and
3. enhance the quality of high school cybersecurity courses.

The graduate certificate initially included 12-credit hours and expanded to 18-credit hours to support dual enrollment requirements. To date, 64 teachers matriculated in 2022 and have completed the graduate certificate, 20 matriculated in 2023 and will graduate in summer 2025, and 38 teachers matriculated in summer 2024 and will graduate in summer 2026.

In 2024 the NCTA coalition expanded to include Dakota State University, the University of Arizona, the University of Maryland Global Campus, and Worcester Polytechnic Institute and formed the National Cybersecurity Teaching Coalition (NCTC). NCTC will continue to offer NCTA graduate certificates with 175 scholarships available in 2025 and another 175 scholarships in 2026.

An eight-credit course based on the CSEC Supplement will be implemented in the 2025–2026 academic year at four high schools in Arkansas and at the University of Arkansas at Little Rock. This implementation will pilot test the application of the CSEC Supplement for dual credit in the United States. In addition, the new cohort of NCTA teacher scholars will learn the foundations of cybersecurity expressed in the CSEC supplement in summer 2025 so that NCTAC can launch additional dual credit cybersecurity courses in the 2026–2027 academic year.

7 Conclusion

Building educational opportunities in cybersecurity is important to developing a sustainable supply chain of cybersecurity talent. The United States educational system has focused on expanding post-secondary educational programs over the past 25 or more years. As cybersecurity has matured into a discipline, this expansion included not only more programs, but growth in the types of programs. Specifically, cybersecurity is now found 1) in a variety of disciplines, such as computer science, computer engineering, information systems, information technology and business, and 2 at a variety of levels, such as baccalaureate, associate, and now secondary. The growth is exciting but also presents challenges in that there are no clear pathways for students to follow across disciplines and levels. The updated CSEC 2017 guidelines that specify the foundations of cybersecurity are well-poised to support educational pathways in the U.S.

Acknowledgments. This work was supported by an award from the ACM. Any opinions, findings, and conclusions or recommendations expressed in this material are those of the author(s) and do not necessarily reflect the views of the ACM or any other organization.

Disclosure of Interests. The authors have no competing interests to declare that are relevant to the content of this article.

References

1. ACM Committee for Computing Education in Community Colleges (CCECC): Bloom's for Computing: Enhancing Bloom's Revised Taxonomy with Verbs for Computing Disciplines. ACM, New York, NY, USA, August 2023. https://doi.org/10.1145/3587276
2. ACM Task Group: Supplement to CSEC 2017: foundational cybersecurity content and instructional guidance for secondary and postsecondary cybersecurity education. Technical report. ACM, New York, NY, USA, January 2025
3. ACM/IEEE-CS/AIS SIGSEC/IFIP WG 11.8 Joint Task Force: Cybersecurity curricula 2017: Curriculum guidelines for undergraduate degree programs in cybersecurity. Technical report, Version 1.0. ACM, New York, NY, USA, December 2017. https://doi.org/10.1145/3184594
4. National Initiative for Cybersecurity Careers and Studies: Explore terms: a glossary of common cybersecurity words and phrases, April 2024. https://niccs.cisa.gov/cybersecurity-career-resources/vocabulary
5. Dark, M., Daugherty, J.: E3C: a report of early college cybersecurity credit. Technical report, Dark Enterprises, Inc., West Lafayette, IN, USA, May 2024. https://teachcyber.org/e3c/
6. Dark, M., et al.: Cybersecurity education: availability & access in public high schools, December 2023. https://cybersupply.org/
7. Fisher, D.: The use of instructional time in the typical high school classroom. Educ. Forum **73**(2), 168–176 (2009). https://doi.org/10.1080/00131720902739650
8. Gartner, I.: Forecast: public cloud services, worldwide, 2022-2028, 2q24 update. Technical report 5541595, Gartner Research, June 2024. https://www.gartner.com/en/documents/5541595
9. Kumar, A.N., et al.: Computer Science Curricula 2023. ACM, New York, NY, USA, January 2024. https://doi.org/10.1145/3664191
10. Statista: Artificial intelligence (2023). https://www.statista.com/outlook/tmo/artificial-intelligence/worldwide
11. Wolanin, T.R.: The student credit hour: an international exploration. New Dir. High. Educ. **2003**(122), 99–117 (2003). https://doi.org/10.1002/he.113
12. Tims, J.L., Tucker, C.S., Weiss, M.A., Zweben, S.H.: Student enrollment and retention in 2022-23 U.S. undergraduate computing programs. ACM Inroads **15**(4), 20–46 (2024). https://doi.org/10.1145/3700774

Gamification in Cybersecurity Education

Loss Aversion and Fixed Reward in Gamified Cyber Security Training

Nicole Carle[1], Jacques Ophoff[1,2(✉)], and Lynsay Shepherd[1]

[1] Abertay University, Dundee, UK
{1902468,j.ophoff,lynsay.shepherd}@abertay.ac.uk
[2] University of Cape Town, Cape Town, South Africa

Abstract. Cyber threats continue to evolve yet research indicates that existing cyber security training programmes are often ineffective, leaving users feeling discouraged rather than empowered. As a result, there is a pressing need to redesign these programmes to enhance both engagement and learning outcomes. This study investigates the impact of two points-based gamification mechanisms, loss aversion (LA) and fixed reward (FR), on cyber security knowledge and user engagement. We developed two gamified web applications to implement LA or FR respectively, while incorporating identical core content alongside additional gamification elements, such as scenario-based learning and exploration. A total of 27 participants completed the training and evaluated the applications through an initial and end cyber security knowledge assessment, and a user engagement survey. Findings indicate that while LA was more effective in improving cyber security knowledge, FR received higher scores for user engagement. These results suggest that both LA and FR offer distinct advantages, with suitability depending on the specific training context.

Keywords: Gamification · Cyber Security Training · SETA · Loss Aversion · Fixed Reward

1 Introduction

While many workplaces provide cyber security awareness training, its delivery is often perceived as monotonous and overwhelming [1]. Employees frequently regard such training as a burdensome obligation rather than a valuable learning opportunity. Recent studies examining employee perspectives on security, education, training, and awareness (SETA) programmes indicate widespread dissatisfaction with both the content and instructional methods. These programmes are commonly criticised for adopting a one-size-fits-all approach that fails to present information in a relatable or memorable manner [2–4].

While technological measures (e.g., packet-filtering firewalls and intrusion detection systems) can enhance cyber security, training for end-users remains a critical component. In 2021, global expenditures on SETA materials and related security products were

Published by Springer Nature Switzerland AG 2026
L. Drevin et al. (Eds.): WISE 2025, IFIP AICT 742, pp. 109–123, 2026.
https://doi.org/10.1007/978-3-031-94924-1_8

estimated to exceed $1tn [3]. However, given widespread dissatisfaction with traditional SETA methods and their limited effectiveness, the value of this investment might be questioned, prompting an exploration of alternative training approaches.

Despite the availability of numerous cyber security training programmes, many adopt a standardised format that may not align with the needs of diverse audiences, potentially reducing their effectiveness in fostering essential security skills [1]. To address these limitations, gamified training methods have been introduced and trialled. Research, particularly in the context of phishing awareness, has demonstrated positive participant feedback, highlighting increased engagement and enjoyment while also enhancing vigilance. Various gamification techniques have been successfully implemented, including role play [5], level progression [6], feedback, and exploration-based training [7]. These studies have yielded promising results, suggesting that further refinement of gamified training should be pursued.

This study extends prior work by incorporating the psychological concept of loss aversion (LA) [8] and gamification mechanic of fixed reward (FR) in a gamified SETA context. LA is a psychological bias where "changes for the worse (losses) loom larger than equivalent changes for the better" [9, p. 119]. An FR is given to users upon completion of predefined actions, which reinforces progression and achievement [10]. While both approaches may be used to enhance engagement within SETA programmes, their relative effectiveness and suitability remain uncertain. We pose the following research question: *How do loss aversion and fixed reward compare in terms of their effectiveness in enhancing cyber security knowledge and their impact on user engagement in gamified training?*

To address this research question, the paper first presents a literature review to examine how LA and FR can be effectively integrated into cyber security training. It then details the development of two cyber security training web applications – one incorporating LA and the other using FR. Through an experimental approach, the study evaluates the impact of each technique. The findings suggest that while both approaches are effective, their suitability varies depending on the specific training context. Since statistical significance is not demonstrated for all tests, further evaluation with a larger number of participants is recommended.

2 Background

Gamification is a technique which involves adding a game element to an application where it is otherwise unnecessary. If the game element were to be removed the underlying application would still be able to function independently. Although points, badges, and leaderboards are the most well-known game elements many others have been proposed [e.g., 11]. In this context both LA and FR extend the points element to provide feedback to the user.

2.1 Loss Aversion

One of the primary challenges associated with implementing LA in training environments is managing the psychological impact of the 'loom' or 'aversion factor'. If participants do not perceive a potential loss as more significant than a potential gain, the aversion factor fails to exert its intended influence [12, 13]. Conversely, excessive pressure associated with potential losses can lead to a phenomenon known as decision paralysis, in which individuals become so overwhelmed that they are unable to act [14].

Although commonly examined in psychological research, the aversion factor also influences real-world cyber security behaviours. For example, a study conducted in Indonesia found that high-income individuals were more likely to enable two-factor authentication (2FA) for their bank accounts than lower-income individuals. This disparity arose because high earners perceived a greater potential loss in the event of a security breach, whereas lower-income individuals felt that the inconvenience of 2FA was not justified by their perceived level of risk [15].

The impact of LA on decision-making has also been observed in gambling-related studies. Research measuring response times found that individuals making high-risk decisions with low confidence exhibited the slowest response times, whereas those with higher confidence responded more quickly. One potential method to mitigate decision paralysis is to introduce time constraints that limit the duration of a task, thereby preventing excessive deliberation. However, findings suggest that time pressure in LA-based scenarios may reduce the emotional impact of loss [16]. In the context of cyber security training, prolonged response times could indicate deeper engagement with the material, leading to more thorough information processing.

Overall, when supported by additional mechanisms to enhance the aversion factor, LA has the potential to be an effective tool for motivating users and encouraging careful consideration of cyber security-related decisions. However, its implementation must be carefully designed to avoid overwhelming users, as excessive information or complex decision-making processes may trigger decision paralysis and undermine the effectiveness of the training.

2.2 Fixed Reward

Numerous studies on gamification in cyber security have incorporated FR mechanics in some form. However, the use of FR elements such as points, badges, and leaderboards has been critiqued as an overused approach [17]. To address this, researchers frequently combine FR with additional techniques to enhance engagement and effectiveness.

One early example is 'Anti-Phishing Phil', a game developed in 2007 that integrated FR alongside level progression [6]. In this game, users earned points by correctly distinguishing between legitimate and phishing URLs. To reinforce learning, users were required to replay a level if they did not meet the minimum required score. This design ensured that participants developed sufficient phishing identification skills before advancing to more challenging examples. A later study compared Anti-Phishing Phil to embedded training and email notices [2]. The embedded training approach provided users with phishing-related education during routine email interactions. Although this method had previously been shown to be more effective than email notices, the game-based training group demonstrated superior performance when assessed on their ability to recognise phishing websites.

More recently, the effectiveness of context-based micro-training (CBMT) was evaluated in comparison to game-based training [7]. The study utilised an existing phishing training tool provided by Google, in which users received a point for each correctly identified phishing attempt, with a final tally displayed at the end. While game-based training improved user behaviour in interactions with phishing emails, only CBMT led to improved classification of emails as legitimate or phishing attempts. The authors speculated that this was due to CBMT's 'awareness-increasing mechanism'. They concluded that an optimal training approach might combine CBMT with game-based elements. However, it could be argued that CBMT had an inherent advantage in this comparison, as it was specifically developed for training, whereas the game-based tool was pre-existing. This argument is further supported by findings that generic SETA programmes are less effective than those intentionally designed for a specific purpose.

2.3 Additional Gamification Elements

While this study primarily compares the consequences of using LA and FR in gamified cyber security training, it also incorporates additional elements from Marczewski's [18] 'Periodic Table of Gamification Elements' to mitigate motivational burnout associated with the points, badges, and leaderboards fallacy [17]. These elements include:

- Narrative: Scenario-based learning (SBL) has been shown to enhance engagement and learning outcomes in gamified environments. By embedding training within a narrative, users can better relate to the material, particularly in areas they may initially perceive as irrelevant to their own experiences [1, 19]. This approach helps maintain engagement and encourages deeper learning.
- Exploration: Providing users with opportunities to investigate and interact with content has been found to positively impact learning [20]. For example, phishing awareness training that allows users to actively explore emails (e.g., by revealing hidden information like the true destination of links) reinforces critical thinking. By linking exploratory actions to consequences, exploration-based training strengthens the message of exercising caution in potentially risky situations.
- Feedback mechanism: The timing and quality of feedback are crucial in shaping user behaviour. Immediate and detailed feedback is essential for correcting mistakes, as it enables users to quickly associate errors with the appropriate corrective action [21]. However, feedback must be carefully designed to strike a balance between guidance and autonomy. It should be detailed enough to direct users toward the correct response without being discouraging or overwhelming, as excessive feedback could reduce exploratory behaviour and engagement [20].

3 Methodology

This study followed a design science research (DSR) paradigm where an artefact is created to solve a real-world problem [22]. A software instantiation was produced as artefact [23] and its design and development are described in Sects. 3.1 and 3.2. We evaluated the artefact using a quick and simple strategy [24] which considers efficacy, in the form of cyber security knowledge, and user engagement properties. The summative evaluation metrics are described in Sect. 3.3.

Following the DSR paradigm two web-based applications (hereafter referred to as apps) designed for gamified cyber security training were developed. While both apps featured similar educational content, they differed in their scoring mechanisms and implementation of either LA or FR. These apps were database-driven and developed using JavaScript, Ajax, HTML5, PHP, and SQL. The following sections will provide an overview of the educational content, differences in gamification, and evaluation approach.

3.1 Content and Design

To achieve a balance between breadth and depth, key cyber security issues were identified, including account security (passwords), social engineering, website security, and malicious software (malware). As a result, the content of the apps focused on these topics. While some elements included widely recognised security practices (e.g., avoiding the opening of suspicious files from unknown senders), all educational material was grounded in recent guidance from authoritative government institutions such as CISA, NCSC, and NIST to enhance credibility and trust.

Each app featured interactive sections dedicated to these cyber security topics, drawing on insights from previous studies and real-world scenarios. Since SBL has been found to be particularly effective [e.g., 5], users assumed the role of a character named Alex, a newly hired security employee. Although the project was not specifically designed for IT professionals, this storyline enabled the inclusion of a wide range of cyber security topics that might otherwise be perceived as irrelevant. This approach aimed to mitigate the issue of user disengagement due to a lack of perceived relevance [19]. Alex's storyline was developed to ensure that the learning experience was purposeful and effectively conveyed key cyber security concepts.

To maintain clarity and accessibility, each section was designed to be informative without overwhelming the user. Efforts were made to present information concisely, utilising bullet points whenever possible. Additionally, key terms and critical information (e.g., an example of a strong passphrase) were highlighted in bold red text. The use of such visual cues has been shown to enhance SETA initiatives [25].

Passwords. This section introduced Alex's scenario and provided an accessible introduction to cyber security concepts (see Fig. 1). As part of the interactive component, users were required to create a strong password for a new account. While this section incorporated the NCSCs recommendation of using passphrases, it also aligned with common password requirements, which typically mandate the inclusion of at least one uppercase letter, one number, and one symbol. To enhance security further, an AJAX-based check was implemented to compare the user-entered password against a database of commonly compromised passwords.[1] If a match was detected, the password was classified as weak, regardless of whether it satisfied other complexity requirements.

Social Engineering. This section incorporated a phishing inbox simulator to allow users to apply their knowledge and reinforce key cyber security concepts (see Fig. 2). The design of this simulator was informed by existing online training examples,[2,3] and

[1] https://github.com/danielmiessler/SecLists.

[2] https://g.co/phishingquiz.

[3] https://www.phishingbox.com/.

findings from previous studies [2, 7]. Users were required to assess whether emails sent to Alex were legitimate or phishing attempts. The phishing emails included real-world examples as well as those sourced from phishing awareness training platforms. The simulation closely mirrored the experience of interacting with a real email inbox. If a user made an incorrect selection, an alert box provided immediate feedback, highlighting the error and indicating specific details they had overlooked. After reviewing all emails, users were given the option to upload their score to a leaderboard. If they chose to participate, they were assigned a user number and shown the leaderboard, which was unique to each application. Alternatively, if they opted not to upload their score, they were simply presented with their result.

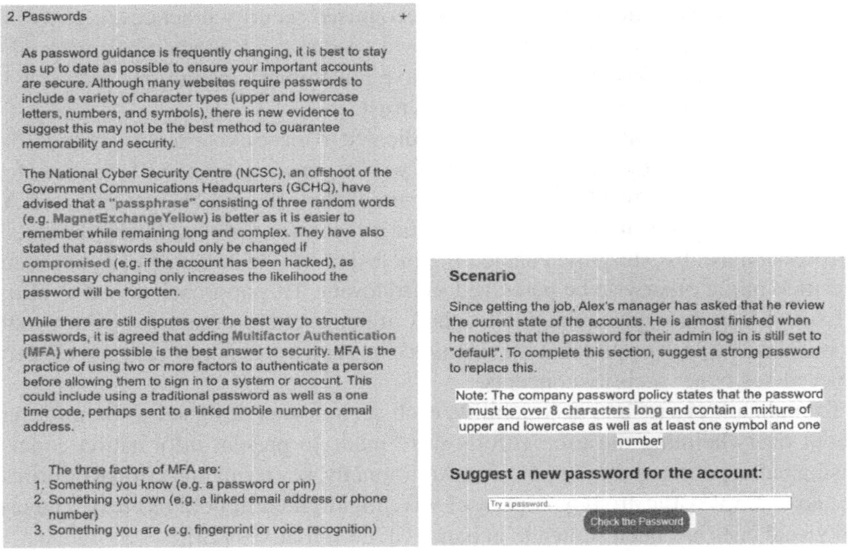

Fig. 1. Passwords training (left) and scenario (right)

Website Security. This section provided users with information on the risks associated with man-in-the-middle attacks and fraudulent schemes (see Fig. 3). It was included due to the prevalence of social engineering scams, particularly phishing and smishing, which often direct users to counterfeit websites. To engage users, the section featured a video depicting Alex's experience, followed by a quiz assessing their understanding of the content. The video's narrative centred on Alex attempting to purchase a discounted smartphone, ultimately falling victim to a scam. The product description featured in the video was initially generated using ChatGPT[4] with the prompt, *"Generate a product description for the iPhone 15"*. It was then modified to include intentional misspellings, making the fraudulent website's poor design more apparent. Upon completing the quiz, users received their result, along with a review of any incorrect answers and their corresponding explanations.

[4] https://chatgpt.com/.

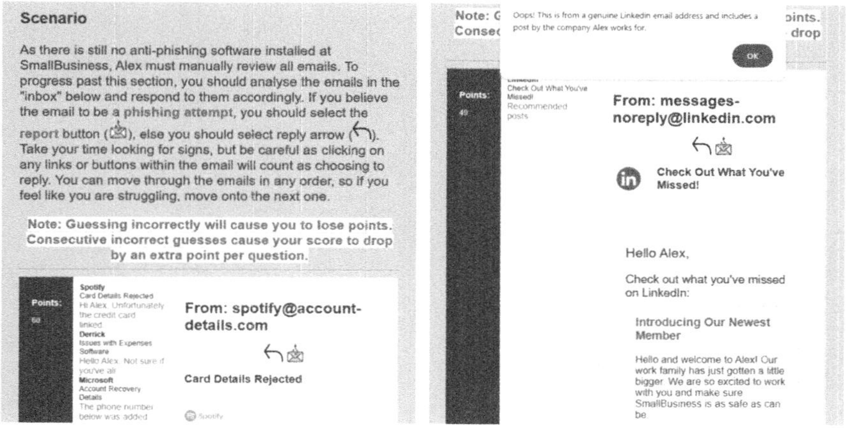

Fig. 2. Social engineering scenario (left) and feedback alert (right)

Malicious Software. This section introduced more detailed cyber security concepts while attempting to maintain accessibility for users without technical expertise (see Fig. 4). The gamified element followed a structure like the phishing inbox simulation but focused on Alex assisting colleagues in resolving malware-related issues. To progress through the scenario, users were required to identify both the type of malware and the appropriate solution. Upon making a correct selection, Alex would 'type' a response to the colleague, providing a detailed explanation of the issue and its resolution. This response was displayed gradually to ensure users had sufficient time to read and absorb the information. Given that malware-related threats were likely less familiar to users, a limit was placed on the number of attempts allowed before the correct answer was revealed. In both versions of the app, users were permitted up to three guesses before the correct response was displayed. This approach aimed to minimise frustration while ensuring that users still received the relevant educational content.

3.2 Implementation of Gamification, LA, and FR

Both apps incorporated a points-based system and leaderboard to enhance engagement through gamification. The implementation of LA and FR involved a custom scoring mechanism for two of the topics.

- Social engineering scenario: In the LA version, users lost 10 points for each incorrect answer, whereas in the FR version no points were deducted for incorrect answers. Additionally, in the FR version, users who answered multiple questions correctly in succession triggered a streak bonus, earning an extra point for each consecutive correct answer, with a maximum possible score of 60. Conversely, in the LA version, consecutive incorrect answers also triggered a streak mechanism, but in this case, the penalty increased by one additional point for each successive mistake.
- Malware scenario: In the LA version, users began with the maximum available points and lost one point for every incorrect guess. This score was displayed in the sidebar,

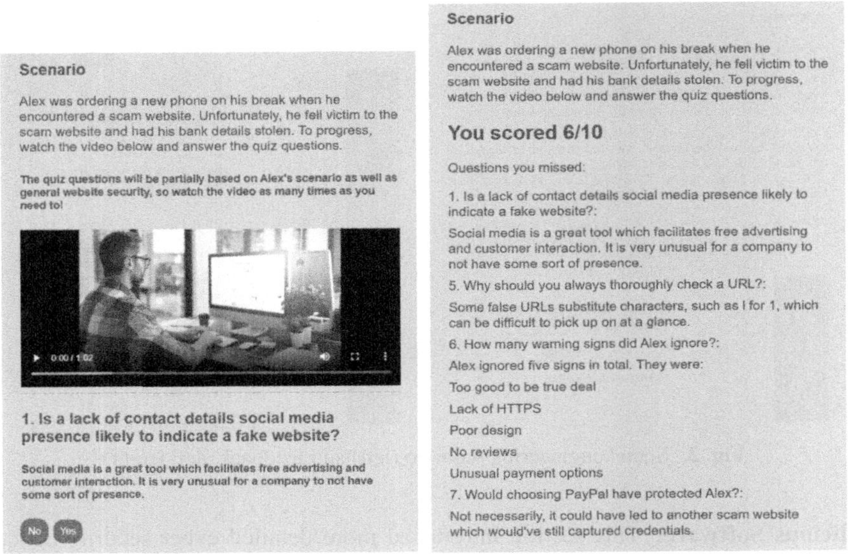

Fig. 3. Website security scenario (left) and quiz feedback (right)

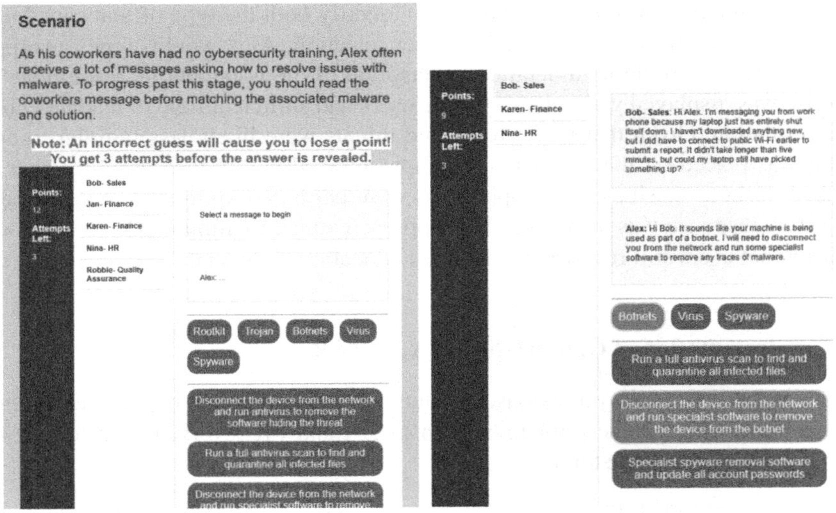

Fig. 4. Malicious software scenario (left) and feedback message (right)

allowing users to see their points decrease, which was intended to encourage more careful examination of the provided information. To prevent users from selecting the same incorrect answer multiple times, previously selected options were visually distinguished with an orange outline. In contrast, the FR version rewarded users with three points for a correct answer on their first attempt, with the score decreasing by one point for each subsequent incorrect attempt. This approach incentivised users to answer accurately on their first attempt. If a user failed to provide the correct answer within the allowed number of attempts, no points were awarded.

The implementation of LA and FR were restricted to these topics since they required the most cognitive effort and interaction. The instructions displayed to the user are shown in Table 1.

Table 1. LA vs FR messages

Topic	Loss Aversion (LA)	Fixed Reward (FR)
Passwords	-	-
Social Engineering	Guessing incorrectly will cause you to lose points. Consecutive incorrect guesses cause your score to drop by an extra point per question. (Starting points = 60)	Answering multiple emails correctly in a row will result in a streak, which will increase your score by an extra point for each consecutive correct answer. (Starting points = 0)
Website Security	-	-
Malicious Software	An incorrect guess will cause you to lose a point! You get 3 attempts before the answer is revealed. (Starting points = 12)	You have 3 attempts to match each message with the correct malware and resolution before the answer is revealed. Getting the answer correct on the first attempt will reward 3 points, second attempt 2 points, and third attempt 1 point. (Starting points = 0)

3.3 Evaluation

To evaluate the apps an experimental survey approach was chosen. A convenience sampling method was used to recruit participants through personal contacts and social media. All participants were over the age of 18 and resided in the UK. A total of 27 participants were randomly assigned to either the LA-based app (n = 13) or FR-based app (n = 14). The evaluation process consisted of three stages: 1) an initial cyber security knowledge survey, 2) completion of the app-based training, and 3) an end cyber security knowledge and user engagement survey. Ethical approval for the study was granted by the Abertay University Ethics Committee (EMS8940).

Cyber Security Knowledge. Consistent with prior research, the study assessed participants' cyber security knowledge before and after training to assess learning [5–8, 21]. Both surveys covered all training topics, with two questions per topic, resulting in a total of eight questions per survey. Each question presented multiple answer choices, requiring participants to select the correct response. For example, one question asked: *"Which password is stronger?"* with the answer options: *Password1234/P@5swOrd!/BlueFishSwim.*

User Engagement. This was assessed using the short-form user engagement scale (UES-SF) [26], which evaluates four key dimensions: focused attention (FA), perceived usability (PU), aesthetic appeal (AE), and reward (RW). Each category contained three questions measured on a five-point Likert scale, resulting in a total of 12 questions. The recommended approach was followed to calculate an overall engagement score. Additionally, optional open-ended questions were included to allow participants to provide qualitative feedback if desired.

4 Analysis and Results

This section will start by presenting the cyber security learning results, followed by the user engagement results. Since no demographic data were collected, the results are limited to the survey responses.

4.1 Cyber Security Learning

LA Group. In the initial knowledge assessment, there was an average of 3.31 correct answers, ranging from 2–6 correct answers per participant. Overall, the group answered 41.35% (43/104) of the questions correctly. Following the training the end knowledge assessment showed an improvement, with an average of 5.38 correct answers, ranging from 3–7 correct answers per participant. Overall, the group answered 66.35% (69/104) of the questions correctly. A comparison of correct answers per topic area is shown in Fig. 5.

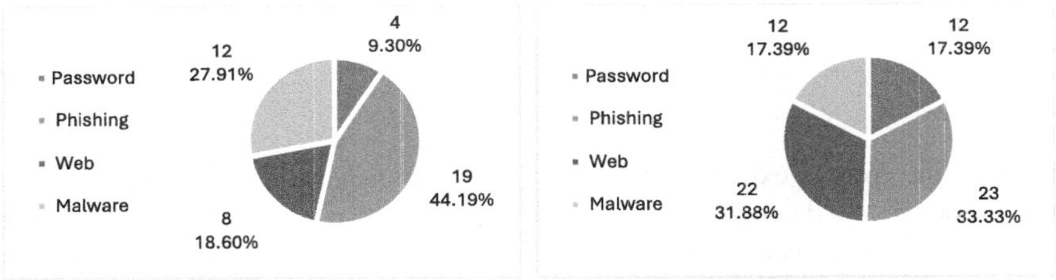

Fig. 5. LA group initial (left) vs end (right) knowledge by topic

A significant overall improvement of knowledge was observed (paired samples *t*-test; $t(12) = 4.999$, $p < .001$). An improvement was evident for the passwords, social engineering, and website security topics.

FR Group. In the initial knowledge assessment, there was an average of 4.07 correct answers, ranging from 3–6 correct answers per participant. Overall, the group answered 42.86% (58/112) of the questions correctly. Following the training the end knowledge assessment showed an improvement, with an average of 5.5 correct answers, ranging from 4–7 correct answers per participant. Overall, the group answered 68.75% (77/112) of the questions correctly. A comparison of correct answers per topic area is shown in Fig. 6.

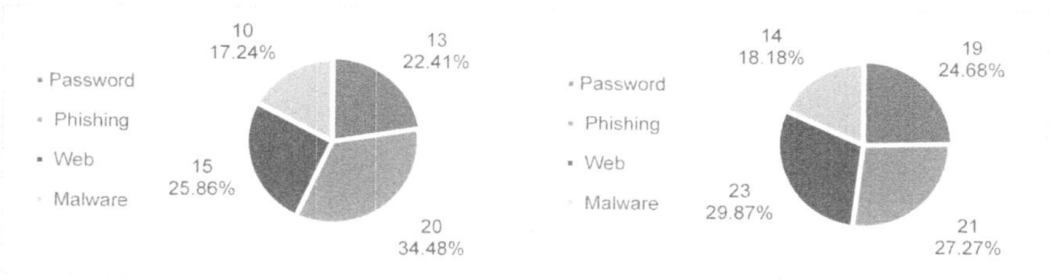

Fig. 6. FR group initial (left) vs end (right) knowledge by topic

A significant overall improvement of knowledge was observed (paired samples t-test; $t(13) = 4.372$, $p < .001$). An improvement was evident across all topics.

4.2 User Engagement

LA Group. An overall UES-SF score was calculated across 12 participants, showing an average score of 3.7 (there was one missing response). The scores per category are shown in Fig. 7 (left). An additional comment made by a participant is *"I found it interesting and learned some new information. It highlighted how little I know about cyber security."*

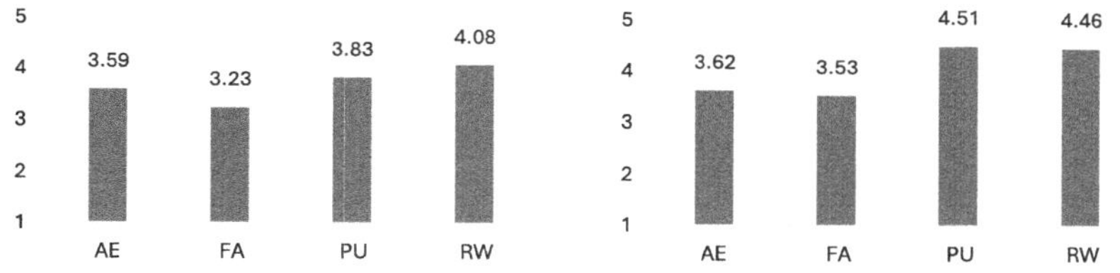

Fig. 7. User engagement by category for LA group (left) and FR group (right)

FR Group. An overall UES-SF score was calculated across all participants, showing an average score of 4.05. The scores per category are shown in Fig. 7 (right). An additional comment made by a participant is *"It just showed me how much I did not know."*

4.3 Group Comparisons

A comparison of overall cyber security knowledge improvement between the LA and FR groups revealed no statistically significant difference (independent samples t-test; $t(25) = 1.236$, $p = 0.228$). This result is further illustrated by the boxplot in Fig. 8 (left), which depicts the average improvement in correct scores, with groups coded as LA (0) and FR (1).

Similarly, there was no significant difference in user engagement between the two groups (independent samples t-test; $t(6) = -1.087$, $p = 0.319$). This outcome is visualised in the boxplot of average user engagement scores presented in Fig. 8 (right).

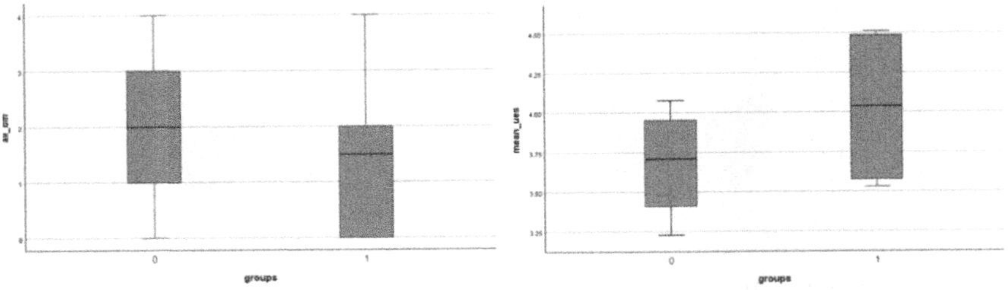

Fig. 8. Boxplots for group cyber security knowledge (left) and user engagement (right)

5 Discussion

Participant feedback from both groups indicated that the training was well received. Additionally, some participants noted that they initially overestimated their level of cyber security awareness, suggesting that the training helped them recognise gaps in their knowledge.

Overall, the findings demonstrate that gamified training, whether incorporating LA or FR, was effective in promoting learning and improving cyber security knowledge. Participants displayed a higher initial understanding of social engineering (and particularly phishing) compared to other topics. This may be attributed to the widespread awareness of phishing threats. Conversely, initial knowledge of password security was the lowest among all topics but showed substantial improvement following the training. The knowledge gains evidenced through correct responses are visualised in Fig. 9, which suggests that the website security scenario was particularly effective in enhancing participant understanding.

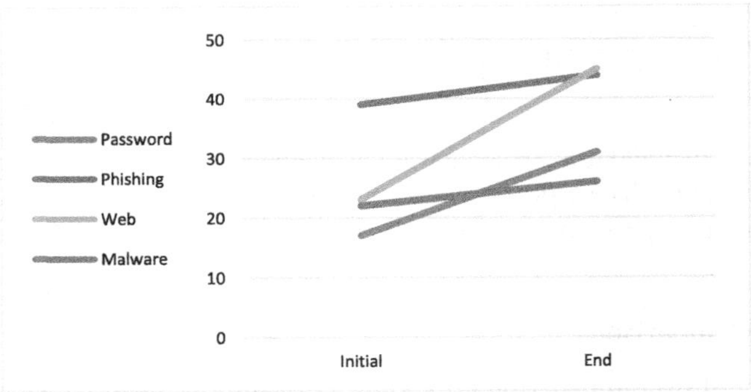

Fig. 9. Cyber security knowledge improvement

The observed learning improvements for the FR group align with findings from previous SETA studies [4], while the LA group demonstrated even greater gains. Although both groups showed increased cyber security knowledge, the improvement was more pronounced among LA participants. The initial knowledge gap between the LA and FR groups (0.76) narrowed to 0.12 after training, suggesting that LA may be more effective in enhancing participant knowledge.

Regarding user engagement, results from the UES-SF indicated strong scores across both groups. However, FR participants consistently reported higher engagement levels in all categories, with particularly notable differences in perceived usability (0.68 higher), reward (0.38 higher), and focused attention (0.3 higher). These findings suggest that FR participants found the training experience more intuitive, immersive, and rewarding. In contrast, the lower engagement scores for LA may indicate that the approach introduced additional cognitive strain, potentially reducing enjoyment during training.

While these findings should be interpreted cautiously due to the small sample size, the study provides further evidence supporting the effectiveness of gamified training. Additionally, it highlights the potential benefits of more nuanced implementations, such as a customised points system based on LA or FR. Future research could focus on increasing the number of participants and collecting demographic data to examine potential variations in the effectiveness of LA and FR across different user groups.

Based on the results in Fig. 9, the malicious software scenario appeared to be less effective in improving cyber security knowledge. Furthermore, focused attention received the lowest scores among all engagement categories for both groups (see Fig. 7). These findings suggest that future research should explore refinements in design and educational content to enhance engagement and knowledge retention.

6 Conclusion

This study successfully enhanced participants' cyber security knowledge through gamified training. The overall positive feedback further indicates that the developed apps serve as effective tools for SETA. The findings suggest that both LA and FR offer distinct advantages. While the LA-based app resulted in greater knowledge improvement, it received lower scores on the UES-SF compared to the FR-based app. Conversely, the FR-based approach was more effective in fostering user engagement. These results suggest that FR may be the preferred approach when the primary objective is to maximise user engagement, whereas LA may be more suitable when the primary goal is to improve cyber security knowledge acquisition.

References

1. Reeves, A., Calic, D., Delfabbro, P.: "Get a red-hot poker and open up my eyes, it's so boring" 1: employee perceptions of cybersecurity training. Comput. Secur. **106**, 102281 (2021). https://doi.org/10.1016/j.cose.2021.102281
2. Kumaraguru, P., Sheng, S., Acquisti, A., Cranor, L.F., Hong, J.: Teaching Johnny not to fall for phish. ACM Trans. Internet Technol. **10**, 7:1–7:31 (2010). https://doi.org/10.1145/1754393.1754396
3. Reeves, A., Calic, D., Delfabbro, P.: "Generic and unusable": understanding employee perceptions of cybersecurity training and measuring advice fatigue. Comput. Secur. **128**, 103137 (2023). https://doi.org/10.1016/j.cose.2023.103137

4. Sikolia, D., Biros, D., Zhang, T.: How effective are SETA programs anyway: learning and forgetting in security awareness training. J. Cybersecur. Educ. Res. Pract. **2023** (2023). https://doi.org/10.32727/8.2023.13
5. Fatima, R., Yasin, A., Liu, L., Wang, J.: How persuasive is a phishing email? A phishing game for phishing awareness. J. Comput. Secur. (2019). https://doi.org/10.3233/JCS-181253
6. Sheng, S., et al.: Anti-phishing Phil: the design and evaluation of a game that teaches people not to fall for phish. In: Proceedings of the 3rd Symposium on Usable Privacy and Security, pp. 88–99. Association for Computing Machinery, New York, NY, USA (2007). https://doi.org/10.1145/1280680.1280692
7. Kävrestad, J., Hagberg, A., Nohlberg, M., Rambusch, J., Roos, R., Furnell, S.: Evaluation of contextual and game-based training for phishing detection. Future Internet **14**, 104 (2022). https://doi.org/10.3390/fi14040104
8. Kahneman, D., Tversky, A.: Prospect theory: an analysis of decision under risk. Econometrica **47**, 263–291 (1979)
9. Novemsky, N., Kahneman, D.: The boundaries of loss aversion. J. Mark. Res. **42**, 119–128 (2005). https://doi.org/10.1509/jmkr.42.2.119.62292
10. Marczewski, A.: Introduction to gamification Part 7: rewards and reward schedules – gamified UK. https://www.gamified.uk/2019/04/10/rewards-and-reward-schedules/. Accessed 12 Feb 2025
11. Toda, A.M., et al.: Analysing gamification elements in educational environments using an existing gamification taxonomy. Smart Learn. Environ. **6**, 16 (2019). https://doi.org/10.1186/s40561-019-0106-1
12. Gal, D., Rucker, D.D.: The loss of loss aversion: will it loom larger than its gain? J. Consum. Psychol. **28**, 497–516 (2018). https://doi.org/10.1002/jcpy.1047
13. Massar, S.A.A., Pu, Z., Chen, C., Chee, M.W.L.: Losses motivate cognitive effort more than gains in effort-based decision making and performance. Front. Hum. Neurosci. **14** (2020). https://doi.org/10.3389/fnhum.2020.00287
14. Manolică, A., Guţă, A.-S., Roman, T., Dragăn, L.M.: Is consumer overchoice a reason for decision paralysis? Sustainability **13**, 5920 (2021). https://doi.org/10.3390/su13115920
15. Pratama, A.R., Firmansyah, F.M.: Until you have something to lose! Loss aversion and two-factor authentication adoption. Appl. Comput. Inf. **21**, 53–64 (2021). https://doi.org/10.1108/ACI-12-2020-0156
16. Clay, S.N., Clithero, J.A., Harris, A.M., Reed, C.L.: Loss aversion reflects information accumulation, not bias: a drift-diffusion model study. Front. Psychol. **8** (2017). https://doi.org/10.3389/fpsyg.2017.01708
17. Chou, Y.: Actionable Gamification: Beyond Points, Badges, and Leaderboards. Packt Publishing Ltd. (2019)
18. Marczewski, A.: The periodic table of gamification elements - gamified UK. https://www.gamified.uk/2017/04/03/periodic-table-gamification-elements/. Accessed 14 Feb 2025
19. He, W., et al.: Improving employees' intellectual capacity for cybersecurity through evidence-based malware training. J. Intellect. Cap. **21**, 203–213 (2019). https://doi.org/10.1108/JIC-05-2019-0112
20. Goodman, J.S., Wood, R.E., Hendrickx, M.: Feedback specificity, exploration, and learning. J. Appl. Psychol. **89**, 248–262 (2004). https://doi.org/10.1037/0021-9010.89.2.248
21. Nicholson, J., Coventry, L., Briggs, P.: Can we fight social engineering attacks by social means? Assessing social salience as a means to improve phish detection. In: Proceedings of the Thirteenth USENIX Conference on Usable Privacy and Security, pp. 285–298. USENIX Association, USA (2017)
22. Hevner, A., Chatterjee, S.: Design Research in Information Systems: Theory and Practice. Springer US, Boston, MA (2010). https://doi.org/10.1007/978-1-4419-5653-8

23. Hevner, A.R., March, S.T., Park, J., Ram, S.: Design science in information systems research. MIS Q. **28**, 75–105 (2004). https://doi.org/10.2307/25148625
24. Venable, J., Pries-Heje, J., Baskerville, R.: FEDS: a framework for evaluation in design science research. Eur. J. Inf. Syst. **25**, 77–89 (2016). https://doi.org/10.1057/ejis.2014.36
25. Carle, N., Ophoff, J.: Using visual cues to enhance phishing education for children. In: Drevin, L., Leung, W.S., von Solms, S. (eds.) Information Security Education - Challenges in the Digital Age, pp. 21–35. Springer, Cham (2024). https://doi.org/10.1007/978-3-031-62918-1_2
26. O'Brien, H.L., Cairns, P., Hall, M.: A practical approach to measuring user engagement with the refined user engagement scale (UES) and new UES short form. Int. J. Hum. Comput. Stud. **112**, 28–39 (2018). https://doi.org/10.1016/j.ijhcs.2018.01.004

Improving Cyber Security Incident Response: A Collaborative Tabletop Game Approach

Andreas Seiler(✉) and Ulrike Lechner

Universität der Bundeswehr München, 85579 Neubiberg, Germany
{Andreas.Seiler,Ulrike.Lechner}@unibw.de
https://www.unibw.de

Abstract. This paper explores the potential of a collaborative tabletop game called Operation Raven to improve incident response processes for critical infrastructure. The game material consists of a game board representing the IT network of a critical infrastructure, various cards, and structured response cards to simulate cyber security incident scenarios. The game introduces hypotheses as a collaborative basis for response actions. Operation Raven is based on de facto standards such as the MITRE ATT&CK Framework and the incident response phases outlined by SANS and NIST. Players are exposed to real-world scenarios and challenges, and playing means training in incident response tasks, communication, and decision-making. The game design encourages players to think critically, analyze available information, collaborate, and make informed decisions. The article presents the game design and the results of the game evaluation after three design iterations and ten game events.

Keywords: serious game · tabletop exercise · critical infrastructure · incident response

1 Introduction

The risk of cyber threats, such as ransomware and targeted attacks [2], combined with complex system ecosystems with Information Technology (IT), Operational Technology (OT), and supply chain dependencies, makes it necessary for organizations to have effective incident response processes in place. The question is no longer whether a company will be breached, but when, how quickly it can be detected, and whether the organization is prepared to respond to the incident [1,4,9]. Although critical infrastructures or larger organizations often have established incident response processes to mitigate the impact of cyber security incidents, smaller companies often lack the necessary security measures and processes to react effectively to incidents [8]. Even within organizations with incident response plans, training and refinement of these processes often fall short due

Published by Springer Nature Switzerland AG 2026
L. Drevin et al. (Eds.): WISE 2025, IFIP AICT 742, pp. 124–139, 2026.
https://doi.org/10.1007/978-3-031-94924-1_9

to the heavy workload of the involved roles and a lack of resources for training activities.

This article introduces the serious game Operation Raven, a collaborative tabletop game designed to improve incident response processes. It is a game for groups of 3–6 players and a game master. The game master emulates a ransomware attack, players collaborate and define or refine their activities in incident response process. The game is played in rounds, and each round marks an action of ransomware. In each round, players define identification, containment, eradication, and recovery actions. The game Operation Raven serves multiple purposes, including defining a collaborative procedure, establishing communication paths, and facilitating decision making. By engaging participants in the game, the objective of the game is to produce applicable results, improve the effectiveness and efficiency of incident response, and make responsibilities and expectations transparent. In addition, the game fosters discussions and knowledge sharing among the practitioners involved. Two Research Hypotheses guide our work:

- *A serious game in the form of a physical tabletop exercise is a good method to leverage the knowledge of practitioners on good incident response processes.*
- *Game material based on best practices and agreed standards helps to ensure the applicability of game results to improve the effectiveness and efficiency of incident response processes.*

For this paper, we use the definition of Luttgens et al. [13] concerning the goals and effectiveness of incident response: Investigate by determining the initial attack vector, the tools used, the affected assets and the time frame. The efficiency is defined by the usage and usefulness of information and tasks within the remediation of the incident.

This article is organized as follows. We discuss background and related work, present the research design, the game Operation Raven, and results from game evaluations. The article concludes with a discussion of the results in design and evaluation, limitations, and findings.

2 Background and Related Work

The problem this paper discusses is a cross-sectional problem through the domains of cyber security incident response, serious games, education, and training.

In the area of incident response, we use recognized and fundamental concepts. The NIST Computer Security Incident Handling Guide [7] emphasizes the importance of regular training, relationships, and communication between stakeholders in the incident response process. We also use different frameworks in terms of adversary modeling [15] like MITRE ATT&CK. MITRE ATT&CK is a knowledge base of adversary tactics and techniques based on real-world observations [21]. These models need to be adapted to the size and resources of an organization. Here, the focus is on **what** should be done in the event of an incident. Our tabletop game forms the bridge to practice here by focusing on **how**.

Looking at serious games within the domain of cyber security and incident response, several attempts have been made. Young and Farshadkhah [25] using the card game Backdoors & Breaches to teach students about incident response foundations by providing a frame and further information by playing cards. We incorporated this simple and easy-to-implement game mechanic into our game. In contrast to this game, we focus not only on awareness and learning, but also on the game's results. Rieb et al. [16,17] use a gamified workshop to analyze different attack scenarios on IT infrastructures. Similarly, we incorporate the idea of creative analysis based on a central game board depicting infrastructures. In this research, the focus was on the challenges of the blue team vs. the red team. We modeled the red team part through a game master and are focusing on the blue team and their solution, given their resources. Shostack [20] maintains a list of different tabletop and card games for security, but those focus on awareness. Denning et al. [5,6] developed and evaluated a tabletop card game to raise awareness and alter perceptions regarding computer security. Other games like Dungeons & Dragons [24] use collective creative processes and ideas to design possible responses. From this game, we have adopted the collective creative process and the idea of designing cards that significantly influence the game process.

Angafor et al. [3] review different tabletop exercises and games in the context of incident response. This paper showed that there are games that facilitate the understanding of incident response and emergency processes or encourage communication and collaboration. Still, none implement interfaces to use the results for further improvement or define processes.

Having a community of people who are committed to the same goals is essential for game design to ensure commitment and meaningful interactions [10]. We foster this foundational requirement by designing a game with the collective purpose of defining good responses to cyber security incidents and stressing the communication and dependencies between the players and their roles within that process. Further research shows that game challenges have a positive effect on participation, as well as perceived learning [11,14].

3 Research Design

The method used for the research presented is the Design Science approach according to Hevner et al. [12]. The heart of the Design Science research framework are the activities to design and build and to justify and evaluate artifacts. We take inspiration from the method of action design research [19], that is, design sciences research which tries to solve organizational problems by designing artifacts and where there is a research process that is embedded in an organizational, industrial context. The principle of concurrent and authentic evaluation from Action Design Research guides or approach to design and evaluation of the game artifact.

The design process of the game is structured in three main iterations with several game events per design iteration for evaluation. Ten game sessions were conducted, as shown in Table 2. The core game mechanics and the game idea have been introduced in version 1.0 (see Table 1), a new type of card was added for game version 1.1 and the game mechanics was enriched by hypotheses as basis for facilitating critical thinking in incident response. Version 1.2 saw a new game board and the introduction of various stakeholder perspectives that the players to encourage the players to encounter perspectives beyond the incident response teams. Version 1.3 has introduced more variety in game cards representing the incident scenario. Note that Version 1.2 has not been played; it is a mere design iteration.

Table 1. Game Versions

Version	Game Material	Mechanics
1.0	network diagram, scenario cards	scenario list, response board
1.1	goal sheet	use of hypotheses
1.2	new game board	stakeholder perspectives
1.3	more variation in cards	feedback questionnaire

Table 2. Game Sessions

ID	Date	Players	Ver.	Description and Roles
1	26.07.2023	5	1.0	evaluation of core game idea with 5 researchers
2	03.08.2023	3	1.1	practical session with 1 IH, 2 IR
3	03.08.2023	3	1.1	practical session with IH, BR, BCM
4	08.02.2024	9	1.3	stakeholder and response focus with 2 IR, 2 IH, OT, ISO, BR, DPO, BCM
5	06.03.2024	7	1.3	evaluation of new game version with 4 researchers, 2 IR, 1 IH
6	26.03.2024	5	1.3	session with focus on forensic processes with 2 IH, 3 IR
7	26.03.2024	8	1.3	session with focus on recovery processes with 3 IT and 5 OT
8	13.05.2024	6	1.3	training session with diverse team of 2 IT, IR, BCM, OT, IH
9	13.05.2024	6	1.3	training session with diverse team of 2 IT, IR, OT, IH
10	14.-15.05.2024	18	1.3	session integrated in a cyber range training with 4 IR, 2 IH, 4 IT, 3 OT, ISO, BR, DPO, BCM, CM

Evaluation in game sessions 1–3 is qualitative, in the form of participative observations and an open-ended focus group discussion after the tabletop game.

As the game designed matured (sessions 4–9), evaluation was done in form of participatory observations, group discussions after the game, and a structured, anonymous survey using a 5-point Likert scale to evaluate game material, game play, game content, and the usefulness of the game (see Fig. 4).

4 Design of Operation Raven

The idea for the tabletop game came from feedback from participants of cyber range trainings: they needed another form of training or workshop to be able to improve their processes instead of just testing them. For the initial design (V1.0), we took inspiration from the incident response card game Backdoors & Breaches [26] and the structured storytelling and creative player responses of the game Dungeons & Dragons [22].

The following questions and answers formed the basis for the first game iterations. *What is the goal of the game and the winning condition?* The overall goal of the game is to collectively train incident response scenarios and extract and document the response knowledge of practitioners and experts. To achieve this goal, the winning condition of the game is uncovering of the adversary tactics, techniques, and procedures through definition of response tasks, communication, and decisions in as few rounds as possible.

Should we use a digital or analog game? We deliberately opted for a face-to-face setting for two reasons: Agile prototyping processes and experiencing collaboration is easier with a tabletop exercise, and in-person events are better for longer group discussions.

Can we combine the elements of board games, card games, and workshops? The game setting is designed to facilitate discussions and bring together different stakeholders. The gamification of incident response in such format leaves room for an after-action review and refinement of the game results. The game material is easy to use, and many players have an intuitive understanding of the game logic and the game material.

How can we keep the game modular and flexible? A round-based game cycle allows us a flexible approach, adapts to the attack vector model with the variety of technical methods used by ransomware in every step, and modularizes the discussion. The game master can choose the adversary actions to steer the game in a direction that serves the training purpose and the needs of players, and the organizations involved.

4.1 Game Scenario

The scenario of the game captures a ransomware attack on an energy provider as a critical infrastructure. It includes the IT and OT infrastructures of the energy provider with networks, key technology for operations, and cyber security technologies. Different tactics, techniques, and procedures (TTP) of the adversary are modeled through cards depicting its actions from initial access to encryption of critical assets. The scenario also incorporates internal and external stakeholders (Version 1.2 and later).

The adversary actions are captured in a master scenario event list (MSEL) in the form of TTPs affecting different assets. Each line in the MSEL documents a possible step of the threat actor in their campaign to compromise the players' company, encrypt their data, and hold them for ransom. These steps are depicted in cards that the game master uses to unfold the story to the players. The players aim to limit the impact of the incident through the definition of response tasks, communication, and decisions for identification, containment, eradication, and recovery.

4.2 Game Roles and Players

A game master orchestrates the game. The game master is responsible for the game progression, acts as a referee, and is the one who knows the whole scenario.

Starting with the most apparent role, the **incident responder (IR)** is an operational and tactical role responsible for the analytical processing of the incident. The **incident handler (IH)** is responsible for ensuring a high-level status of the incident and ensuring that everyone is aware of the current hypothesis. They coordinate and orchestrate communication with stakeholders and document information about decisions. **IT Administrators (IT)** and **OT Administrators (OT)** support the identification and scope of the incident and perform containment tasks within the incident process. The **Information Security Officer (ISO)** is the main responsibility for information security within the company. He advises on business decisions and makes risks transparent. Many communications and decisions in an attempt to mitigate or end an intrusion are risk-based and need the advice, responsibility, and decisions of **business responsible (BR)**. Another key player in incidents involving personal data is **data protection officer (DPO)**. To ensure that data protection laws are adhered to, timely and accurate reporting to the authorities is essential. The **business continuity manager (BCM)** is responsible for managing processes for business resilience, redundancies, and backup strategies. The **legal advisor (LA)** is required when external partners are involved or law enforcement is consulted. Whenever official statements are required or information needs to be sent to partners or customers, the **communication manager (CM)** must be consulted. Observers support the game master in documenting relevant observations and player reactions and feedback regarding game design.

4.3 Game Material

This section describes the developed game material. The **Master Scenario Event List (MSEL)** is a table of adversary actions that describe a specific attack scenario that the game master uses to manage the progression of the game and provide information to the players. Each line in the MSEL describes details of the implementation of a MITRE ATT&CK technique in the given game scenario, the affected assets, and the corresponding IOCs. In the current scenario of the game, this ranges from spearfishing mails, malware execution, and persistence techniques to data encryption for impact. The game master presents this information to players in the form of cards. The **TTP cards** depict all the tactics, techniques, and procedures defined within a given scenario. For example, there are cards with information on how the adversary would achieve initial access to the player's network or different means of data exfiltration.

The **game board** includes a network diagram of the most valuable and critical incident response assets. This infrastructure comprises "crown jewel" information systems, trust borders, interfaces, and security controls. As the first game sessions were conducted with an energy provider, the infrastructure can range from traditional separated IT/OT networks to cloud-based zero-trust architectures. The game board is depicted in Fig. 1 in an early version, and in Fig. 2 in the current version.

Fig. 1. Game board in version 1.0.

Another deck of cards that is used are the so-called **IOC cards**. Those cards depict indicators of compromise (IOC) and are clues and rewards for players after each round.

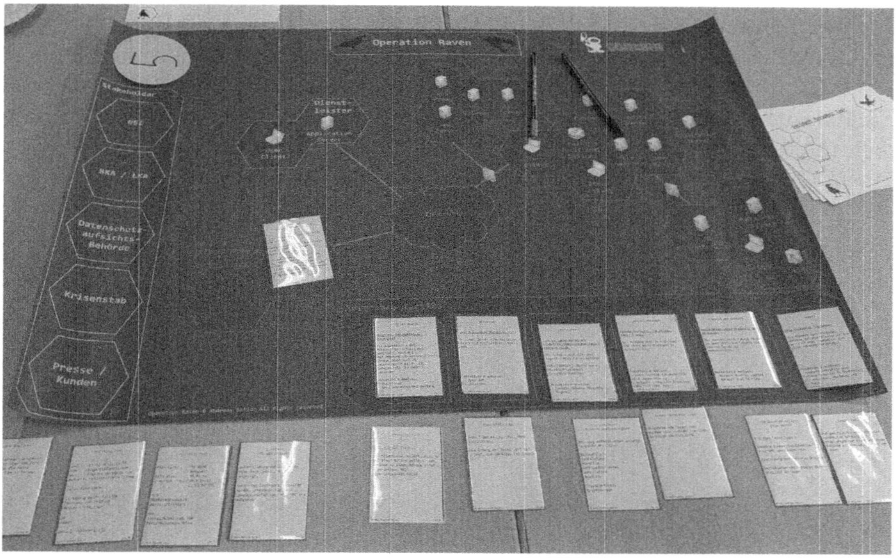

Fig. 2. Game board version 1.3.

The players document their actions on structured **response cards**. These are DIN A5 cards with different types: hypotheses, incident response tasks, communication, and decisions. Metadata such as round number, incident response phase, responsible role, used tools, and affected assets make it easier for players to document relevant information and allow better analysis of responses after game sessions.

The last element is the **response board**, a whiteboard, structured into different sections where the response cards are sorted and pinned down for everyone to read. Those sections are places for the hypothesis cards, and one section for each of the phases within the incident response process: identification, containment, eradication, and recovery.

4.4 Gameplay

We decided to use an open method for gameplay that encourages the players' creativity, engagement, and involvement. The gameplay of Operation Raven is round-based [18]. First, the game master describes a scenario and hands out IOC cards to the players to get them started. Then players use the given information (cards and game board) to collectively come up with responses with the objective of unveiling the tactics, techniques, and procedures the adversary uses in the given attack scenario. These responses are documented via response cards on the response board to identify what happens, contain the attack, eradicate the adversary's foothold, and recover compromised systems and disrupted services. At the end of each round, the game master assesses the players' responses and provides them with corresponding IOC cards or revealed TTP cards for the next round. For the assessment, the game master evaluates players' responses in perspective to the MSEL and progression of the game. Then the game cycle repeats with the new cards given to the players. The players win the game when the ransomware is contained or eradicated and recovery is on the way. The players aim to achieve this in as few rounds as possible.

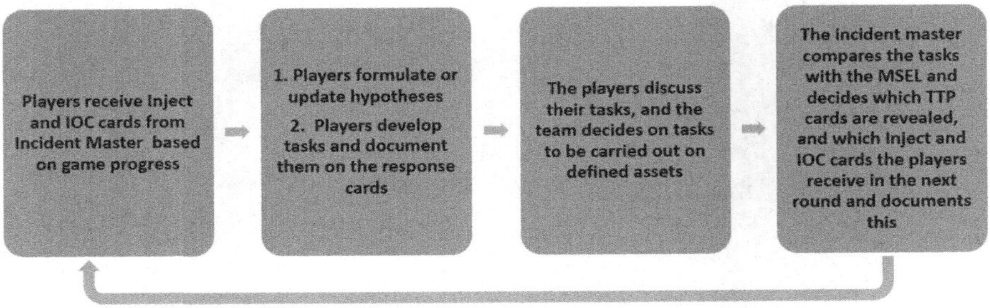

Fig. 3. Game flow.

4.5 Development and Versions

This section presents a brief description of the development, changes, and refinements based on the evaluations presented in Sect. 5.

The focus of the first version of the game was on game scenario and main gameplay. Based on a cyber threat analysis of different ransomware groups and malware reports, the MSEL and the corresponding TTP cards were created. The design decision to use different card decks was made to keep the serious game modular and to be able to expand the content with other scenarios or new TTP in the future. This allows us to tailor the game to different levels of expertise and focus topics - according to the needs of the players and the organization. In the game version 1.0, as depicted in Fig. 1, we used color-coded paper sheets for player responses: red cards for emergency tasks, blue cards for incident response tasks, yellow cards for communication, and green cards for decisions.

Based on the feedback of the first evaluation, we designed version 1.1. With this version, only smaller changes were incorporated because it was the initial assessment game. The game board was printed larger for a better overview, and a die was used to indicate the current round of the game to the players. Furthermore, we designed a cheat sheet, which states the focus and goals of the four different incident response phases to support less experienced players. Concerning the response board, we rearranged the way the response cards are displayed. The first row is for the hypothesis cards that were added to the game. Under the hypotheses, the whiteboard is divided into the four phases of incident response. The response cards are then displayed chronologically. Version 1.1 was played in game sessions 2 and 3.

With the development of the first card decks, cyber kill chains and adversary frameworks were analyzed to identify the relevant steps within an incident that are crucial for the defender and had to be part of the game. Due to the existing open-source information and wide acceptance within the incident response community, the choice fell on a subset of the MITRE ACK&CK [23] categories: Initial access, Execution, Persistence, Lateral Movement, Command and Control, and Impact. These are concepts and terminology that the players know from their daily work and are used to, which increases acceptance and ensures applicability. The next question was how to help players discuss the adversary steps, what is impacted, and how best to visualize what can be done to contain the incident. For this purpose, we designed a generic network infrastructure diagram as the main board. Players can use this to mark compromised systems or networks, and it facilitates discussions about adjacent assets or networks.

The first major upgrade for version 1.3 was a newly designed game board as shown in Fig. 1. The network diagram depicts a more detailed network with different sub-networks and external partners. In addition, the adversary tactics field was incorporated into the board and a newly added section was added for stakeholders. As the first three game sessions showed, it was necessary to come up with a solution for roles that are not present and for modeling crucial external parties that need to be taken into account for incident response, such as authorities, law enforcement, press, and customers.

5 Evaluation

The data base for the evaluation of Operation Raven consists of the game results of ten game events with more than 30 h of gameplay with 70 participants (see Table 2) and the data from the feedback discussions and surveys.

The evaluation of the game session was carried out using qualitative and quantitative evaluation methods, depending on the maturity of the game design. Game sessions 1, 2, and 3 were evaluated through open discussion and feedback sessions. From session 4 to session 9, we added a quantitative evaluation in the form of a questionnaire that used a 5-point Likert scale to measure the satisfaction of the players, ranging from very dissatisfied to very satisfied. In addition to the scale, the players were given an open comment and feedback field to express their thoughts. The questionnaire consisted of 17 questions that assessed four key areas (see Fig. 4). The first questions evaluate the game material, the second set of questions the gameplay, the game content part addresses the soft factors of collaboration of the various roles, the communication, the decisions that have been simulated in the approach, and the fourth set of questions as for the transfer to the real world and whether players expect that the experience is beneficial for effectiveness and efficiency in incident response.

5.1 Qualitative Evaluation: Sessions 1–3

The qualitative evaluation is based on the first three game sessions, using versions 1.0 and 1.1. In session 1, five players with a background in information security and serious game research played five rounds for three hours to evaluate the initial game idea. Game sessions 2 and 3 were conducted in parallel with one technical and one management-focused team of three players each. These sessions focused on game testing and reviewing existing incident response processes.

The result of the discussion and feedback sessions was that players liked the game material and game play. The combination of a game board, cards, and response documentation is appealing to players and helped them to have a structured, playful way to think about incident response. The feedback showed that the hypothesis cards helped the players to agree on a common starting position each round. Further feedback for improvement stated that the game board was too small and a broader view of the infrastructure components and interfaces to other stakeholders was missing. Also, the objectives of the game were not clear to all players. These sessions clearly showed that the color-coded response cards need to be more structured to document more meta-information for further analysis of the results. Another finding was that differentiating between emergency actions and response tasks is more irritating than helpful.

We observed that players, who had responsibility for incident response in their current job, are more engaged than players who are not involved with incident response in their job.

5.2 Quantitative and Qualitative Evaluation: Sessions 4, and 6–9

This section presents results from the overall quantitative evaluation of all game sessions and discusses the improvements of the game by analyzing the evaluation of game event 4 and 8. Figure 2 shows the median of each Likert scale per question, as well as the total median, variance, and standard deviation per question for the game sessions 4, 6, 7, 8 and 9. Game sessions 5 and 10 had no quantitative evaluation but qualitative feedback from peer researchers in the context of a research project meeting (sessions 5), and from practitioners (session 10) in the context of a cyber range training. Game session 4 involved the first utilization of the version 1.3 game, with a total of nine players of various backgrounds, three observers, and lasted 3.5 h. This session aimed to provide a more comprehensive depiction of various roles, emphasizing the importance of effective communication and stakeholder interfaces, such as business owners and government authorities. Sessions 8 and 9 were run in parallel as 3-hour introduction courses on the first day of a one-week cyber range training. It was an introduction to the existing ransomware incident response process for a diverse team of a company within the critical infrastructure department. The players were split into two teams with 6 players each and with a focus on diversification of roles within each team. In addition, each team had two observers. Game session 10 was integrated with a cyber range training.

When we look at the overall evaluation results of the questionnaires, we observe that over time, the responses in the survey get more favorable, indicating that the game material and the game play improved over time. The minimum median value in the entire evaluation is 3.7 and all the total median values per question is higher than 4, which shows that the game is at a good maturity

Question/ Session	4	6	7	8	9	total Ø	σ^2	σ
1. What is your overall impression of the game material?	4.33	4.40	4.50	4.83	5.00	4.57	0.39	0.62
1.1 How do you rate the game board?	4.22	4.20	4.67	4.83	4.50	4.44	0.32	0.57
1.2 How do you rate the incident cards?	3.78	4.20	5.00	4.67	4.75	4.28	0.60	0.78
1.3 How do you rate the response cards?	4.56	4.60	4.33	4.80	4.25	4.54	0.40	0.63
2. What is your overall impression of the gameplay?	4.00	4.60	3.75	4.83	4.75	4.36	0.52	0.72
2.1 How do you rate the session length?	4.33	4.60	4.33	4.60	4.00	4.38	0.39	0.62
2.2 How do you rate the round length?	3.89	4.60	4.33	4.60	4.00	4.23	0.49	0.70
2.3 How do you rate the game cycle?	3.78	4.60	4.00	5.00	4.50	4.32	0.72	0.85
3. What is your overall impression of the game content?	4.67	4.80	4.67	5.00	4.75	4.78	0.17	0.42
3.1 Does the game contribute to defining a common approach to incident response?	4.67	4.40	4.75	5.00	4.75	4.71	0.20	0.45
3.2 Does the game help to create transparency regarding responsibilities and processes?	4.67	4.80	4.00	4.83	5.00	4.68	0.36	0.60
3.3 Does the game help to make expectations transparent?	4.44	4.80	4.25	4.83	4.25	4.54	0.39	0.63
3.4 Does the game help define communication channels?	4.33	4.60	4.50	5.00	4.50	4.57	0.39	0.62
3.5 3.3 Does the game help to clearly define decisions?	4.33	4.00	4.25	4.83	3.75	4.29	0.63	0.80
4. What is your overall impression of the realisticness and applicability of the results?	4.33	4.40	4.00	4.83	4.00	4.36	0.30	0.55
4.1 Does the game contribute to making incident response processes more effective? (We do the right things.)	4.33	4.60	4.67	5.00	4.50	4.59	0.39	0.62
4.2 Does the game contribute to making incident response processes more efficient? (We do things right.)	4.11	4.60	4.33	4.83	4.75	4.48	0.40	0.63

Fig. 4. Session median and total median values for each evaluation question including variance and standard deviation.

level since session 4. The total median values over all game sessions show that the players are very satisfied with the game content (such as the scenario and contents of the game cards). The most room for further improvement is seen in the length of the rounds and sessions (players gave the feedback that these were partly too long). When analyzing the variance and standard deviation, we see that the responses scattered the most on the questions concerning the game cycle, decisions, and incident cards. Yet again, the low variance and standard deviations on the questions that evaluated the game content and joint approach further show that most players agree on the value of our game in these fields.

With the overall evaluation in mind, let's take a deeper look into sessions 4 and 8. We picked those two sessions, because session 4 was the one with the most versatile team concerning the roles and session 8 was played by the team with the most practical incident response experience compared to the other team within our game sessions. After analysis of the sessions 4 questionnaires, comments, and feedback session, the following main improvements were identified. If there are too many players, there is no good view on the IOC and TPP cards. Given the state of the game material and game play 3 to 6 players per session is optimal. The game rounds should not be too long, because discussions emerge where there is further information on internal processes or technical implementations of the company needed. Rounds of 20 to 30 min and 6 rounds per session is the maximum.

Question / Player	1.	1.1	1.2	1.3	2.	2.1	2.2	2.3	3.	3.1	3.2	3.3	3.4	3.5	4.	4.1	4.2
1	4	3	5	5	3	4	3	4	5	5	5	4	4	4	4	3	4
2	5	4	4	3	5	5	3	3	5	5	5	5	5	5	5	5	4
3	4	5	4	4	4	3	3	4	4	4	5	5	4	4	5	4	4
4	5	4	4	5	4	4	5	4	5	4	4	3	3	4	4	4	3
5	5	5	4	5	4	5	5	4	5	5	5	5	5	5	4	5	5
6	4	5	3	5	4	5	4	3	5	5	5	5	5	5	5	5	5
7	3	4	2	4	3	4	4	5	4	4	3	3	3	2	3	3	3
8	4	4	3	5	4	5	4	3	5	5	5	5	5	5	4	5	4
9	5	4	5	5	5	4	4	4	4	5	5	5	5	5	5	5	5
median	4.33	4.22	3.78	4.56	4.00	4.33	3.89	3.78	4.67	4.67	4.67	4.44	4.33	4.33	4.33	4.33	4.11

Fig. 5. Likert scale of game session 4 evaluation.

When analyzing the questionnaire of session 4 (see Fig. 3) most players strongly agree that the game helps to "define a common approach to incident response" (question 3.1) as well as "create transparency for responsibilities and processes" (question 3.2). Also, most players strongly agreed that the game helps to "make expectations transparent" (question 3.2) between the different roles and responsibilities. Concerning the game material, the structured incident response cards, newly implemented in this version, satisfied most of the players (question 1.3) and might be a reason for the result on transparency for responsibilities and processes (question 3.1). These ratings also correspond with the overall quantitative evaluation.

An interesting finding was that the most experienced incident response team gave the overall best evaluation in session 8 (see Fig. 4). Here too, we see a corresponding and very good ratio to the joint approach on incident response as well as the transparency the game provides for the roles, responsibilities, and processes. In this evaluation, the players also pointed out that the training and documentation are applicable to their day-to-day work and improve the effectiveness of their tasks and processes.

Question / Player	1.	1.1	1.2	1.3	2.	2.1	2.2	2.3	3.	3.1	3.2	3.3	3.4	3.5	4.	4.1	4.2
1	5	5	5	5	5	4	4	5	5	5	4	5	5	5	5	5	5
2	5	5	5	5	5			5	5	5	5	5	5	5	5	5	5
3	4	4	4	4	5	5	5	5	5	5	5	5	5	5	5	5	5
4	5	5	4	5	4	5	5	5	5	5	5	5	5	5	5	5	5
5	5	5	5	5	5	5	5	5	5	5	5	4	5	4	4	5	4
6	5	5	5		5	4	4	5	5	5	5	5	5	5	5	5	5
median	4.83	4.83	4.67	4.80	4.83	4.60	4.60	5.00	5.00	5.00	4.83	4.83	5.00	4.83	4.83	5.00	4.83

Fig. 6. Likert scale of game session 8 evaluation.

Within the commentary fields and discussions, the players of session 8 pointed out several interesting points. They stated that the game is a very good opportunity to train specific incident response scenarios and to see other colleagues' thinking and roles, viewpoints, and decisions. They also discussed that engagement, course of the game, and results are highly dependent on the players' roles and experience. This agrees with our observation that engagement depended on whether the players had a connection to their roles in the real world or not.

The evaluations are positive, and according to the quantitative and qualitative evaluation, players perceive the experience to be useful and enjoy the experience. Players are willing to participate in multiple sessions, and management and business units support the initiative and provide the necessary resources.

6 Discussion and Conclusion

This paper presents the serious game "Operation Raven". This serious game aims to increase the effectiveness and efficiency in incident response. It captures the design process and the evaluation of the game in various events. The article presents the design rationale and justifies design decisions using de facto standard frameworks and the round-based game logic. The target groups of the game is technical experts in the field of cyber security, and more management-oriented roles and other stakeholders. The evaluation results improved throughout the research process, indicating that design and evaluation are well-designed and goal-oriented. The players find the game useful and a good experience. The idea to gamify incident response in the form of Operation Raven seems to work.

The limitations of our approach are inherent to the design science and serious games in cyber security. First, other design decisions would yield a different serious game, and we cannot claim that our game is the best solution for the problem of how to prepare for a ransomware attack. In this industrial context, we need to be respectful of the resources and the privacy of the employee. This has an impact on the number of participants, the evaluation, and the effort spent on the evaluation. Also, in this setting, it is hardly possible to work with interventions and control groups, and we need to believe the experts' opinions on the usefulness of serious games for improving incident response.

This paper and our research contribute an artifact, the game Operation Raven, and an evaluation that demonstrates that it indeed improves the skills of the players. The distinguishing characteristics of our approach are the domain incident response and the target audience of professionals and experts. It closes a gap between technical exercises, e.g. in cyber ranges, and introductory games. Comparing Operation Raven to introductory games like Backdoors & Breaches [25] or Operation Digital Chameleon [17] shows that not only beginners or intermediate but also experts can profit from serious games. Our contribution to practitioners is a lightweight and customizable tabletop game that experts can use for regular training of incident response scenarios and applicable documentation of developed solutions using structured response cards.

Future work includes refinement of the game material and game flow, improving the validation of the game sessions, and follow-up on the documented results of the game sessions. For validation, we plan to document further important information about the players, such as experience, job role, and other diversification attributes, and improve the validation of the usefulness of the game.

Concerning the documented results of game sessions, we plan to design a process to follow up on the game results. In this process, reference models for incident response and playbooks for individual organizations and incident responders will be developed.

Acknowledgments. The research in this paper was conducted within the framework of the German-Austrian research project CONTAIN. The authors acknowledge funding for CONTAIN from the German Federal Ministry of Education and Research (BMBF) (grant numbers 13N16581-13N16587) as part of the SIFO program, and from the Austrian Research Promotion Agency (FFG) (grant number FO999902707).

References

1. Ahmad, A., Hadgkiss, J., Ruighaver, A.B.: Incident response teams-challenges in supporting the organisational security function. Comput. Secur. **31**(5), 643–652 (2012)
2. Al-Rimy, B., Maarof, M.A., Shaid, S.: Ransomware threat success factors, taxonomy, and countermeasures: a survey and research directions. Comput. Secur. **74**, 144–166 (2018)
3. Angafor, G.N., Yevseyeva, I., He, Y.: Game-based learning: a review of tabletop exercises for cybersecurity incident response training. Secur. Priv. **3**(6), e126 (2020)
4. Bundesamt für Sicherheit in der Informationstechnik: BSI-Standard 100-4 Notfallmanagement. Technical report, Bundesamt für Sicherheit in der Informationstechnik (2008). www.bsi.bund.de/gshb
5. Denning, T., Lerner, A., Shostack, A., Kohno, T.: Control-alt-hack: the design and evaluation of a card game for computer security awareness and education. In: Proceedings of the 2013 ACM SIGSAC conference on Computer & communications security, pp. 915–928 (2013)
6. Denning, T., Shostack, A., Kohno, T.: Practical lessons from creating the {Control-Alt-Hack} card game and research challenges for games in education and research. In: 2014 USENIX Summit on Gaming, Games, and Gamification in Security Education (3GSE 14) (2014)
7. Grance, T., Kent, K., Kim, B.: NIST computer security incident handling guide. Special Publication (NIST SP), Gaithersburg, MD, USA (2004)
8. Greiner, M., et al.: Scared? Prepared? Toward a ransomware incident response scenario. In: International Conference on Innovations for Community Services, pp. 289–320. Springer (2024)
9. Grobauer, B., Schreck, T.: Towards incident handling in the cloud: challenges and approaches. In: Proceedings of the 2010 ACM Workshop on Cloud Computing Security Workshop, pp. 77–86 (2010)
10. Hamari, J., Koivisto, J.: Social motivations to use gamification: an empirical study of gamifying exercise. In: ECIS, vol. 105, pp. 18–19 (2013)
11. Hamari, J., Shernoff, D.J., Rowe, E., Coller, B., Asbell-Clarke, J., Edwards, T.: Challenging games help students learn: an empirical study on engagement, flow and immersion in game-based learning. Comput. Hum. Behav. **54**, 170–179 (2016)
12. Hevner, A.R., March, S.T., Park, J., Ram, S.: Design science in information systems research. MIS Q., 75–105 (2004)

13. Luttgens, J.T., Pepe, M., Mandia, K.: Incident Response & Computer Forensics. McGraw-Hill Education Group (2014)
14. Majuri, J., Koivisto, J., Hamari, J.: Gamification of education and learning: a review of empirical literature. In: Proceedings of the 2nd International GamiFIN Conference, GamiFIN 2018. CEUR-WS (2018)
15. Naik, N., Jenkins, P., Grace, P., Song, J.: Comparing attack models for IT systems: Lockheed Martin's cyber kill chain, MITRE ATT&CK framework and diamond model. In: 2022 IEEE International Symposium on Systems Engineering (ISSE), pp. 1–7. IEEE (2022)
16. Rieb, A., Gurschler, T., Lechner, U.: A gamified approach to explore techniques of neutralization of threat actors in cybercrime. In: Schweighofer, E., Leitold, H., Mitrakas, A., Rannenberg, K. (eds.) APF 2017. LNCS, vol. 10518, pp. 87–103. Springer, Cham (2017). https://doi.org/10.1007/978-3-319-67280-9_5
17. Rieb, A., Lechner, U.: Towards a cybersecurity game: operation digital chameleon. In: Critical Information Infrastructures Security: 11th International Conference, CRITIS 2016, Paris, France, 10–12 October 2016, Revised Selected Papers 11, pp. 283–295. Springer (2017)
18. Seiler, A., Lechner, U., Strussenberg, J., Hofbauer, S.: Operation raven: design of a cyber security incident response game. In: International Conference on Innovations for Community Services, pp. 337–347. Springer (2024)
19. Sein, M.K., Henfridsson, O., Purao, S., Rossi, M., Lindgren, R.: Action design research. MIS Q., 37–56 (2011)
20. Shostack, A.: Games for security (2023). https://shostack.org/games
21. Strom, B.E., Applebaum, A., Miller, D.P., Nickels, K.C., Pennington, A.G., Thomas, C.B.: MITRE ATT&CK: design and philosophy. Technical report. The MITRE Corporation (2018)
22. Wizards Rpg Team, et al.: Player's Handbook (Dungeons & Dragons). Wizards of the Coast (2014)
23. The MITRE Cooporation: MITRE ATT&CK cloud matrix (2020). https://attack.mitre.org/versions/v8/matrices/enterprise/
24. Veldthuis, M., Koning, M., Stikkolorum, D.: A quest to engage computer science students: Using dungeons & dragons for developing soft skills. In: Proceedings of the 10th Computer Science Education Research Conference, pp. 5–13 (2021)
25. Young, J., Farshadkhah, S.: Backdoors & breaches: using a tabletop exercise game to teach cybersecurity incident response. In: Proceedings of the EDSIG Conference, vol. 2473, p. 4901 (2021)
26. Young, J., Farshadkhah, S.: Teaching cybersecurity incident response using the backdoors & breaches tabletop exercise game. Cybersecur. Pedagogy Pract. J. (2022)

Gamified Defence: Practical Guidelines for Combating Social Engineering Attacks

Amandla Mpanza, Tapiwa Gundu(✉), and Lynn Futcher

Nelson Mandela University, Gqeberha, South Africa
{s223269042,tapiwag,lynn.futcher}@mandela.ac.za

Abstract. This study explores the potential of gamification as an effective method to simulate social engineering attacks and enhance cybersecurity awareness among employees. Given the increasing sophistication of social engineering tactics, traditional security training needs to be improved, prompting a need for innovative approaches. The objective of this research is to develop guidelines for using gamification to simulate social engineering attacks, focusing on methods that increase employee engagement and improve their ability to recognize and respond to these threats. This study employed a systematic literature review to examine current gamification techniques and lay the groundwork for developing these guidelines. The search criteria initially identified 232 papers and after screening, only 12 papers were reviewed. Findings indicate that gamification techniques, such as simulations, challenges, and reward systems, hold substantial promise in enhancing cybersecurity awareness.

Keywords: Gamification · Social Engineering · Cybersecurity Awareness · Employee Training · Simulation · Human Vulnerabilities · Business Security

1 Introduction

Cybersecurity has become a top concern for companies everywhere in the digital era, as malicious attackers increasingly exploit human weaknesses to get beyond complex technological protections [1]. Because social engineering relies more on human psychology than on technological flaws, it is still one of the most challenging types of cyber threats to overcome [2]. Social engineering is a strategy that manipulates human behaviour to obtain unauthorised access or extract sensitive information [3]. The "human element" of cybersecurity is the focus of this type of attack, which gets past even the most advanced technological protections. In acknowledgement of this vulnerability, businesses have spent much in cybersecurity awareness and training; however, traditional approaches often fail to give employees the efficient training they require to identify and respond to social engineering attacks.

Gamification, or the use of game-design concepts outside of gaming contexts, is a promising approach to increase training engagement and knowledge retention [4]. Gamified training transforms passive learning environments into active, engaging ones

Published by Springer Nature Switzerland AG 2026
L. Drevin et al. (Eds.): WISE 2025, IFIP AICT 742, pp. 140–151, 2026.
https://doi.org/10.1007/978-3-031-94924-1_10

by adding elements like challenges, rewards, and simulations. According to current research, gamification can be advantageous in many areas, including business training and education, because it may increase employee engagement and improve learning outcomes. Despite this promise, more is needed about how gamification might be explicitly used in cybersecurity training [5], especially for simulating social engineering attacks. By evaluating how gamification may be used to effectively simulate social engineering attacks and its effects on employee awareness and response to such attacks, this study seeks to close this gap.

The objective of this study is to develop guidelines for gamifying cybersecurity training to improve employees' understanding of social engineering. This objective will be achieved by performing a thorough literature analysis of techniques for gamification. To develop a more resilient workforce to identify and thwart social engineering threats, this research ultimately seeks to give organisations guidelines for incorporating gamified simulations into cybersecurity awareness training.

The rest of the paper is structured as follows: Following this introduction, we discuss the related literature. Next, we outline the methodology used to develop the guidelines, followed by a discussion of the results from the systematic literature review. We then present the proposed guidelines, and finally, we conclude with a summary and future directions.

2 Related Literature

The information technology landscape has changed rapidly over the last ten years, affecting every aspect of our everyday lives [3]. Technology has become the field that drives progress in many necessary fields in a very short time. Both private and public businesses have fully embraced this change to the digital paradigm and implemented technology into their daily operations, using internet connectivity to improve services and maintain a competitive edge [6].

Information technology has advanced, making network environments more complex and posing more severe challenges to network security [7]. As technology advances, social engineering attacks pose an increasingly severe cybersecurity threat. Social engineering is defined by Wang et al. [8] as exploiting human vulnerabilities through social interaction to compromise cybersecurity. Cusack and Adedokun [9] define social engineering as the practice of deceiving individuals to obtain information. These attacks have become prominent threats due to their reliance on human weaknesses. A social engineering attacker seeks access to sensitive information or financial gain, manipulating victims to achieve their malicious objectives [10].

Social Engineering has gained significant attention because of its effectiveness in bypassing technical security [8]. According to Abu Hweidi and Eleyan [11], financial losses on the internet are caused mainly by social engineering attacks, which comprise a significant percentage of all cybercrimes. Social engineering was shown to be the most common kind of cyberattack in the ISACA report from 2021, surpassing other types of cybercrimes [12]. About 98% of cybercrimes were related to social engineering, as stated in Purplesec [13] cybersecurity statistics report. Businesses and individuals are particularly vulnerable to ransomware and phishing attacks, primarily using social media and email as their primary distribution methods [3]. Microsoft, for example, notes that phishing emails are a common social engineering tactic in business settings and present severe difficulties for enterprises [14]. This is further corroborated by IBM's Threat Intelligence Index 2023, which shows that 41% of occurrences used phishing emails, making them the most common attacks [15].

Because victims are always unaware of preventative techniques, models, and frameworks, attackers looking to obtain sensitive data or financial assets can easily manipulate them. How well an attacker can create discomfort for the victim determines how successful a social engineering attack will be, which can cloud their judgment and make it easier to disclose private information [10]. Social engineering attacks rely on preying on human emotions like fear, curiosity, trust, and greed to succeed. The primary way by which the attackers deceive the victim into divulging information or gaining access to private or restricted data is through their interactions with them [16, 17]. The ability to mislead or deceive a target into divulging personal information is necessary for social engineering attacks to be successful [18].

This means that social engineering continues to be among the most dangerous types of cybersecurity attacks, having consequences for private individuals and companies [3]. Attackers using social engineering use more advanced tools and strategies to trick their victims as technology develops. Generative artificial intelligence (AI) is one such tool that has attracted much interest lately [19]. It has, however, also discovered a dark niche in the realm of cyberattacks, where it is utilised to increase the effectiveness and possibility of social engineering attacks [8]. Organisations face a big issue with social engineering. Businesses of all sizes are becoming increasingly concerned about the threat posed by social engineering attacks [14].

Businesses are becoming more aware of how important human behaviour is to cybersecurity and the risk it may cause to protecting information [20]. Internal sources account for a large percentage of security issues in organisations, and figures show that user error, mishaps, and ignorance account for at least 70% of these events [21]. Studies like the one conducted by Khando et al. [22] emphasise that, despite implementing several technological security measures, people still need to improve their attempts to secure systems and networks. As stressed by Goodman [23], relying on technologically based security measures often fails the vital human component of cybersecurity. Businesses may be exposed to dangers that technical solutions could better mitigate if human factors are ignored in security initiatives entirely.

To reduce the risks related to cyberattacks, it is now crucial for businesses to foster a culture of security awareness [24]. As noted by Ribeiro et al. [14], enhancing social engineering resilience requires the implementation of behavioural interventions such as user awareness training. User education and training programs are essential to minimise the likelihood of these attacks. Studies like Sankhwar, et al. [25] and Trumbach [26] indicate that these kinds of interventions can considerably lower the likelihood that social engineering attacks will be effective.

This is in line with the definition of cybersecurity awareness provided by Qusa and Tarazi [27], which is having the ability to recognise and prevent security-compromising activities. Moreover, Khan et al. [28] emphasise the importance of providing employees with cybersecurity awareness training to identify, report, and mitigate security threats properly. Employees might need to be made aware of security dangers or receive proper training, leaving them ill-prepared to respond. Businesses can improve security awareness and lower the likelihood of successful cyberattacks by strengthening their security posture and offering targeted training.

Within this context, gamification approaches have emerged as a potentially effective way to raise security awareness [29]. Putz et al. [4] define gamification as the practice of introducing elements or techniques from games into non-gaming contexts. Based on Sodikin and Hikmawan [30] research, gamification components have much potential to improve cybersecurity education, particularly when addressing the complexity of today's threats and attacks. Serious games, gamified learning, or gamification are innovative approaches that can assist in achieving the necessary awareness individually. Qusa and Tarazi [27] talk about the idea of using games to achieve educational goals in addition to having a good time Qusa and Tarazi [27].

The latest technology-based training approach is called simulation, a type of gamification. Using technology-driven approaches, participants can explore real-life scenarios [31]. It is a helpful tactic for improving teamwork [32]. Research indicates that using digital simulations can improve employee effectiveness [33].

3 Methodology

This study conducts a Systematic Literature Review (SLR) to determine current gamification techniques that could be used to simulate social engineering attacks. A systematic literature review is a special literature review with several important benefits. According to Siddaway et al. [34], it entails a methodical approach to answering a particular topic by methodically locating, picking, and assessing pertinent research and collecting and analysing data from the included studies. By systematically reviewing and analysing relevant literature, this study aims to provide an understanding of how gamification can be leveraged to enhance business security awareness. The insights gained from this review will contribute to the development of guidelines for using gamification as a tool to simulate social engineering attacks, thereby supporting the primary objective of the research.

This section explains the systematic review process undertaken to identify and evaluate relevant articles related to gamification techniques for simulating social engineering attacks. Figure 1 illustrates the detailed steps involved, from the selection of databases and formulation of search strategies to the inclusion and exclusion criteria used to filter the most pertinent studies.

The systematic literature review process began with the selection of reputable databases to ensure coverage of relevant studies. ScienceDirect, IEEE Xplore, and Emerald were chosen as primary sources due to their extensive collection of relevant papers.

Studies were included if they focused on simulation, were written in English, appeared in journals or conference proceedings, and were published between 2018 and 2024 to capture recent developments. Additionally, studies within the computer science field that addressed social engineering and gamification techniques or methods were considered. The following exclusion criteria were applied: article summaries, panels, posters, book chapters, and publications in languages other than English.

Only full-text, peer-reviewed journal and conference papers published in English were included in the search results. These criteria were selected based on the premise that research findings from journals and conferences undergo rigorous peer review, making them more reliable and innovative than those from other sources. Publications related to information security or awareness, including book chapters, news articles, non-technical magazines, brief abstracts, and annual reports, were excluded.

The search query on ScienceDirect was ("Social Engineering Attacks") AND ("Gamification"). This search retrieved a large number of results, many of which were outside the scope of the study. The objective was to identify articles that explore gamification techniques applicable to simulating social engineering attacks. The term "Simulation" was included separately in the keyword list to focus on gamification techniques specifically used for simulating social engineering attacks rather than gamification in general. Inclusion was based on access type, while exclusion criteria included publication year, and relevance was determined by reviewing abstracts.

On IEEE Xplore and Emerald, the search query used was (("Social engineering") AND (("Gamification technique" OR ("Gamification Method")) AND (Simulation)). Inclusion and exclusion criteria were based on publication year, full-text or open-access availability, and language (English). Abstracts were scanned to determine whether papers were relevant or outside the study scope.

The keywords used in this study were "Social Engineering Attack," "Simulation," "Gamification technique," and "Gamification method." The search queries were structured to align with the research objectives, ensuring the inclusion of both broad and targeted research topics. For example, the term "Social engineering" was combined with general terms like "gamification techniques" as well as more specific terms like "Simulation."

4 Results

This section presents the results of the SLR by describing the concept-centric map resulting from the analysis. A concept-centric map is a structured framework used in literature reviews to organize and synthesize research findings around key concepts rather than simply listing studies in chronological order. It helps to identify relationships, trends, gaps, and contradictions within a body of research (Table 1).

5 Gamification Guidelines

Based on the findings of the systematic literature review, we propose 11 key guidelines designed to enhance security awareness and engagement through structured, gamified, and interactive learning approaches. These guidelines address identified challenges and leverage best practices to ensure an effective and sustainable implementation. Each element plays a crucial role in fostering motivation, participation, and knowledge retention. The following sub-sections provide a detailed discussion of each guideline, explaining its purpose, implementation strategies, and expected impact.

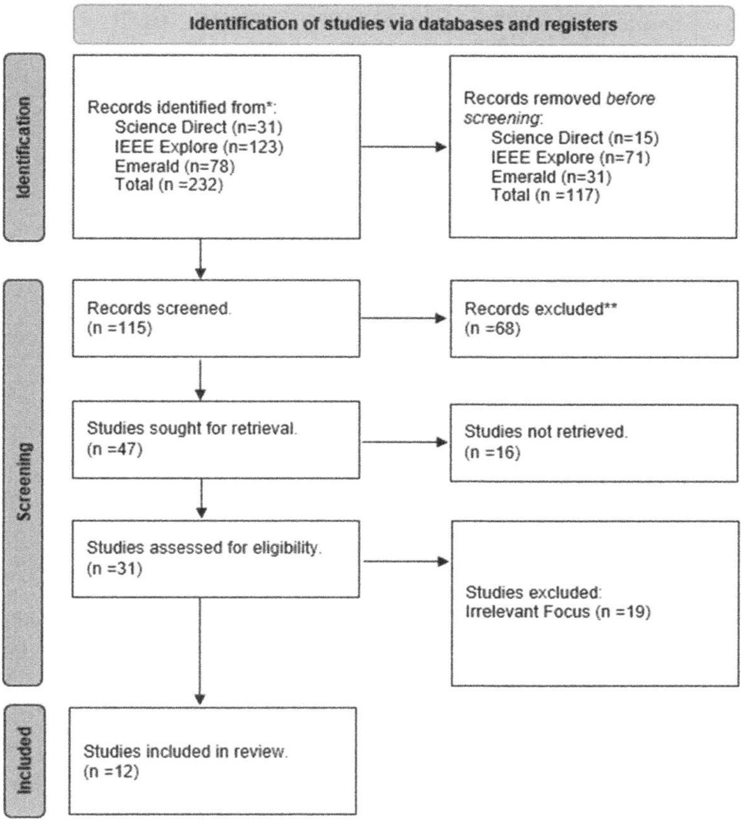

Fig. 1. Systematic Literature Review Process

5.1 Points

Diaz Redondo et al. [40] and Al-Karaki et al. [37] explain that in gamified systems, participants receive points according to their actions and task accomplishment, which helps them reach milestones and unlock levels. A key element of game design, this pontification system must be fair, consistent, and transparent to maintain participants' engagement [37]. Points technique increases learning and encourages engagements [5, 40, 43, 44]. Point systems are a classic gamification design strategy that is widely acknowledged for its capacity to increase engagement. Yasin et al. [35], for instance, the winner of the game is determined by a points system.

5.2 Challenge

The challenge technique is essential to gamification because it introduces a game conflict that requires competitors' active engagement, making the experience entertaining and engaging. While Zainuddin et al. [43] highlight that the challenge technique gives

Table 1. Corpus of papers analysed

Techniques	[35]	[36]	[37]	[38]	[39]	[40]	[5]	[41]	[42]	[43]	[44]	[45]	Total
Points	X		X			X	X			X	X		6
Challenge	X									X			2
Levels			X		X	X	X			X			5
Achievements	X				X		X						3
Collaborations	X						X					X	3
Live Activities		X											1
Simulations		X					X					X	3
Badges					X	X	X	X		X			5
Leaderboards					X	X	X		X	X	X		6
Progress Bar						X				X	X		3
Learning Man System					X								1

interactions with games in nongaming contexts rather than repeating the game itself, Yasin et al. [35] note that this conflict is crucial for engaging players. This aligns with the more general concept that gamification is about leveraging game-like characteristics to improve user experiences and accomplish objectives rather than playing games.

5.3 Levels

The concept of "levels" in gamification is crucial in engaging participants by integrating gaming elements into learning environments. The approach draws participants in and improves their educational experience, which eventually results in higher achievement [37, 39]. Higher levels must be unlocked in a way that reflects the skills and talents that students have gained, and they must appeal to participants' cognitive, emotional, and social components [40]. In this context, "gamification" refers to the use of game design patterns and concepts to boost motivation in a variety of contexts, whether they are digital or not [5]. Likewise, levels are frequently used to encourage this participation in contexts other than games [43].

5.4 Achievements

The achievement technique solves problems, encourages behaviour, engages individuals, and promotes learning [5, 39]. Yasin et al. [35] is an example of this, as participants attempt to create a precise and well-balanced phishing email. Those who complete this work successfully will accumulate the most points during the evaluation stage, ultimately resulting in a game win. This illustration shows how the accomplishment strategy can successfully promote learning and engagement in a simulated setting.

5.5 Collaborations

The goal of collaborative learning is to combine participants' informal and formal learning experiences while overcoming group problems [5, 45]. Yasin et al. [35] game is meant to be played in groups, where players can exchange ideas and expertise. Incorporating deliberate discussions and constructive criticism sessions improves teamwork and knowledge sharing even more, especially when creating and assessing different attack scenarios. This method emphasizes how crucial cooperation is when modelling social engineering assaults.

5.6 Live Activities

Workman et al. [36] discusses the use of live activities, like hackathons or capture-the-flag competitions, which take learning beyond simulation by immersing students in situations where they compete to breach and protect systems. Workman et al. [36] further emphasizes that these practical tests of participants' understanding make these live engagements an excellent teaching tool. This method fosters a reciprocal learning process that improves comprehension through active engagement by highlighting areas for growth and reinforcing what is effective. This method is crucial to the gamification process since it offers a practical experience that mimics real-world difficulties like social engineering attacks.

5.7 Simulations

Simulations are essential for establishing a connection between mental representations and physical settings, improving efficiency, and encouraging positive changes in behaviour in cybersecurity procedures [36, 45]. They give participants a safe environment to experiment and learn by experience. They enhance cognitive cueing and metacognitive awareness by enabling participants to evaluate their development and go over content again when necessary. Workman et al. [36] conclude that cybersecurity simulations greatly improve practical learning compared to traditional classroom or lab study alone. Furthermore, Ingvarsson et al. [5] emphasize how team members can learn particular duties more successfully by utilizing virtual reality and game-like scenarios. Simulations foster original thought and provide superior results than traditional techniques.

5.8 Badges

In gamified apps, badges are a popular form of reward intended to draw in participants and improve learning outcomes by encouraging performance [39]. These badges, which represent the degree of skill gained or the kind of mission completed, are given out upon doing tasks or reaching intermediate objectives [5, 39, 40, 43]. They support and encourage students by giving them constructive criticism and acknowledgement from their peers as they strive toward predetermined goals. Badge completion rates in the context of Kiyaslio, a gamified mobile crowdsourcing application, are determined by user activity [41]. The badges are given out in phases, each of which builds on the one before it, making the transition between them a difficult task rather than a quite simple one.

5.9 Leaderboards

Leaderboards, as discussed in [5, 39, 40, 42–44], are tools that display the relative positions of students compared to their peers. They are effective in motivating students by appealing to their emotional and social aspects. Leaderboards can foster friendly competition among participants, encouraging engagement and driving performance. By highlighting individual standings, they serve as a powerful motivator in gamified environments, promoting continuous improvement and participation.

5.10 Progress

The progress bar is acknowledged as a crucial gamification tool that provides participants with feedback on the tasks they have completed and the remaining tasks to complete before achieving their next goal, as stated in Diaz Redondo et al. [40]. Progress bars keep participants motivated and goal focused, which engages users and aids in problem-solving in the real world [43, 44]. This method is essential for preserving user interest, which makes it a useful tool for modelling situations like social engineering assaults.

5.11 Learning Management System

According to Anannya et al. [39], a learning management system (LMS) is a platform or piece of software intended for the administration, tracking, and delivery of training courses. It offers instructors tools to create and organize course content, deliver it to students or learners, administer assessments, track progress, and manage various aspects of the learning process. Understanding the role of an LMS is essential for identifying gamification techniques that can be integrated to simulate social engineering attacks effectively.

6 Conclusion

The study aimed to develop guidelines for using gamification to simulate social engineering attacks and improve employee cybersecurity awareness. The literature reviewed provided detailed insights into the types of social engineering tactics, human vulnerabilities, and existing countermeasures. The systematic literature review used for this study highlighted effective gamification techniques, including simulations, leaderboards, and interactive learning.

This study contributes valuable theoretical insights into the application of gamification in cybersecurity training. The research lays a foundation for businesses to develop more engaging and practical training programs by identifying effective gamification techniques and linking them to social engineering scenarios. These programs can enhance awareness and resilience among employees, addressing the human factor often the weakest link in cybersecurity.

The limitation of this study is the limited number of papers reviewed in the SLR. Future studies could expand on the systematic literature review by expanding on the database suite and explore pilot implementations of gamification-based training to observe their effectiveness in practice. Expanding this research to include qualitative feedback from training participants could provide deeper insights into user experiences and further refine the proposed guidelines.

References

1. Gundu, T., Modiba, N.: Building competitive advantage from Ubuntu: an African information security awareness model. In: ICISSP, pp. 569–576 (2020)
2. Lugo, R.G., Juozapavicius, A., Lapin, K., Ask, T.F., Knox, B.J., Sütterlin, S.: Human-centric approach to cyber threat identification: the role of cognition, experience, and education in decision-making. JCIT **27**, 1–13 (2025). https://doi.org/10.4018/JCIT.368220
3. Fuertes, W., et al.: Impact of social engineering attacks: a literature review. In: Rocha, Á., Fajardo-Toro, C.H., Rodríguez, J.M.R. (eds.) Developments and Advances in Defense and Security, pp. 25–35. Springer, Singapore (2022). https://doi.org/10.1007/978-981-16-4884-7_3
4. Putz, L.-M., Hofbauer, F., Treiblmaier, H.: Can gamification help to improve education? Findings from a longitudinal study. Comput. Hum. Behav. **110**, 106392 (2020). https://doi.org/10.1016/j.chb.2020.106392
5. Ingvarsson, C., Hallin, A., Kier, C.: Project stakeholder engagement through gamification: what do we know and where do we go from here? IJMPB **16**, 152–181 (2023). https://doi.org/10.1108/IJMPB-07-2022-0170
6. Alkhazi, B., Alshaikh, M., Alkhezi, S., Labbaci, H.: Assessment of the impact of information security awareness training methods on knowledge, attitude, and behavior. IEEE Access **10**, 132132–132143 (2022). https://doi.org/10.1109/ACCESS.2022.3230286
7. Lin, J., Yu, W., Zhang, N., Yang, X., Zhang, H., Zhao, W.: A survey on internet of things: architecture, enabling technologies, security and privacy, and applications. IEEE Internet Things J. **4**, 1125–1142 (2017). https://doi.org/10.1109/JIOT.2017.2683200
8. Wang, Z., Sun, L., Zhu, H.: Defining social engineering in cybersecurity. IEEE Access **8**, 85094–85115 (2020). https://doi.org/10.1109/ACCESS.2020.2992807
9. Cusack, B., Adedokun, K.: The impact of personality traits on user's susceptibility to social engineering attacks. In: Australian Information Security Management Conference (2018). https://doi.org/10.25958/5C528FFA66693
10. Syafitri, W., Shukur, Z., Mokhtar, U.A., Sulaiman, R., Ibrahim, M.A.: Social engineering attacks prevention: a systematic literature review. IEEE Access. **10**, 39325–39343 (2022). https://doi.org/10.1109/ACCESS.2022.3162594
11. Abu Hweidi, R.F., Eleyan, D.: Social Engineering Attack concepts, frameworks, and Awareness: a Systematic Literature Review. IJCDS **13**, 691–700 (2023). https://doi.org/10.12785/ijcds/130155
12. ISACA: Threat landscape, security operations and cybersecurity maturity (2021)
13. PurpleSec: Cyber security statistics: the ultimate list of stats, data trends (2021)
14. Ribeiro, R., Mateus-Coelho, N., Mamede, H.: Improving social engineering resilience in enterprises: a systematic literature review. ARIS2-J. **3**, 34–65 (2023). https://doi.org/10.56394/aris2.v3i1.30
15. IBM: Threat Intelligence Index 2023 (2023)
16. Alves, F., Mateus-Coelho, N., Cruz-Cunha, M.: Encryption file system framework - proof of concept. Procedia Comput. Sci. **181**, 1237–1246 (2021). https://doi.org/10.1016/j.procs.2021.01.322
17. Saraiva, M., Mateus-Coelho, N.: CyberSoc framework a systematic review of the state-of-art. Procedia Comput. Sci. **204**, 961–972 (2022). https://doi.org/10.1016/j.procs.2022.08.117

18. Junger, M., Montoya, L., Overink, F.-J.: Priming and warnings are not effective to prevent social engineering attacks. Comput. Hum. Behav. **66**, 75–87 (2017). https://doi.org/10.1016/j.chb.2016.09.012
19. Kaur, R., Gabrijelčič, D., Klobučar, T.: Artificial intelligence for cybersecurity: literature review and future research directions. Inf. Fus. **97**, 101804 (2023). https://doi.org/10.1016/j.inffus.2023.101804
20. Shaw, R.S., Chen, C.C., Harris, A.L., Huang, H.-J.: The impact of information richness on information security awareness training effectiveness. Comput. Educ. **52**, 92–100 (2009). https://doi.org/10.1016/j.compedu.2008.06.011
21. McIlWraith, A.: Information security and employee behaviour: how to reduce risk through employee education, training and awareness, New York, London (2022)
22. Khando, K., Gao, S., Islam, S.M., Salman, A.: Enhancing employees information security awareness in private and public organisations: a systematic literature review. Comput. Secur. **106**, 102267 (2021). https://doi.org/10.1016/j.cose.2021.102267
23. Goodman, S.: Information security: policy, processes, and practices. Routledge (2016). https://doi.org/10.4324/9781315288697
24. Hart, S., Margheri, A., Paci, F., Sassone, V.: Riskio: a serious game for cyber security awareness and education. Comput. Secur. **95**, 101827 (2020). https://doi.org/10.1016/j.cose.2020.101827
25. Sankhwar, S., Pandey, D., Khan, R.A., Mohanty, S.N.: An anti-phishing enterprise environ model using feed-forward backpropagation and Levenberg-Marquardt method. Secur. Priv. **4**, e132 (2021). https://doi.org/10.1002/spy2.132
26. Trumbach, C.C., Payne, D.M., Walsh, K.: Cybersecurity in business education: the 'how to' in incorporating education into practice. Ind. High. Educ. **37**, 35–45 (2023). https://doi.org/10.1177/09504222221099389
27. Qusa, H., Tarazi, J.: Cyber-hero: a gamification framework for cyber security awareness for high schools students. In: 2021 IEEE 11th Annual Computing and Communication Workshop and Conference (CCWC), pp. 0677–0682. IEEE (2021). https://doi.org/10.1109/CCWC51732.2021.9375847
28. Khan, A.H., Bahl Sawhney, P., Das, S., Pandey, D.: SartCyber security awareness measurement model (APAT). In: 2020 International Conference on Power Electronics & IoT Applications in Renewable Energy and its Control (PARC), Mathura, Uttar Pradesh, India, pp. 298–302. IEEE (2020). https://doi.org/10.1109/PARC49193.2020.236614
29. Lampropoulos, G., Sidiropoulos, A.: Impact of gamification on students' learning outcomes and academic performance: a longitudinal study comparing online, traditional, and gamified learning. Educ. Sci. **14**, 367 (2024). https://doi.org/10.3390/educsci14040367
30. Sodikin, R.A., Hikmawan, R.: Analysis of gamification in cybersecurity education for students: a systematic literature review. Jurnal Educ. **8**, 147 (2023). https://doi.org/10.30983/educative.v8i2.7513
31. Guo, Z., et al.: Robust spammer detection using collaborative neural network in internet-of-things applications. IEEE Internet Things J. **8**, 9549–9558 (2021). https://doi.org/10.1109/JIOT.2020.3003802
32. Wada, R.K., et al.: Simulation-based pediatric interprofessional team training to facilitate end-of-life discussions. Clin. Simul. Nurs. **78**, 27–33 (2023). https://doi.org/10.1016/j.ecns.2023.02.010
33. Kulkarni, P.M., Appasaba, L.V., Gokhale, P., Tigadi, B.: Role of digital simulation in employee training. Global Trans. Proc. **3**, 149–156 (2022). https://doi.org/10.1016/j.gltp.2022.04.014
34. Siddaway, A.P., Wood, A.M., Hedges, L.V.: How to do a systematic review: a best practice guide for conducting and reporting narrative reviews, meta-analyses, and meta-syntheses. Annu. Rev. Psychol. **70**, 747–770 (2019). https://doi.org/10.1146/annurev-psych-010418-102803

35. Yasin, A., Fatima, R., JiangBin, Z., Afzal, W., Raza, S.: Can serious gaming tactics bolster spear-phishing and phishing resilience?: Securing the human hacking in Information Security. Inf. Softw. Technol. **170**, 107426 (2024). https://doi.org/10.1016/j.infsof.2024.107426
36. Workman, M.D., Luevanos, J.A., Mai, B.: A study of cybersecurity education using a present-test-practice-assess model. IEEE Trans. Educ. **65**, 40–45 (2022). https://doi.org/10.1109/TE.2021.3086025
37. Al-Karaki, J.N., Itradat, A., Mekonen, S.: Immersive cybersecurity teaching/training using gamification on the metaverse: a hands-on case study*. In: 2023 IEEE International Conference on Dependable, Autonomic and Secure Computing, International Conference on Pervasive Intelligence and Computing, International Conference on Cloud and Big Data Computing, International Conference on Cyber Science and Technology Congress (DASC/PiCom/CBDCom/CyberSciTech), Abu Dhabi, United Arab Emirates, pp. 0101–0108. IEEE (2023). https://doi.org/10.1109/DASC/PiCom/CBDCom/Cy59711.2023.10361297
38. Davis, N., Grant, E.S.: Simulated phishing training exercises versus gamified phishing education games. In: 2022 Fourth International Conference on Emerging Research in Electronics, Computer Science and Technology (ICERECT), Mandya, India, pp. 1–8. IEEE (2022). https://doi.org/10.1109/ICERECT56837.2022.10060595
39. Anannya, T.T., Mahmud, &S.R., Khan, S.R., Zaman, S.R., Jalal, Md.S., Sharmin, S.: From blackboards to byteboards: adapting to the digital age in undergraduate education on campus. In: 2023 17th International Conference on Signal-Image Technology & Internet-Based Systems (SITIS), Bangkok, Thailand, pp. 54–61. IEEE (2023). https://doi.org/10.1109/SITIS61268.2023.00018
40. Diaz Redondo, R.P., Ktena, A., Kunicina, N., Zabasta, A., Patlins, A., Mele, D.E.: Advanced practices: micro learning, practice oriented teaching and gamified learning. In: 2020 IEEE 61th International Scientific Conference on Power and Electrical Engineering of Riga Technical University (RTUCON), Riga, Latvia, pp. 1–7. IEEE (2020). https://doi.org/10.1109/RTUCON51174.2020.9316555
41. Macakoğlu, ŞS., Alakuş Çınar, B., Peker, S.: Kiyaslio: a gamified mobile crowdsourcing application for tracking price dispersion in the grocery retail market. IJWIS **18**, 55–75 (2022). https://doi.org/10.1108/IJWIS-09-2021-0089
42. Lyons, R.M., Fox, G., Stephens, S.: Gamification to enhance engagement and higher order learning in entrepreneurial education. ET **65**, 416–432 (2023). https://doi.org/10.1108/ET-05-2022-0204
43. Zainuddin, Z., Rasyidin, R., Zanzibar, Z., Aruni, F., Nurmasyahyati, N.: Andragogical principles in a gamification concept: how does it work for adult learners in an online class? JARHE **15**, 1632–1648 (2023). https://doi.org/10.1108/JARHE-04-2022-0127
44. Mohanty, S., Christopher, B.P.: A study on role of gamification elements in training outcomes: comparing the mediating effect of intrinsic and extrinsic motivation. TLO **30**, 480–500 (2023). https://doi.org/10.1108/TLO-08-2022-0098
45. Patrício, R., Moreira, A.C., Zurlo, F.: Enhancing design thinking approaches to innovation through gamification. EJIM **24**, 1569–1594 (2021). https://doi.org/10.1108/EJIM-06-2020-0239

Lucky the Fish Teaches Children About Phishing

Given Mnisi, Günther Richard Drevin(✉), and Lynette Drevin

School of Computer Science and Information Systems, North-West University, Potchefstroom, South Africa
{gunther.drevin,lynette.drevin}@nwu.ac.za

Abstract. Digital technologies have become an integral part of everyday life, making them unavoidable for people, particularly children who grow up surrounded by them. Today, most households have at least one digital device, making it challenging to keep children away from these technologies and exposing them to online risks including cyberbullying, phishing, and deepfakes. Given that many children are predominantly engaged with gaming, it has emerged as an effective tool for educating them about cybersecurity and fostering positive digital habits. This paper reports on a study where a serious game was developed aimed at raising phishing awareness among preschool children. The game is designed as a collaborative tool for children and their caregivers, encouraging discussions and activities that extend beyond merely restricting technology use. The design science research methodology, in conjunction with qualitative methods, was employed. Eleven expert reviewers evaluated the game regarding the usability, engagement, and design elements of the game. The findings indicated favourability towards enhancing digital well-being and cybersecurity awareness.

Keywords: Digital well-being · Preschool children · Cybersecurity · Awareness · Phishing · Serious games

1 Introduction

In the contemporary digital era, children are immersed in a world saturated with digital media, including smartphones, tablets, television, video games, and social media. This digitalisation presents new ways of how children interact and develop.

This prevalent digital environment makes it challenging to protect children from its influence. Children's inherent need for attention is increasingly satisfied through digital technologies rather than through interactions with their peers and caregivers, which include parents, guardians, teachers, educators, and childcare providers. From an early age, many children are introduced to digital technologies, with their first encounter with screen time occurring as early as four

Published by Springer Nature Switzerland AG 2026
L. Drevin et al. (Eds.): WISE 2025, IFIP AICT 742, pp. 152–167, 2026.
https://doi.org/10.1007/978-3-031-94924-1_11

months. This early exposure enables them to interact with distant family members and become accustomed to screen time by the time they reach preschool age [1,2].

While traditional games such as hide-and-seek, marbles, kite flying, and hopscotch remain integral to children's childhoods, digital devices provide new avenues for connecting with peers online.

Although digital technologies offer significant benefits to users, such as learning, acquiring information, and entertainment, they also present potential risks, including cyberbullying, phishing, malware, viruses, and deepfakes. This is particularly concerning regarding children, who may lack the knowledge and experience to protect themselves [3,4].

Maintaining positive digital well-being is similar to maintaining a healthy lifestyle in the physical world. This involves an individual's ability to identify potential threats and opportunities, behave responsibly, and align their digital and physical behaviour to ensure safety [4].

Among several forms of digital media, video games are also prevalent among preschoolers, as indicated by numerous studies [2,5–9]. Gaming is a popular activity for children, offering various benefits, including fostering creativity, improving social skills, providing relaxation, improving cognitive abilities, and creating learning opportunities [10]. Furthermore, games have been identified as valuable tools for cultivating digital well-being awareness in children and play a significant role in enhancing cybersecurity and digital well-being awareness in this age group [3,11].

Although most video games are primarily designed for entertainment purposes, a distinct category known as serious games is specifically developed for educational purposes. They extend beyond conventional teaching methods by integrating behaviour change theories, empowering users to apply acquired knowledge proactively [12].

The primary objective of this paper is to *culminate in the development of a serious game intervention aimed at enhancing digital well-being and cybersecurity awareness among preschool children.*

The methodology followed in this study was design science, during which an artefact was developed; in this case, a serious game, and evaluation was conducted using qualitative methods, particularly purposive sampling, to gather feedback from expert reviewers.

The remainder of this paper is structured as follows: Sect. 2 presents a review of the literature on cybersecurity, cybersecurity awareness, cybersecurity for preschool-age children, and serious games. In Sect. 3, the developed proof-of-concept serious game is discussed. The results and findings of the expert reviewers are provided in Sect. 4. Finally, in Sect. 5, the conclusion and potential directions for future research and development are presented.

2 Literature Review

In this section, an overview of the pertinent literature related to two primary aspects of this study: cybersecurity and serious games, is provided. In

Sect. 2.1, background information on cybersecurity, particularly phishing, is provided. Section 2.2 discusses two approaches to enhancing cybersecurity awareness. Section 2.3 outlines the key stakeholders whose involvement is essential for the effectiveness of these strategies, along with the learning methods suitable for children. Finally, Sect. 2.4 presents the critical design elements necessary for developing a successful game, along with design elements specifically tailored for preschool-aged children.

2.1 Cybersecurity

The widespread adoption of mobile devices among children has become increasingly common, as numerous caregivers allow their use during mealtimes as a means of encouraging them to eat, calming them down, or as a distraction while working. However, caregivers may not be aware of the potential consequences that these devices have on their children's digital well-being [13,14].

Although anyone can be a victim of various risks associated with the digital world, children are the most vulnerable demographic due to their inexperience and inquisitive nature [15]. As a result, cybersecurity for children has gained significant attention and is becoming a prominent topic driven by the increased accessibility of the Internet for children and their subsequent exposure to various online threats, including phishing, cyberbullying, password security, online strangers, identity theft, financial scams, and privacy [3].

This paper specifically focuses on phishing, as it is often underestimated and perceived as a problem affecting mainly adults [16]. Phishing is a type of attack in which an attacker uses deception and disguise techniques to gain access to confidential information of a user online [17]. In layman's terms, a phishing attack does not obtain a victim's sensitive information by compromising them but deceives a person into willingly providing it. These attacks can be carried out for personal gain or to steal someone's identity.

2.2 Cybersecurity Awareness Attempts

A study was conducted to develop strategies that have been shown to be effective in increasing cybersecurity awareness and promoting the digital well-being of children, including the implementation of digital applications and early intervention measures [18].

Digital Applications

Anti-Phishing Phil is an educational game that teaches players about phishing attacks and how to prevent them. Players control Phil, a young fish that distinguishes between real and fake worms, guided by his experienced father. The game covers phishing recognition and safe online practices [19].

Digital Compass[1], developed by Common Sense Education, teaches children about digital citizenship and the consequences of online behaviour. Players navi-

[1] https://www.digitalcompass.org/.

gate scenario-based situations, including avoiding phishing scams and protecting personal information, where they must make wise choices in the digital world.

Google developed an interactive digital game called *Interland*[2] that educates children about digital safety and citizenship. Players navigate four floating islands to help Internauts combat bullies, hackers, and phishers.

CyberAware is a digital application that teaches preschoolers about cybersecurity. It covers various topics such as email spam filters, security updates and patches, antivirus software, and firewalls through simulations, interactive lessons, and quizzes [20].

Tanzanite Collector is a mobile game developed for African contexts, focusing on Tanzania. Players control *Tanzanite Collector*, collecting genuine tanzanite stones while avoiding malicious ones. The game incorporates numerous phishing concepts such as emails, phone calls, and message-based attacks [15].

Although these games have been proven effective in promoting digital well-being and cybersecurity among children, they have their own limitations, particularly for preschool-aged children.

Anti-Phishing Phil lacks cognitive development, as many children may find it difficult to identify URLs, which can also be complex for adults. In addition, it lacks contextual learning and does not have a level selector that could structure the challenges for players. While *Digital Compass* offers contextual learning, it lacks sufficient choices for players. In addition its long playtime, combined with instances of being solely in a text-based format, may limit engagement for some children who have not yet developed reading skills.

Although *Interland* includes content that may be challenging for children to grasp, it requires caregiver involvement to reinforce the concepts presented. Similar to the other games, *Tanzanite Collector* lacks a difficulty selector and does not encourage caregiver engagement, which is critical for child development. Finally, *CyberAware* can be challenging for children due to the high speed of the balls and time limitations that may restrict engagement, and the information provided within the game may be insufficient for players to progress.

Early Intervention Campaigns

Early intervention programs that have been shown to be effective in improving children's digital well-being and providing cybersecurity awareness training include the implementation of a school curriculum, using digital comics, interactive storytelling, and educational videos, essentially incorporating educational resources [3].

There are key components necessary for fostering early intervention campaigns aimed at developing children's digital well-being and cybersecurity awareness. These components include consistency, simplicity, engaging content, and appropriateness [21]. Some of the resources designed specifically for children include an interactive educational e-book titled *Cyberheroes*[3], which teaches

[2] https://beinternetawesome.withgoogle.com/en_us/interland.

[3] https://www.leahzhangkennedy.com/cyberheroes.

children about online anonymity, password security, cyberbullying, and location sharing. This e-book facilitates discussions about online privacy between caregivers and children and includes a discussion guide for caregivers [22].

Chicken Clicking, is a children's book that discusses online safety. It follows a young chick who discovers a farmer's laptop and explores cyberspace. The chick unknowingly shops online for the farm and eventually befriends an individual on the Internet. As the chick shares personal information and arranges a meeting, the friend turns out to be different than expected [23].

Digital Wellnests: Let us play in safe nests! is a book designed to enhance digital well-being and cybersecurity awareness among preschoolers. It features 14 poems with animal characters, each containing a lesson, and questions for children to ask their caregivers [24].

This resource is the main focus of this study as it addresses various cybersecurity and digital well-being topics, including phishing, hacking, cyberbullying, password ontology, and other related topics. The book introduces new concepts with clear explanations and uses simple language that is suitable for all readers, including non-native English speakers. The events occur in a fictional animal world, with characters familiar to African children such as fish, cats, snails, and sheep using various digital technologies [25]. The book is divided into four parts: a foreword, explanations of technology-related terminology, poems, and 14 short messages. More information can be found in [24].

2.3 Cybersecurity in Preschool Education

For the two approaches, digital applications and early intervention campaigns, to be successful, it is essential to have involvement and support from various stakeholders to ensure their effectiveness. This includes [26]:

- Government: setting up systems that promote and assist in creating a secure online environment;
- Law: establishing legislation to protect children from cybercrime;
- Schools: conducting and creating initiatives centred on digital well-being and cybersecurity awareness;
- Teachers: being well-equipped in terms of cybersecurity education and digital well-being;
- Caregivers: supervising their children when they use the Internet, as they have a direct impact on how it is used; and
- Peers: motivating and assisting their friends.

While this is feasible, it requires a significant amount of time, as well as commitment, especially in developing countries where resources are scarce. To promote digital well-being and cybersecurity awareness among children, it is essential to understand their learning preferences and optimal approaches. Children learn in various ways, with play being a central component in their early childhood development. Play is a multifaceted concept observed not only in humans but also across various species, allowing individuals to hone their skills [27,28].

Playing allows children to explore, observe, and make sense of their surroundings. Some ways in which children learn include hands-on experience, trial and error, social interaction, parental involvement, and self-directed learning [29].

Additional learning methods may include inquisitiveness and auditory learning [21]. It is important to note that not all children learn in the same way. Some may learn through listening, while others may learn through building structures, and some may require assistance from their caregivers. Integrating these components into a game can be a beneficial and captivating method that enhances children's overall learning experiences and helps achieve the desired objective.

2.4 Serious Games

Games have long been a popular recreational pursuit across generations. A game is defined as a competition, whether mental or physical, that is played according to predetermined guidelines for the purpose of entertaining the player [30]. They have been identified as a valuable solution for raising awareness of digital well-being among children [11]. Although most video games are designed primarily for entertainment purposes, there is a distinct category called serious games, which serve a "serious goal."

Serious games are a type of video game in which the main objective goes beyond mere amusement [31]. They can take on various forms, such as educational games, role-playing games, and simulations, and are designed to achieve specific objectives, which can include promoting health, providing training, facilitating education, and raising awareness [32].

Design Elements for Serious Games

Developing serious games can be challenging because it involves integrating different game design principles to make them successful [33]. The fundamental principle of developing an optimal serious game is to make it both entertaining and educational. However, there are various design principles or elements that contribute to the overall quality of a serious game and distinguish it from other games. Several studies have identified optimal design principles [34–38].

The game principles relevant to this paper are those discussed in [35,36,38]. These studies explored the guiding principles for developing serious games for preschool-age children, analysed commonly used design principles in twenty-two cybersecurity serious games, and examined the characteristics for an effective game, respectively. The design principles include competition and goals, rules, choice, challenge, fantasy (also known as narrative), aesthetics, simplicity, feedback, and rewards.

Serious Game Development for Preschool Children

When developing serious games for preschool children, there are additional design elements that align with their unique cognitive abilities, as they process information differently compared to older individuals. Since their cognitive memory is still developing, preschool children typically have shorter attention spans and limited visual processing capabilities and hand-eye coordination. Incorporating these elements can harness the natural enjoyment of play and establish a successful medium for their learning experience [39]. The elements of game design that meet the needs of preschoolers include: engaging visuals, quality feedback mechanisms and reward systems, structured challenges, physical interactions, balanced simplicity and complexity, short playtime and quality interactions [40].

The elements mentioned above are essential for developing a game specifically for preschool children. These elements are incorporated into the serious game as they have the potential to effectively meet the needs of preschool-age children.

3 Overview of the Game: Lucky the Fish

In this section, the developed serious game is presented. The story of Lucky the Fish was chosen to raise awareness about phishing among preschool children, using design elements and additional elements suited for this age group.

The game was developed using the Godot game engine[4] and its built-in scripting language, GDScript. The visuals were edited with Paint.NET[5] and the animations were created using Synfig[6].

The game consists of four main scenes: the main menu, poem, quiz, and game scene. The main menu scene, as presented in Fig. 1, serves as the initial interface for the user, allowing them to select a poem.

Fig. 1. Main Menu scene for game selection.

Each poem is accompanied by a corresponding quiz and game. When the game begins, all the poems are animated; however, the animations are only

[4] https://godotengine.org/.
[5] https://getpaint.net/.
[6] https://www.synfig.org/.

active once a specific game is selected. These animations are designed to capture the child's attention. The left and right arrow buttons are used to navigate between the various poems in the main menu. The settings include sound configurations, credentials, and assets; additional settings will be incorporated into future versions of the game.

Upon selecting a poem from the main menu, players are directed to the poem scene. In this scene, the chosen poem is presented visually and audibly (read to the player). Players can progress through the text by clicking anywhere on the screen, allowing them to advance to subsequent paragraphs or pages. If a player clicks on the wrong poem, they can return to the main menu using the back button.

Fig. 2. Lucky the Fish poem scene.

The primary objective of this scene is to raise awareness about phishing in an engaging and entertaining manner. The specific poem presented in Fig. 2 addresses the topic of phishing. A fish named Lucky receives a message informing it that it has won a prize and should click on the link to claim it, even though it knows it has not entered any competition. However, its friend Sunny advises it to delete the message as it might be a trick.

The quiz scene is the third scene that the player encounters, following the poem scene as presented in Fig. 3. The objective of this scene is to assess the player's comprehension of the problem presented in the poem by requiring them to answer four random questions related to the topic, thereby introducing an element of replayability.

The progress of the game is not contingent upon the player's performance; even if the player achieves suboptimal results, they advance to the next scene.

Fig. 3. Quiz scene presenting four random questions based on the poem.

This scene aims to raise awareness of a specific topic in an engaging manner, rather than providing formal education. It can also serve as a collaborative tool for children and their caregivers.

The game scene is the final scene that the user encounters. Each poem is paired with a distinct game, which serves as a reward for the player after completing the poem and quiz. In Fig. 4a, a snapshot of the game menu containing instructions is presented to the player and read aloud.

(a) **Lucky the Fish game instructions** (b) **Lucky the Fish game**

Fig. 4. Lucky the Fish game scenes, including the instructions and the mini-game.

In Fig. 4b, the game featured is the "Lucky the Fish" game. The objective of this game is to raise awareness when it comes to distinguishing between safe emails, indicated by a green checkmark and safety signs, and unsafe emails, represented by caution and phishing signs, as they appear from the bottom of the screen.

The player must collect twenty safe emails to achieve victory; however, clicking on three unsafe emails results in a loss. The game enhances hand-eye coordination, thus improving fine motor skills. In addition, it educates players on the importance of identifying secure and malicious messages, promoting awareness, and promoting digital well-being. The inclusion of a level slider encourages players to replay the game in order to improve their skills.

Upon completion of the game, players receive visual and auditory feedback that informs them of their win or loss. The player has the choice to replay the game or return to the main menu to explore additional poems.

The Lucky the Fish game extends beyond existing digital applications in terms of its target audience, combining storytelling with interactive animations in the poem scene. This makes the learning process engaging and allows for collaboration between caregivers and children in the quiz scene. As a result, it serves as a great tool for contextual learning, providing an immediate feedback mechanism through auditory and visual feedback. After the quiz, players receive additional feedback. In addition, this game offers players choices, such as a difficulty level selector, which most existing games lack.

4 Findings

In this section, the results obtained from the expert reviewers are presented. Expert reviewers were selected through purposive sampling, a technique that involves selecting participants based on specific expertise or knowledge related to the subject matter.

A questionnaire was distributed to eleven expert reviewers. They included experts in preschool education (teachers), game design and development, academia, engineering, cybersecurity, and software development. Preschool teachers assessed the content and educational value, while the other experts evaluated the technical aspects of the game. The questionnaire consisted of multiple choice, open-ended, Likert scale, and dichotomous questions. Subsequently, expert reviewers were asked about their background, cybersecurity and digital well-being education, digital technologies, usability of the game, game evaluation, and game elements. This feedback was required as part of the evaluation phase of the design science approach.

Reviewer Background

The questionnaire responses revealed the following educational background among the reviewers: one had a high school education, one had a diploma, five had bachelor's degrees, and four had honours degrees. In terms of experience in their field, six of the reviewers had between one and three years, three had four to six years, and the remaining two had less than one year.

Feedback on Cybersecurity Education

Ten of eleven reviewers indicated their familiarity with cybersecurity and digital well-being. When it comes to usage of resources, two of the reviewers reported using CyberPatriot, Common Sense Education books, and other guides to educate their children. All the reviewers emphasised the importance of educating children about these topics. Nine of the eleven respondents believed guardians do not teach their children about cybersecurity awareness and digital well-being.

This perspective is primarily motivated by the fact that in developing countries, caregivers often lack an understanding of cybersecurity and digital well-being, making it challenging for them to educate their children. Some parents provide their children with digital technologies to occupy them while they work, without monitoring their usage. Some of the expert reviewers noted that cybersecurity and digital well-being concepts are not prioritised in parenting. However, two reviewers stated that they were taught these concepts prior to using the Internet and implemented limits on their screen time.

These findings highlight the need for intentional parenting regarding cybersecurity and digital well-being awareness. Ten of the experts suggested incorporating these topics into the basic curriculum to raise awareness and equip children with essential knowledge and skills to navigate the Internet. One reviewer responded that it can be time consuming and suggested that rather than being part of the curriculum, it could be an extracurricular activity.

Feedback on Digital Technologies

Reviewers were presented with questions regarding digital technologies to gather information about the role of digital technologies in children's daily lives, particularly focusing on the digital landscape to which preschoolers are exposed and its implications for their safety and well-being. The reviewers rated it on a Likert scale of 5, with a score of 3.7 indicating that children are exposed to various digital technologies, including tablets and smartphones, while a smaller proportion use gaming consoles, computers, and smart TVs. Eight of the eleven of reviewers believed that this exposure is concerning and supported their concerns with the following statements:

- *"Too much exposure to the wrong kind of content on the Internet can affect young children's critical thinking development and can even lead to mental disorders."*
- *"As they spend more time online, children become more vulnerable to cyber threats such as phishing, cyberbullying, and inappropriate content."*

While the majority of reviewers expressed concern, a minority did not find it concerning, asserting that children should be familiar with the latest technology to avoid difficulties in the future and that parents should establish boundaries and limit the use of digital technologies. These findings show that while the use of technology is predominant in this generation, it should be used responsibly and with parental guidance. The final question revealed that seven of the reviewers believe that parents do not monitor their children's digital technology usage, which can increase the risk of cybersecurity threats, while the remaining four reviewers believe that parents do supervise their children's online behaviour.

This underscores the importance of cybersecurity and digital well-being awareness, as the majority of children are exposed to digital technologies, and a substantial proportion of parents do not supervise this usage. Consequently, the development of a game that addresses the gap in spreading awareness among children and their parents is crucial, fostering healthy habits when it comes to using digital technologies.

Game Evaluation

The game evaluation used a five-point Likert scale and an open-ended question. The game received a score 4.4 for introducing fundamental cybersecurity and digital well-being concepts, 3.9 for age-appropriate scenarios, 4.5 for promoting cybersecurity awareness and digital well-being, and 4 for children's retention of the lessons taught. Some responses to the open-ended question to support the previous answer were:

- *"The concepts being presented, even though they are from a very technical field, are presented in a very simple and gamified way. The fact that the game is narrated or read by a child makes it even more appropriate for pre-schoolers."*
- *"The game is engaging, interactive, and age-appropriate."*

These findings indicate that the game is generally effective in disseminating cybersecurity and digital well-being awareness. Notably, this game is serves as a collaborative tool for children and their parents. In instances where children encounter difficult scenarios due to their age, their guardians can provide further explanations, thereby enhancing educational impact of the game.

Game Usability and Engagement

Regarding the usability and engagement of the game, a five-point Likert scale and an open-ended question were presented. The questions covered various aspects, including participation in the game, suitability of animal characters, storylines, design of the game for the target audience, clear objectives, easy-to-understand rules, gameplay structure, and interface. These questions received scores ranging from 4.1 to 4.8. An open-ended question was posed to gain deeper insights on the usability and engagement of the game, with the following responses:

- *"Introducing a pointer or indicator to prompt the user to touch the screen for additional lines could be helpful."*
- *"Making it web based so it is more accessible."*

These findings indicate that the game is well received, but suggest areas of improvement in future development, including accessibility and the user interface.

Game Design Elements and Effectiveness

For game design elements, another five-point Likert scale was used. The structured levels for children scored 3, whilst the rewarding elements of the game to maintain children motivated and engaged received 3.7. The simplicity of the game scored 4.8, its effectiveness in promoting cybersecurity and digital well-being scored 4.2 as indicated in Fig. 5a, and its ability to foster collaboration between children and their caregivers scored 4.5. Expert reviewers scored 4.5 for recommending the game to educators and guardians who work with children, as shown in Fig. 5b.

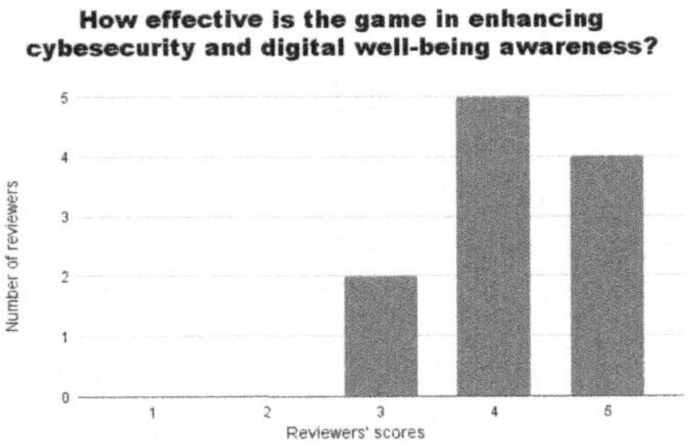

(a) Effectiveness of the game

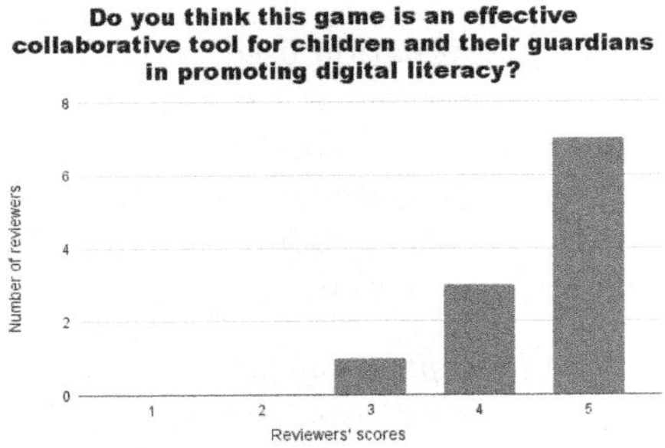

(b) Recommendation of the game

Fig. 5. Reviewer's overall perception of the game.

The experts reviewers indicated that engaging visuals, appropriate interface, balanced simplicity and complexity are the most well integrated serious game elements for children, whilst quality feedback mechanisms and reward systems, quality interactions and structured challenge should be improved to enhance the game's engagement for preschool children.

In response to the open-ended question, reviewers commended the game's engaging visuals and appropriate interface while suggesting improvements in the feedback mechanism and quality of interactions. The final question was about sharing their feedback and suggestions on the game's educational value; this included the following:

- *"The game does an excellent job of presenting the concepts of cybersecurity and digital well-being through a gamified approach, which is an effective way to engage children."*
- *"The game has strong educational points. It is ideal for parents and educators to engage with their children when playing the game".*

5 Conclusion and Future Work

The primary contribution of this paper is *in the development of a serious game intervention aimed at enhancing digital well-being and cybersecurity awareness among preschool children.* The findings revealed that the serious game is effective in enhancing cybersecurity and digital well-being awareness and serves as a collaborative tool for children and their guardians. It is positively received by the expert reviewers in terms of engaging, easy to play and overall interface.

Future developments include incorporating the remaining poems into games to create a complete game, improving the serious game elements, adding multilingual support, and allowing the target audience to play the game to gain better insights into its real-world efficacy.

Acknowledgments. The author acknowledges Fischer, R. and von Solms, S. (2016) for allowing the use of the content from the book Digital Wellnests: Let us play in safe nests!. To my colleagues at the Council for Scientific and Industrial Research (CSIR), thank you for your invaluable support and insightful contributions to this study. This study was sponsored by the CSIR.

References

1. Swider-Cios, E., Vermeij, A., Sitskoorn, M.M.: Young children and screen-based media: the impact on cognitive and socioemotional development and the importance of parental mediation. Cogn. Dev. **66**, 101319 (2023). https://doi.org/10.1016/j.cogdev.2023.101319
2. Bacil, E., da Silva, M.P., Martins, R.V., da Costa, C.G., de Campos, W.: Exposure to smartphones and tablets, physical activity and sleep in children from 5 to 10 years old: a systematic review and meta-analysis. Am. J. Health Promot. **38**(7), 1033–1047 (2024). https://doi.org/10.1177/08901171241242556
3. Quayyum, F., Cruzes, D.S., Jaccheri, L.: Cybersecurity awareness for children: a systematic literature review. Int. J. Child Comput. Interact. **30**, 100343 (2021). https://doi.org/10.1016/j.ijcci.2021.100343
4. Mnisi, G., Drevin, G., Drevin, L., Esterhuizen, J., Croucamp, C.: Digital wellness of preschool children: the story of cyber-cat and the consequences of hacking. In: Yang, X.S., Sherratt, S., Dey, N., Joshi, A. (eds.) Proceedings of Ninth International Congress on Information and Communication Technology, pp. 635–646. Springer, Singapore (2024). https://doi.org/10.1007/978-981-97-3559-4_51
5. Konca, A.S.: Digital technology usage of young children: screen time and families. Early Child. Educ. J. **50**, 1097–1108 (2022). https://doi.org/10.1007/s10643-021-01245-7
6. Neumann, M.: Young children and screen time: Creating a mindful approach to digital technology. Aust. Educ. Comput. **30**(2) (2015)
7. Kabali, H.K., et al.: Exposure and use of mobile media devices by young children. Pediatrics **136**(6), 1044–1050 (2015). https://doi.org/10.1542/peds.2015-2151
8. Panjeti-Madan, V.N., Ranganathan, P.: Impact of screen time on children's development: cognitive, language, physical, and social and emotional domains. Multimodal Technol. Interact. **7**(5), 52 (2023). https://doi.org/10.3390/mti7050052
9. Vedechkina, M., Borgonovi, F.: A review of evidence on the role of digital technology in shaping attention and cognitive control in children. Front. Psychol. **12** (2021). https://doi.org/10.3389/fpsyg.2021.611155
10. Scott, F., et al.: An ecological perspective on children's play with digital technologies in South Africa and the United Kingdom. Int. J. Play **12**(3), 349–374 (2023). https://doi.org/10.1080/21594937.2023.2235466
11. Kritzinger, E.: Enhancing cyber safety awareness among school children in South Africa through gaming. In: 2015 Science and Information Conference (SAI), pp. 1243–1248 (2015). https://doi.org/10.1109/SAI.2015.7237303

12. Chen, T., Stewart, M., Bai, Z., Chen, E., Dabbish, L., Hammer, J.: Hacked time: design and evaluation of a self-efficacy based cybersecurity game. In: Proceedings of the 2020 ACM Designing Interactive Systems Conference, pp. 1737–1749. ACM, New York, NY, USA (2020). https://doi.org/10.1145/3357236.3395522
13. Park, J.H., Park, M.: Smartphone use patterns and problematic smartphone use among preschool children. PLOS ONE **16**(3), 1–12 (2021). https://doi.org/10.1371/journal.pone.0244276
14. Ponti, M.: Screen time and preschool children: promoting health and development in a digital world. Paediatr. Child Health **28**(3), 184–202 (2023). https://doi.org/10.1093/pch/pxac125
15. Panga, R.C.T., Marwa, J., Ndibwile, J.D.: A game or notes? The use of a customized mobile game to improve teenagers' phishing knowledge, case of Tanzania. J. Cybersecur. Priv. **2**(3), 466–489 (2022). https://doi.org/10.3390/jcp2030024
16. Carle, N., Ophoff, J.: Using visual cues to enhance phishing education for children. In: Drevin, L., Leung, W.S., von Solms, S. (eds.) In Information Security Education - Challenges in the Digital Age, WISE 2024. IFIP Advances in Information and Communication Technology, vol. 707, pp. 21–35. Springer, Cham (2024). https://doi.org/10.1007/978-3-031-62918-1_2
17. Alkhalil, Z., Hewage, C., Liqaa, N., Khan, I.: Phishing attacks: a recent comprehensive study and a new anatomy. Front. Comput. Sci. **3** (2021). https://doi.org/10.3389/fcomp.2021.563060
18. Cao, S., Li, H.: A scoping review of digital well-being in early childhood: definitions, measurements, contributors, and interventions. Int. J. Environ. Res. Public Health **20**(4), 3510 (2023). https://doi.org/10.3390/ijerph20043510
19. Sheng, S., et al.: Anti-Phishing Phil: the design and evaluation of a game that teaches people not to fall for phish. ACM Int. Conf. Proc. Ser. **229**, 88–99 (2007). https://doi.org/10.1145/1280680.1280692
20. Giannakas, F., Kambourakis, G., Gritzalis, S.: CyberAware: a mobile game-based app for cybersecurity education and awareness. In: 2015 International Conference on Interactive Mobile Communication Technologies and Learning (IMCL), Thessaloniki, Greece, pp. 54–58. IEEE (2015). https://doi.org/10.1109/IMCTL.2015.7359553
21. Snyman, D.P., Drevin, G.R., Kruger, H.A., Drevin, L., Allers, J.: A wolf, hyena, and fox game to raise cybersecurity awareness among pre-school children. In: Proceedings of the 15th International Symposium on Human Aspects of Information Security and Assurance (HAISA), Virtual, United Kingdom, pp. 91–101 (2021). https://doi.org/10.1007/978-3-030-81111-2_8
22. Zhang-Kennedy, L., Abdelaziz, Y., Chiasson, S.: Cyberheroes: the design and evaluation of an interactive ebook to educate children about online privacy. Int. J. Child Comput. Interact. **13**, 10–18 (2017). https://doi.org/10.1016/j.ijcci.2017.05.001
23. Willis, J.: Chicken Clicking. Random House (2015)
24. Fischer, R., von Solms, S.: Digital Wellnests. African Centre of Excellence for Information Ethics (ACEIE) (2016)
25. von Solms, S., Fischer, R.: Digital wellness: concepts of cybersecurity presented visually for children. In: Eleventh International Symposium on Human Aspects of Information Security & Assurance, HAISA 2017 Digital, University of Plymouth, Adelaide, Australia, pp. 156–166. University of Plymouth (2017)
26. von Solms, S., von Solms, R.: Towards cyber safety education in primary schools in Africa. In: Proceedings of the 8th International Symposium on Human Aspects of

Information Security and Assurance, HAISA, University of Plymouth, Plymouth, UK, pp. 185–197 (2014)
27. Pellis, S., Pellis, V.: The Playful Brain: Venturing to the Limits of Neuroscience. Simon and Schuster (2013)
28. Yogman, M., et al.: The power of play: a pediatric role in enhancing development in young children. Pediatrics **142**(3), e20182058 (2018). https://doi.org/10.1542/peds.2018-2058
29. UNICEF: Learning Through Play: Strengthening Learning Through Play in Early Childhood Education Programmes. UNICEF (2019)
30. Laamarti, F., Eid, M., El Saddik, A.: An overview of serious games. Int. J. Comput. Games Technol. **2014**(1), 1–15 (2014). https://doi.org/10.1155/2014/358152
31. Freire, M., et al.: Game learning analytics: learning analytics for serious games. In: Spector, M.J., Lockee, B.B., Childress, M.D. (eds.) Learning, Design, and Technology: An International Compendium of Theory, Research, Practice, and Policy, pp. 1–29. Springer, Cham (2016). https://doi.org/10.1007/978-3-319-17727-4_21-1
32. Damaševičius, R., Maskeliūnas, R., Blažauskas, T.: Serious games and gamification in healthcare: a meta-review. Information **14**(2), 105 (2023). https://doi.org/10.3390/info14020105
33. Pelser-Carstens, V., Matthew, G.: Conceptualising the educational serious game design space for workshop presentation. In: Proceedings of EdMedia + Innovate Learning 2023, Vienna, Austria, pp. 806–816. Association for the Advancement of Computing in Education (AACE) (2023)
34. Charsky, D.: From edutainment to serious games: a change in the use of game characteristics. Games Cult. **5**(2), 177–198 (2010). https://doi.org/10.1177/1555412009354727
35. Drevin, G., Snyman, D.P., Drevin, L., Kruger, H. A., Allers, J.: The story of safety snail and her e-mail: a digital wellness and cybersecurity serious game for pre-school children. In: Proceedings of the 9th International Conference on Information Systems Security and Privacy - Volume 1: ICISSP, pp. 519–527. SciTePress, INSTICC (2023). https://doi.org/10.5220/0011682200003405
36. Esterhuizen, J., Drevin, L., Drevin, G., Snyman, D.: Design choices among recent security related serious games. In: 16th Annual International Conference of Education, Research and Innovation, ICERI2023 Proceedings, Seville, Spain, pp. 8807–8816. IATED (2023). https://doi.org/10.21125/iceri.2023.2244
37. Lameras, P., Arnab, S., Dunwell, I., Stewart, C., Clarke, S., Petridis, P.: Essential features of serious games design in higher education: linking learning attributes to game mechanics. Br. J. Edu. Technol. **48**(4), 972–994 (2017)
38. Mildner, P., Stamer, N., Effelsberg, W.: From game characteristics to effective learning games. In: Göbel, S., Ma, M., Baalsrud Hauge, J., Oliveira, M.F., Wiemeyer, J., Wendel, V. (eds.) Serious Games, pp. 51–62. Springer, Cham (2015). https://doi.org/10.1007/978-3-319-19126-3_5
39. Callaghan, M.N., Reich, S.M.: Are educational preschool apps designed to teach? An analysis of the app market. Learn. Media Technol. **43**(3), 280–293 (2018). https://doi.org/10.1080/17439884.2018.1498355
40. Callaghan, M.N., Reich, S.M.: Applying a developmental lens to educational game designs for preschoolers. In: Information Resources Management Association (ed.) Research Anthology on Developments in Gamification and Game-Based Learning, pp. 471–487. IGI Global Scientific Publishing (2022). https://doi.org/10.4018/978-1-6684-3710-0.ch022

Innovative Approaches to Cybersecurity Awareness

The Cyber Range Lite

Lightweight Infrastructure for Training and Education

Leonardo A. Martucci(✉), Jonathan Magnusson, Tobias Vehkajärvi, and Jonas Karlsson

Karlstad University, Karlstad, Sweden
{leonardo.martucci,jonathan.magnusson,tobias.vehkajarvi, jonas.karlsson}@kau.se

Abstract. This paper presents the requirements, design, development, and evaluation of a container-based cyber range for cybersecurity training and education named Cyber Range Lite (CRL). CRL is a scalable, lightweight platform with well-defined interfaces tailored to educational contexts. Cybersecurity exercises, or challenges, are described using a YAML-based template and deployed via Docker container images, which simulate a networked environment with a large number of hosts orchestrated by Docker Swarm. Students access the system through WireGuard VPN tunnels. We initially tested CRL using jeopardy-style Capture The Flag (CTF) exercises, comprising independent challenges. We then extended it to a virtual network scenario where students must solve challenges in a prescribed sequence. CRL was deployed and evaluated in an advanced-level ethical hacking course, where we compared its functionality, cost, and student feedback against a previous cyber range implementation based on virtual machines hosted on the Google Cloud Platform. Our results indicate that CRL offers a cost-effective and pedagogically flexible alternative for hands-on cybersecurity education.

Keywords: Cyber range · Ethical hacking · Cybersecurity · Education

1 Introduction

Cyber ranges are interactive, virtual, cloud-based simulated infrastructures used in cybersecurity exercises and training [6]. They enable hands-on practice in realistic scenarios, helping students develop vital cybersecurity skills in a virtual, controlled environment without risking live production systems.

The keystone of our ethical hacking advanced-level course practical element is its cyber range. For the past two years, we have used a cyber range implementation based on virtual machines (VMs) and hosted on the Google Cloud Platform (GCP) [6]. This implementation and choice of hosting platform resulted in an important limitation: students needed to co-exist in the same virtual environment. The implications of students sharing a cyber range are many, e.g., information leaks, tampering with the environment, and shared flags. To mitigate these constraints, its developers added multiple tools and controls to the

L. Drevin et al. (Eds.): WISE 2025, IFIP AICT 742, pp. 171–185, 2026.
https://doi.org/10.1007/978-3-031-94924-1_12

cyber range, negatively affecting the student experience and the completion of the ethical hacking course's learning goals.

In this paper, we introduce Cyber Range Lite (CRL). CRL is a cyber range implementation designed for cybersecurity training and education. CRL is a lightweight, container-based platform that can run on-premise. It offers students individual cyber ranges, simplifies cyber range management, and eliminates administrative checks. Our students in the ethical hacking course started using the CRL in January 2025. This paper reports our initial findings, feedback from the students, and the present limitations of the CRL.

The main contribution of this paper is threefold: (*1*) the CRL architecture and its implementation; (*2*) a comparison between our previous VM-based GCP-hosted environment and CRL; and (*3*) the lessons learned from deploying CRL in an advanced-level ethical hacking course.

We organized the paper as follows. Section 2 revisits cyber ranges and the use of Capture The Flag (CTF) exercises in education. Section 3 lists the limitations of our previous VM-based cyber range deployment. These limitations led us to a set of functional requirements that led us to design a new cyber range, the CRL, described in Sect. 4. We detail the CRL architecture and its implementation in Sect. 5. Our initial findings, the lessons learned, and the CRL limitations are discussed in Sect. 6. Section 7 concludes the paper.

2 Background

We have been offering an advanced-level ethical hacking course since 2023. A key component of our course is a hands-on cybersecurity project in which each student works individually to attack a fictitious corporate computer network hosted in a cyber range. Students access the cyber range through a Virtual Private Network (VPN) connection, which enables them to navigate the virtual network by pivoting between hosts and escalating their privileges. The cyber range contains flags—unique strings placed strategically throughout the infrastructure—in line with competitive CTF community conventions. Finding and retrieving (capturing) these flags demonstrates students' ability to identify and exploit real-world vulnerabilities in a controlled setting.

2.1 Capture The Flag

CTF is a gamified way of learning cybersecurity. Players are rewarded points by solving CTF challenges that can be tracked and compared against others on a scoreboard. The objective of a CTF challenge is to find a hidden string, called a "flag", behind a problem that needs to be solved or a vulnerability that needs to be exploited. The flag has two parts: (*1*) a recognizable prefix, e.g., "flag", and (*2*) and a postfix that is hard to guess, e.g., a hash or a passphrase, within curly brackets. For instance, `flag{c049r49rq09m48qc8urqcqpo4xh}` is a possibly valid flag in a CTF exercise.

The most common CTF game mode is *Jeopardy*, where the challenges are sorted into categories, e.g., Web, Cryptography, Forensics, and Reverse Engineering. Individual players or teams try to solve as many challenges as possible within a time limit to crown a winner.

In recent years, cybersecurity courses in higher education have utilized the gamification from CTF competitions to enhance learning [2]. A penetration test setting sometimes replaces the Jeopardy game mode to increase realism. Such a setting includes virtual networks with vulnerable services, which the students scan, enumerate, exploit, and pivot around the machines to find hidden flags. Students then submit the flags they found to pass the practical assignment.

2.2 Cyber Ranges

Previously, in Sect. 1, we defined cyber ranges rather narrowly as interactive, virtual, cloud-based simulated infrastructures used in cybersecurity exercises. However, cyber ranges can also encompass facilities designed for testing tools and equipment or conducting large-scale, transnational cyber defense exercises. Examples include CR14 NATO CR and the RI.SE [1]

Academic cyber ranges focus primarily on training and educational objectives. Jamk's Realistic Global Cyber Environment (RGCE) [4], Virginia Tech's US Cyber Range,[2], Masaryk University's KYPO [9], the AIT Cyber Range [5], and the Open Cyber Range (OCR)[3] Estonian-Norwegian initiative—are all capable of hosting both forensic exercises and CTF-style challenges. A common aspect of these academic cyber ranges is that are all implemented using VMs.

Closer to our work, are the lightweight implementations of cyber ranges, which are based on containers instead of VMs. Containers are more lightweight than VMs because they share the host OS kernel and eliminate the need for a full OS stack. This results in faster startup times, lower resource consumption, and better scalability compared to VMs, which rely on hardware emulation, hypervisors, and separate OS instances. Like CRL, avatao [1], InCTF [8], CyExec* [7], and Git-based CTF [10] are container-based cyber ranges.

CRL is different from them because (*1*) CRL can host multiple exercises on a single service, (*2*) participants have unique flags, and (*3*) it allows for a large number of hosts and individualized virtual networks that are described using Docker Compose and orchestrated with Docker Swarm (see Sect. 5).

3 Lessons From Our Previous Cyber Range Deployment

In the past two academic years, we have used in our ethical hacking course, a custom cyber range designed and implemented for the online ethical hacking course of the Kungl. Tekniska Högskolan (KTH) [3,6]. We have an established academic collaboration in research and postgraduate education with KTH, and

[1] https://www.cr14.ee/ and https://www.ri.se/sv/cyberrange.
[2] https://www.uscyberrange.org/.
[3] https://documentation.opencyberrange.ee/.

KTH shares its cyber range code and exercises with two Swedish universities that run on-campus ethical hacking courses.

KTH's cyber range (called the Tool With Many Names, or TWMN) is based on virtual machines (VM) and hosted on GCP, with most of its code written in Ansible. Currently, TWMN is Sweden's largest platform for advanced-level university cybersecurity training, with approximately 400 enrolled students across three Swedish universities in 2024. In addition, its ethical hacking course is offered for professional (continuing) education.

TWMN hosts CTF exercises with a set of flags hidden throughout the virtual environment. It uses Canvas, a Learning Management System (LMS), as its student-facing interface for flag submission, tracking progress, and hint purchasing (hints help students solve the exercises). Canvas is also used for distributing access credentials to the environment. A practical limitation of this VM-based range is its high GCP infrastructure cost: around €150 per month per virtual environment (an instance of the cyber range). For example, a course with 100 students would have a monthly cost of €15,000 if each student were assigned an individual environment. This price tag is prohibitive for most universities, so the workaround is to have multiple students share the same environment and, thus, reduce the overall monetary cost. The use of shared environments for running CTF exercises results in a series of limitations that are discussed in Sect. 3.1.

3.1 Shared Environments and Their Problems

In TWMN, up to 10 students are assigned to each virtual environment, which are known as "worlds." Multiple students co-existing in a world result in several problems for managing the cyber range, such as:

- **Concurrent Tests**. Multiple students may simultaneously run computationally demanding tasks—such as password cracking or port scans—within the same environment. High CPU usage and network overhead degrade performance, causing long wait times for all students and negatively affecting their experience.
- **Crashing Machines**. In an ethical hacking course, students are expected to experiment with commands and tools, sometimes causing a target machine to crash. Although this can be a valuable learning experience, it disrupts everyone else in that shared environment. Once a machine is down, it remains unavailable to all co-located students.
- **Littering**. During vulnerability assessments, students often leave behind files, folders, or installed tools on the operating system. In a shared environment, other students may spot these remnants, potentially revealing shortcuts to the flags and undermining the intended challenge.
- **Shared Flags**. Each environment contains a set of flags for students to capture. In a shared setup (akin to a Jeopardy-style CTF), everyone searches for the same flags. Unlike a competitive CTFs, where there is a disincentive to share flags, an educational cyber range does not have this competitive aspect. Sharing a flag is simple, it requires sending a string, allowing other students to bypass the learning process of discovering it themselves.

The designers of TWMN were aware of these problems, so they added a procedure to the cyber range: a periodic system restore. The purpose of a system restore is to return the environment to its initial state and refresh all its flags. This measure mitigates the last three listed problems: the crashed machines return to a functional state, all litter is deleted, and all flags are refreshed. In our ethical hacking course, we restored the machines every 24 h and then changed it to 12 h after our students requested more periodic restores in the second instance of the course. We also maintain a support email list that is forwarded to the teaching staff and support that can start the restore process. These restores do not solve the problems but shrink the time window that the environment is unavailable to the students, provide a periodic cleaning of the system, and set a "best before" timestamp to flags.

The side-effect of returning the system to its initial state is that the student's progress in their worlds is lost when a restore happens. They must retrace their steps, often reinstall tools, and rerun their tests and attacks to return where they were before the restore happened. The side-effect of resetting flags is the need to store a list of all flags and their valid time windows. There are two reasons to do this: (*1*) to verify if a student handed in a valid flag, and (*2*) to detect possible cheating, i.e., students submitting expired flags that can no longer be captured or a flag belonging to another world likely obtained from another student.

The problem of *concurrent tests* could be solved by allocating more resources to individual VMs in the GCP when deploying the cyber range, but that would result in additional costs. Hence, we monitored the use of the VMs and the students' feedback, allocated more resources to VMs on demand, and returned them to their original settings later. High CPU usage and network overhead at specific machines of the cyber range were exacerbated by the synchronous nature of our on-campus ethical hacking course, where synchronous deadlines caused many students to run tests simultaneously.

In contrast, the asynchronous nature of online courses, in which the students solve exercises at their own pace, minimizes the likelihood of simultaneous resource contention in their shared environments and reduces the problem of students bumping into each other while navigating their worlds.

3.2 User Authentication and Credential Management

There are multiple alternatives to give students access to a cyber range. Jamk's RGCE is accessed with a VM that students can download. The ForCyRange proposes using a web interface linked to an LMS to give students access to their environments. TWMN also uses an LMS (Canvas) to authenticate and distribute student access (VPN) credentials. From its architectural perspective, the solution is complex because it requires a four-step protocol: (*1*) Canvas sends the list of registered students to the TWMN, which (*2*) generates VPN credentials for each name in the list and (*3*) returns them to Canvas. (*4*) Canvas sends a message with their VPN credentials to each student. We followed these steps for the past instances of our on-campus ethical hacking course.

4 The Cyber Range Lite Requirements and Design

The root cause of all problems, limitations, and mitigation tools presented in Sect. 3.1 arises from students co-existing and sharing worlds. Considering the GCP-related costs, isolating students in their worlds is ideal but very expensive.

4.1 Requirements

The essential requirements for the new cyber range are to: (*1*) isolate students in their virtual environment (*2*) while offering an ethical hacking course to a large number of students and (*3*) simultaneously making it economically viable to the institution delivering it. All three requirements must be addressed concurrently, and the outcome is that all problems arising from shared environments cease to exist, and so is the need for all mechanisms created to mitigate the problem. As a result, each student could have its set of flags and would be able to reset their environments without affecting other students, resulting in a reduced workload for those teaching and managing the course. A secondary requirement is to simplify the existing process for students to obtain their cyber range access credentials.

4.2 Design

To develop a cyber range that meets the requirements outlined in Sect. 4.1, we first analyzed the economic constraints of providing individual environments under our VM-based, GCP-hosted infrastructure. The main reason is that VM-based ranges are resource-hungry implementations.

The main advantage of hosting a VM-based cyber range on an enterprise cloud service, such as GCP and AWS, is their scalability. However, each VM has a complete operating system, leading to heavier CPU, memory, and storage use. The use of VMs also comes with additional drawbacks: spinning them up is a matter of minutes of downtime, and it is inefficient in handling computational resources, e.g., some VMs may be overloaded while others remain mostly idle.

Therefore, our design is tailored to a lightweight environment virtualization. A container-based solution is both resource-efficient and more flexible than VM-based alternatives. Containers share the host OS kernels, which reduces overhead significantly, can be launched and restarted in seconds, and are easily orchestrated with tools like Docker Swarm or Kubernetes.[4] In summary, a container-based solution fits the needs of educational cyber ranges, where frequent resets, scalability, and budget constraints are critical. Hence, we opted for a container-based solution to base the design of our cyber range.

The design of our cyber range, which we named the CRL, consists of four blocks: (*1*) the CRL orchestrator, (*2*) the Events, (*3*) the Worlds, and (*4*) the Challenges. The CRL design is illustrated in Fig. 1.

[4] https://docs.docker.com/engine/swarm/ and https://kubernetes.io/.

(1) The **CRL** orchestrator provisions and manages the isolated containerized environments. Its goal is to automate deployment, optimize resource usage, and enable fast resets, ensuring scalability while providing minimal administrative overhead. The CRL orchestrator creates one or more events.
(2) An **event** consists of a blueprint, a recipe for setting up virtual environments (worlds), and a pointer to a student front-end. An event is a course or a CTF competition. For example, our ethical hacking course is an event.
(3) Events spawn one or more **worlds**. Each world represents an isolated instance of the event, i.e., a cyber range, for an individual participant.
(4) Worlds have **challenges**, cybersecurity exercises for participants to solve.

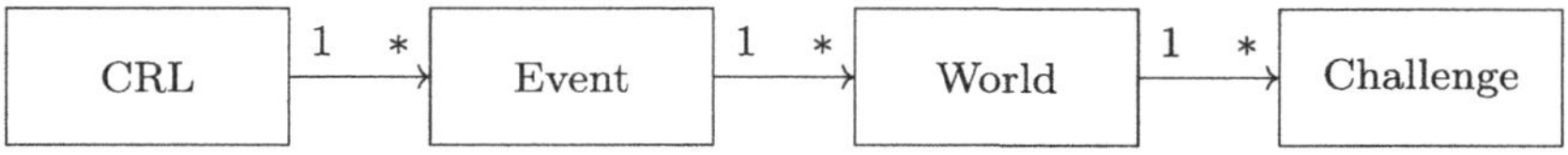

Fig. 1. The design of the Cyber Range Lite. Each event references a blueprint that defines one or more worlds. Each world contains and one or more challenges. The relationships reflect instance counts and deployment structure.

5 The Cyber Range Lite

The CRL is a framework for automating the creation and management of CTF-inspired cybersecurity labs. The framework is based on CTFd and Docker. It is flexible enough to support multiple CTF game modes, including Jeopardy and virtual environments for courses. The CRL code is open-source, released under GPL3 license (https://git.cs.kau.se/csma/cyber-range/crl).

We opted to base the worlds and challenges on Docker, as Docker containers are lightweight and have well-defined file structures. Another benefit of using Docker is that it makes the development environment very close to the production environment. Furthermore, it lets us run and test each component in standalone mode, without CRL. Standalone testing helps to ease the learning curve and, therefore, reduce development time, especially when developing new challenges and blueprint definitions. To explain the anatomy of CRL, we first describe in further detail the blocks introduced in Sect. 4.2.

5.1 Events, Blueprints, and Worlds

An **event** defines a specific named course or competition and specifies (*1*) the blueprint to be used, (*2*) the structure of the flags, and (*3*), the configuration of the front-end which the students use to interact with their worlds.

A **blueprint** is a Docker Compose file.[5] It bundles one or more services (Docker containers, see Sect. 5.2) and specifies the virtual network's content and topology. A blueprint can be used in multiple events, i.e., it can be reused.

A **world** is a Docker Stack deployed in a Docker Swarm. Each Docker Stack is defined by a Docker Compose file, i.e., an instantiation of a blueprint.[6]

5.2 Services and Challenges

A **service** is a Docker container representing a server or machine. By building static container images for each service but allowing flags (and other details) to be injected using environment variables in run-time, we can scale the deployment of multiple service instances effortlessly and much faster than using approaches that must be compiled in all settings at build time. Each service can host one or more challenges. For instance, a service hosting two challenges may require students to solve them sequentially. The first challenge would require students to upload a reverse shell and then capture the first flag on the home directory of "user." The second would need them to escalate their privileges to capture the second flag in the home directory of "root."

A **challenge** is a cybersecurity puzzle or vulnerability, described using a YAML-based template, that students need to solve or exploit to capture its flag, which is unique to the student. Challenges can be simple, such as viewing the HTML source code of a website, or complex, such as exploiting a vulnerability in a Linux system and escalating privileges. Some challenges involve multiple services on different containers, while others may not need services at all, such as flags hidden in `pcap`-files. Challenges have metadata such as name, description, score, author, and hints. Two or more challenge containers can be designed together, creating dependencies and network interactions within a world.

The challenges are kept in separate `git` repository, apart from the CRL code. The challenges repository is meant to be shared privately between teachers and universities so that the library of challenges can be expanded organically.

5.3 CTFd

CTFd is an open-source platform for managing CTF events.[7] It lets students select challenges, take hints, and submit flags for points. CTFd administrators can access REST API endpoints for creating and modifying challenges and to write plugins that change or extend its functionality. CTFd does not support running interactive challenges natively. Its core role is managing submissions and scoring. We have developed four plugins for CTFd to fulfill our requirements:

- An init plugin for setting up CTFd using environment variables, including settings such as event name, event mode, and event authentication. It also sets up an admin account and creates an API key for that user.

[5] https://github.com/compose-spec/compose-spec.

[6] https://docs.docker.com/reference/cli/docker/stack/.

[7] https://ctfd.io/.

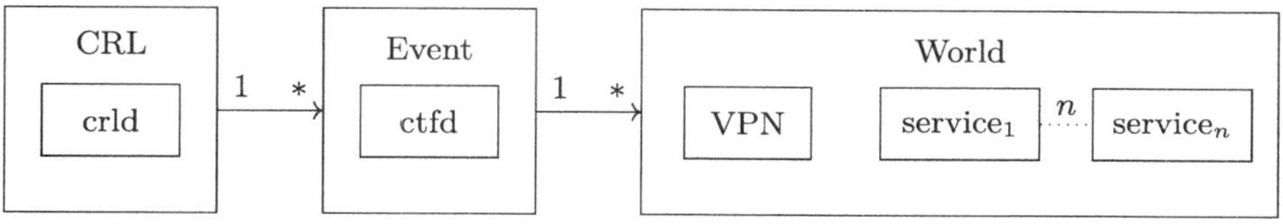

Fig. 2. An overview of the CRL implementation and its components.

- An `OAuth` plugin for allowing players to register/log in using `OAuth` with, e.g., their GitLab account, instead of MajorLeagueCyber.[8]
- A hint plugin that temporarily allows players to get a negative score when grabbing their first hints and presents the hints in the correct order.
- A CRL plugin which allows players to create and reset their CRL instance. A "`create`" button in the (/crl) page generates an instance and its WireGuard config. The subsequent "`reset`" button resets the instance.

5.4 CRLd

To access their world, students must first create them and retrieve their VPN credentials. The CRL plugin from CTFd interacts with CRLd, a daemon responsible for creating and restarting worlds (blueprint instances). Students use the CRL plugin to instantiate their worlds (by pressing the `create` button). The CRL plugin then sends an `API` request to CRLd to instantiate the world. CRLd also provides students with a configuration file for connecting to their world: the VPN credentials and the details of their `IP` subnet.

Figure 2 illustrates the relationship between the CRL implementation and its components. The blueprints and the challenges are not shown in the figure.

6 Discussion and Evaluation

We tested and evaluated CRL in our ethical hacking course, with 42 students enrolled and eight guest participants. The ethical hacking course is a CRL event. In its blueprint, every world has 13 challenges implemented using five services. It also includes 15 "red herring" services and one VPN service, distributed in two overlay networks. Our environment is a Docker Swarm cluster consisting of one manager node and one high-performance worker node. The worker was deployed on a 40-core CPU server with 755 GB of memory, and the manager node on a 20-core CPU machine with 32 GB of memory.

[8] https://www.majorleaguecyber.org/.

6.1 The CRL Deployment in Our Ethical Hacking Course

For our ethical hacking course, we deployed CRL in a penetration-test setting. In order to pass the course, the students need to: (*1*) attend the mandatory lectures and seminars, (*2*) hand in *all* flags in the cyber range, and (*3*) get at least half of the total flag score.

We set up a hint system for the students in CTFd. If they got stuck on a challenge, they could take a hint at the cost of points. If they took all hints for a challenge, they would unlock a step-by-step walkthrough to the flag. The cost of all hints for a challenge would cancel out the score of the flag, resulting in zero points. Figure 3 shows the hint page for one of our challenges.

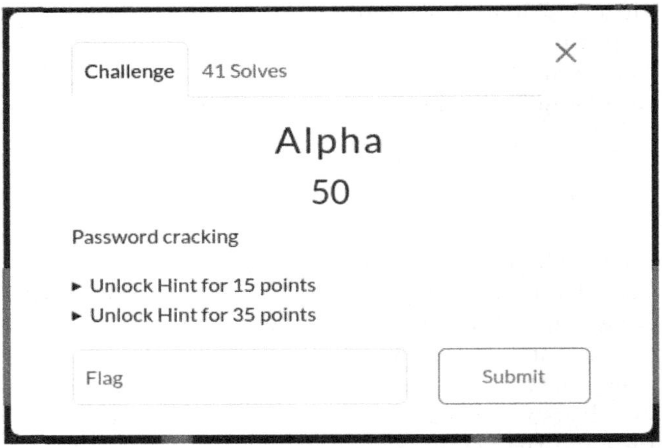

Fig. 3. CTFd hints for a challenge. Taking all hints results in a step-by-step guide, but costs all points.

We demonstrated to them how to create a world and connect to it and published the `https` address of the CTFd platform in our LMS platform. The students signed in using `OAuth`, which set their usernames on the platform to their university student IDs.

Using our CRL CTFd plugin, the students created their cyber range instances by pressing the "`create`" button (see Fig. 4). The button changes to "`reset`" and a WireGuard configuration file is made available with instructions on how to connect, the IP range scope of the world, and which ports are forwarded.

As soon as the world is created, the flags are generated. The flags structure has three parts: (*1*) their first part is the student ID, (*2*) their second part is the name of the challenge, and (*3*) their third part is padded with a random base64 string.[9] This structure guarantees that every flag is unique; students can't share flags, and students can identify the challenge to which the flag belongs.

Once a flag is captured, the students report them on the CTFd page.

[9] `flag{studentID-challengeName-base64}`.

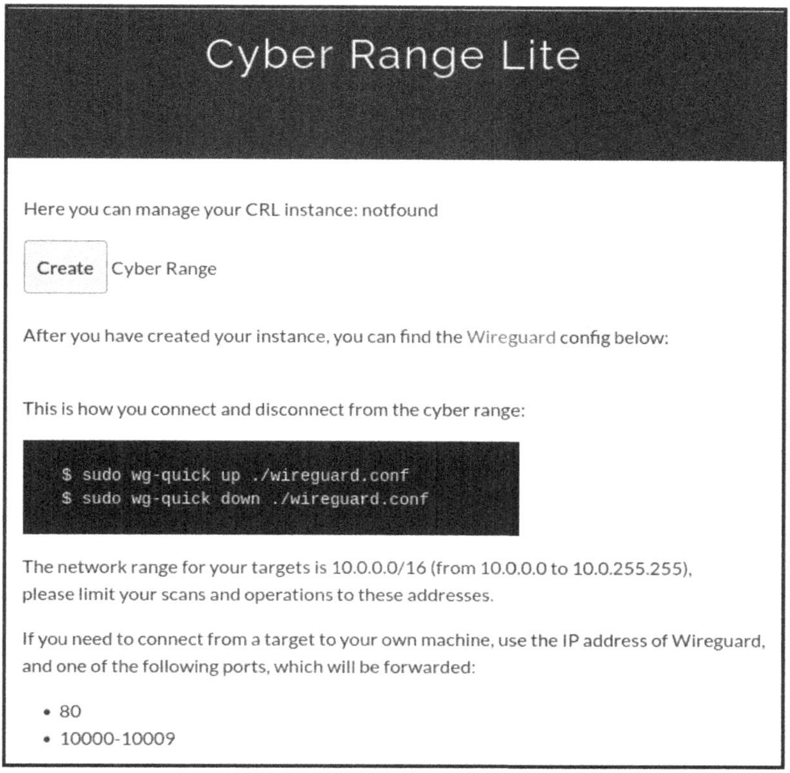

Fig. 4. CRL CTFd plugin for managing your instance of the cyber range.

6.2 Lessons Learned

Running CRL in a course setting with close feedback from the students allowed us to patch urgent issues and detect unintended behaviors for a future update of the infrastructure. In the blueprint for the cyber range, we specified limits for CPU and memory usage for each container. One container had its limits set too low, resulting in crashes whenever a student added too much load against it. After verifying this behavior in the container, we adjusted the resources allocated to it and requested the students reset their instances, which worked flawlessly.

When students reset their cyber ranges, the services were allocated to new private `IP` addresses. This behavior was intended in the implementation, but some students saw this as a point of frustration, having to scan the range for the services yet again. A possible future update of CRL would be to look into static `IP` addresses for the services.

When solving challenges in the cyber range, some students found unintended solutions. Even shortcuts between challenges were found, bypassing some of the designed dependencies. We did not patch any of these during the course but added them to our issue board for future fixes.

CTFd displays hints ambiguously, as seen in Fig. 3. Whenever a challenge had more than three hints, it was difficult for the students to pick which hint to reveal blindly. A first hint might not help if some progress has already been made. This led to some frustration when students paid for useless hints. At the same time, revealing the hint's content without leaking some information about the challenge is difficult. In the future, we want to enhance the hint system in CTFd to tackle this issue.

6.3 Student Feedback

The first instance of our ethical hacking course using CRL ran in mid-January and ended in mid-March 2025. During this period, we collected anecdotal evidence from our students in and out of the classroom, as well as from their weekly written reports (`.md` files stored in their individual `git` repositories). Additional feedback was gathered through a course support email linked to the GitLab issue board. Out of the 100 messages on our issue board, 75 were concerned about the state of the cyber range, most of them linked to three distinct occurrences. Aside from these, CRL generated no additional administrative overhead.

Of the 42 enrolled students, four were repeating the course and, therefore, experienced the evolution of the cyber range. Students reported being very satisfied with the current infrastructure and appreciated having individual cyber ranges and the ability to reset them independently. Many found the idea hard to believe when told that previous course instances relied on shared environments. The complete evaluation analysis is available in the course webpage.[10]

6.4 Performance Evaluation

One of the main drivers for CRL was to reduce the overhead/cost (computational and human effort) of maintaining the cyber range during all its states, i.e., before, during, and after a course. Hence, we measured the performance and hardware required to operate the cyber range in our ethical hacking course.

A blueprint specifies which challenges are included in the event, and every challenge has computational requirements to run its services, e.g., CPU, memory, and interfaces (see Sect. 4). The hardware requirement for an event directly correlates to the blueprint specification and the number of participants in the event (i.e., the number of worlds). Disk space is also directly dependent on the blueprint (i.e., image sizes) but only to a lesser degree on the number of users as Docker, which uses a copy-on-write filesystem to store images and container filesystems by default.

The ethical hacking course deploys 21 services per participant. We limited services to one CPU core and allocated 64 MB to 2 GB of memory each. The ethical hacking course used 20 to 50% CPU and ca. 100 GB of memory in

[10] https://www.kau.se/en/education/programmes-and-courses/courses/DVAD25.

the worker node, i.e., around 2 GB per participant. Hence, we estimated that our server could host 200 to 250 participants. A world reset took ca. 30 s from pressing the reset button until the participant could log on again.

We also stress-tested the cyber range and found that the CRL could host up to 510 worlds, using 683 GB of memory and 50% CPU load on the worker node and 15 GB of memory and 11% CPU load on the manager node. A world reset under these conditions took ca. 200 s. This limit is not caused by hardware limitations but originate from a cap on the number of public IP addresses in the implementation of CRL that we used in the course.

6.5 Limitations

Containers are convenient for deploying cyber ranges but have limitations, too. Docker containers do not provide the same isolation level as traditional VMs. Since containers share the same host kernel, vulnerabilities in the kernel or container escape exploits can potentially allow unauthorized access to the host system. This shared kernel can be a security concern when running untrusted applications or conducting high-risk cybersecurity exercises.

Integrating Windows machines within a Docker-based cyber range is more challenging than running Linux-based containers. Compatibility issues and licensing constraints complicate the inclusion of Windows-based scenarios. We have explored workarounds, such as bridging the Docker network with Windows VMs on a separate network or running Windows via KVM[11].

Networking within Docker presents challenges, particularly when multiple containers need to interact across different subnets or when simulating complex attack scenarios. By default, Docker uses bridge networks, which may not provide sufficient control over traffic flow. Furthermore, enabling advanced routing configurations requires elevated privileges, which could introduce security risks or limit deployment options in specific environments.

7 Conclusion

In this paper, we presented Cyber Range Lite (CRL), a container-based platform designed to address the primary challenges of traditional VM-based cyber ranges: high costs, scalability bottlenecks, and complex administration when handling large cohorts of students. By reducing resource overhead and enabling faster resets, CRL offers individual virtual environments without incurring excessive infrastructure expenses. An initial deployment in our ethical hacking course indicates that CRL effectively replaced the VM-centric solution used in previous years, while simplifying administration and enhancing student experience.

CRL's four-component architecture (orchestrator, events, worlds, and challenges) and its integration with CTFd simplify environment provisioning and user interaction. Its lightweight containerization ensures quicker spin-up times

[11] https://github.com/dockur/windows.

and reduced downtime. CRL supports individualized virtual networks with large numbers of hosts, allows multiple challenges to run on the same containerized service, and generates unique flags per student to prevent sharing. In addition, CRL was locally deployed and ran on-premise, which eliminated external cloud provider-related costs. Throughout a live course deployment with 42 students, we could quickly detect errors, react to spikes of resource utilization and adjust the allocated computational resources.

Our future work includes testing CRL with a larger cohort of students and expanding the blueprint library. We want to test CRL in other modes, like Jeopardy, and for use in laboratory exercises for other courses in Computer Science, such as networking and operating systems. We have a prototype implementation of an advanced logging system that we want to deploy and test on the next instance of our ethical hacking course. Furthermore, we want to look into the security implications of container-based approaches and minimize container-escape risks and other student-driven interferences with the host machines.

In conclusion, CRL's practical and effective design and implementation provides a solid foundation for delivering a virtual environment. We successfully tested in our ethical hacking course and are certain that others teaching hands-on cybersecurity will benefit from it.

Acknowledgments. This study was funded in part by Vinnova's Cybercampus Sweden (ref. 2023-00538) and by the Cross Border Cyber Capacity (CBCC), an Interreg Sverige-Norge cross-border cooperation, innovative environments project, which is co-funded by the European Union.

References

1. Buttyán, L., Félegyházi, M., Pék, G.: Mentoring talent in IT security–a case study. In: USENIX Workshop on Advances in Security Education (ASE 16) (2016)
2. Cole, S.V.: Impact of capture the flag (CTF)-style vs. traditional exercises in an introductory computer security class. In: Proc. of the 27th ACM Conference on Innovation and Technology in Computer Science Education, vol. 1 (2022)
3. Kakouros, N., Johnson, P., Lagerström, R.: Detecting plagiarism in penetration testing education. In: Nordsec, 25th Nordic Conference on Secure IT Systems (2020)
4. Karjalainen, M., Kokkonen, T.: Comprehensive cyber arena; the next generation cyber range. In: Euro S&P Workshops. IEEE (2020)
5. Leitner, M., et al.: AIT cyber range: flexible cyber security environment for exercises, training and research. In: Proceedings of the 2020 European Interdisciplinary Cybersecurity Conference (2020)
6. Martucci, L.A., Magnusson, J., Akil, M.: On-campus hands-on ethical hacking course: design, deployment and lessons learned. In: International Symposium on Human Aspects of Information Security and Assurance, pp. 76–90. Springer (2023)
7. Nakata, R., Otsuka, A.: CyExec*: A high-performance container-based cyber range with scenario randomization. IEEE Access **9**, 109095–109114 (2021)

8. Raj, A.S., Alangot, B., Prabhu, S., Achuthan, K.: Scalable and lightweight CTF infrastructures using application containers. In: USENIX Workshop on Advances in Security Education (ASE 16) (2016)
9. Vykopal, J., Ošlejšek, R., Čeleda, P., Vizvary, M., Tovarňák, D.: KYPO cyber range: design and use cases. In: Proceedings of the 12th Interenational Conference on Software Technology (2017)
10. Wi, S., Choi, J., Cha, S.K.: Git-based CTF: A simple and effective approach to organizing in-course attack-and-defense security competition. In: USENIX Workshop on Advances in Security Education (ASE 18) (2018)

A Car Hacking Mini-unit for High School Cybersecurity Education

Cooper Dean[1], Brian Almaguer[1], Timothy Buck[2], Nichole Kunkle[3], Christian Nguyen[4], Preet Patel[1], Anne Roberts[5], Marti Shirley[6], Huirong Fu[7], Xiaoyan Sun[1], and Jun Dai[1](✉)

[1] Worcester Polytechnic Institute, Worcester, MA, USA
{cjdean,baalmaguer,pnpatel,xsun7,jdai}@wpi.edu

[2] Chesapeake High School, Pasadena, MD, USA
tbuck@aacps.org

[3] Chambersburg Area Senior High School, Chambersburg, USA
nichole.kunkle@casdonline.org

[4] Troy High School, Fullerton, CA, USA
cnguyen@fjuhsd.org

[5] Christian Brothers College High School, St. Louis, USA
RobertsA@cbchs.org

[6] Glenbard East High School, Lombard, USA
marti_shirley@glenbard.org

[7] Oakland University, Rochester, USA
fu@oakland.edu

Abstract. As technology advances, the need for education on the security of these technologies becomes increasingly critical. However, security education predominantly targets post-secondary curricula, leaving high school learners with limited engaging resources. To address the growing demand for high school cybersecurity education, as highlighted by the College Board's AP Career Kickstart Cybersecurity Pilot Program, this paper bridges the gap by introducing a practical and engaging mini-unit focused on autonomous vehicle security. Autonomous vehicles represent a cutting-edge domain with interconnected systems vulnerable to cyberattacks, including remote vehicle control, adversarial attacks on vision systems, and exploits on keyless entry systems. Drawing from teaching experience and feedback from five high school educators, we present nine labs designed to teach cybersecurity concepts through hands-on exploration of autonomous vehicle systems. These labs are divided into three sections—CAN bus security, key fob security, and security with AI road image processors—each with progressive levels of complexity. Students engage in activities ranging from simulations of replay attacks and adversarial manipulations on road signs to experimenting with hacking hardware and programming AI models. High-profile real-world incidents, like the 2015 Jeep Cherokee hack and Tesla Model 3 vulnerabilities, highlight the urgent need to integrate these topics into cybersecurity education. Our hands-on labs bring this critical learning experience to high school students, equipping them with the skills and awareness to tackle emerging challenges, and sparking their interest in postsecondary education and career pathways in the field of cybersecurity.

Published by Springer Nature Switzerland AG 2026
L. Drevin et al. (Eds.): WISE 2025, IFIP AICT 742, pp. 186–200, 2026.
https://doi.org/10.1007/978-3-031-94924-1_13

Keywords: Autonomous Vehicles · Security · Education · High School

1 Introduction

As technological innovation accelerates, the need for education on its security becomes increasingly essential. However, security education has primarily been confined to post-secondary curricula, creating a significant gap at the high school level. In particular, there is a shortage of engaging, hands-on security labs that explore specific subdomains of the technological landscape.

One rapidly evolving technological field is autonomous vehicles, which rely on numerous interconnected systems, each presenting potential vulnerabilities. For instance, a 2015 Jeep Cherokee was found to have a flaw that allowed remote access, enabling hackers to take full control of the vehicle [10]. Similarly, adversarial attacks on road sign recognition systems can mislead autonomous vehicles into misclassifying objects, posing significant safety risks [12]. More recently, Xie et al. discovered that the Tesla Model 3's Key Cards were susceptible to relay attacks [15]. These real-world examples underscore the pressing need to integrate autonomous vehicle security into education, equipping students with both relevant knowledge and awareness, and hands-on learning experiences.

High school cybersecurity education is essential for addressing the growing workforce gap in the field by introducing students to cybersecurity concepts early in their academic journey. While efforts to build the cybersecurity workforce have largely focused on college-level education, expanding these initiatives to high schools can spark students' interest before they choose their majors and career paths. Recognizing this need, the College Board has launched the AP Career Kickstart Cybersecurity Pilot Program [1] for hundreds of high schools to test their cybersecurity frameworks for two new courses: "AP Cyber: Networking" and "AP Cyber: Security". However, the availability of quality and engaging cybersecurity teaching materials remains limited, making it challenging for educators to deliver effective instruction. Many existing resources are either too advanced for high school students or lack the hands-on, interactive components necessary to sustain student interest.

This paper addresses the gap in high school cybersecurity education by introducing a set of nine high school-level labs, newly developed or adapted from existing resources, to teach cybersecurity concepts through the lens of autonomous vehicles. Organized into a structured mini-unit[1], these labs focus on three key components of modern vehicles: the CAN Bus, key fobs, and vision systems. By providing engaging and accessible resources, this initiative aims to equip high school educators with innovative tools to enhance security-related instruction, fostering a deeper understanding of cybersecurity from an early stage.

[1] https://wpi-lions-group.github.io/ADS-Labs/.

2 Background and Related Work

2.1 Autonomous Vehicles

CAN Bus. The Controller Area Network (CAN) Bus serves as the central communication hub, transmitting information between various edge devices within a vehicle. Exploiting vulnerabilities in this system can grant attackers access to critical functions such as braking and steering [3,10,13]. To illustrate these security risks, we introduce two hands-on labs focused on replay attacks targeting the CAN Bus. These labs provide students with a practical understanding of real-world cyber threats in automotive systems, enhancing their grasp of critical security vulnerabilities in modern vehicles.

Key Fobs. Modern key fobs must securely communicate with vehicles to prevent theft. However, hackers can exploit vulnerabilities in key fobs using replay attacks [6], relay attacks [15], and rolljam attacks [5]. To explore these threats, we have introduced three labs focused on key fobs. The first two labs introduce replay and rolljam attacks, while the final lab challenges students to design their own secure key fob, protecting it against the attacks they have studied.

Vision Systems. Autonomous vehicles increasingly depend on computer vision systems to see and interpret their surroundings, which must be continually updated to counter emerging threats. Adversarial attacks on road sign images, for example, can interfere with object classification tasks [12]. To address this, we have included three labs focused on adversarial AI attacks targeting road sign classification, enabling students to explore the vulnerabilities and countermeasures within these critical systems.

2.2 Autonomous Vehicles in Cybersecurity Education

In 2019, Payne [13] developed a car hacking lab as part of a semester-long security course. This lab guides students in using open-source tools to perform a replay attack on a virtual CAN Bus. The lab is designed for undergraduate and graduate students, causing the setup and instructions to be too difficult for our use case. Our *CAN Bus Hacking with ICSim* lab is adapted from Payne's *Advanced Car Hacking Lab Assignment*, with streamlined instructions and reduced setup requirements designed to be taught at the advanced high-school level.

Francia et al. [2] examine curriculum challenges and propose a series of hands-on scenarios using real simulation hardware to exploit a CAN bus. To ensure accessibility for high school students, we opted not to adopt or modify these scenarios due to their specific hardware requirements.

McCall et al. [9] constructed an educational activity in which a Raspberry Pi simulates a CAN bus. Students completed three exercises: analyzing dumped CAN data, performing a replay attack similar to Payne's lab [13], and injecting fake CAN data into the network. Due to the hardware requirements and overlap with Payne's lab, we chose not to adopt or modify these exercises.

Grover et al. [4] explore the integration of AI and Machine Learning in cybersecurity education. After conducting two workshops, they received positive feedback from teachers on incorporating AI into high school classrooms. Similarly, we introduce a set of labs focused on security issues with AI vision systems.

3 Labs

We have introduced a series of nine labs that together form a mini-unit on autonomous vehicle security. These labs are structured into three sections, each focusing on a critical component of an autonomous vehicle: CAN Bus, Key Fobs, and AI Road Image Processors. Each section includes three labs, designed to provide targeted, in-depth exploration of security challenges in that area. We present the labs in our recommended teaching sequence, as outlined in Table 1.

Table 1. The mini-unit plan in recommended sequence

Lab	Section	Version
Hands-On Hack and Defense for an Autonomous Vehicle	Can Bus	Low Tech
CAN Bus Replay Attack Simulation	Can Bus	Med Tech
CAN Bus Hacking with ICSim	Can Bus	High Tech
Real-World Key Fob Cloning	Key Fobs	High Tech
Rolljam Attack Simulation	Key Fobs	Med Tech
Designing a Smart Key Fob Prototype	Key Fobs	Low Tech
Simulating Road Sign Attack with Adversarial Images	AI	Low Tech
Road Sign Recognition with Google Teachable Machine	AI	Med Tech
Real-Time Adversarial Attack on Road Sign Recognition	AI	High Tech

Three of these labs are designed to be completed without the use of a computer or laptop. Instead, they focus on group discussions and creative thinking activities. While some setup with printed materials and art supplies may be needed, these activities emphasize conceptual engagement over technical execution. In Table 1, we designate these labs as "Low Tech" (LT).

Three of these labs are fully online simulations, accessible for free. To support these activities, we have developed two static websites hosted on GitHub Pages, demonstrating different ways to hack a car. Additionally, one lab utilizes Google's Teachable Machine to simulate AI-based road sign recognition. In Table 1, we designate these labs as "Med Tech" (MT).

The final three labs are designed for more advanced students or require specialized equipment, making them a more realistic alternative to the free simulation labs. These labs provide hands-on experience with hardware hacking, working within a virtual machine, and programming an AI model. In Table 1, we designate these labs as "High Tech" (HT).

Please be advised that the three key fob labs should be completed in reverse order. This approach ensures a smoother learning progression, beginning with the High-Tech lab, which is the easiest to grasp conceptually. The Low-Tech lab is introduced later, as it builds on foundational knowledge of key fob security.

3.1 Hands-On Hack and Defense for an Autonomous Vehicle

This lab serves as an introduction to the mini-unit plan and does not necessarily need to cover the CAN Bus. However, it is included in this section since the topic will likely be new to students, serving as an effective starting point. We created the lab with this in mind, using the CAN Bus in some of our examples.

This lab spans two days, beginning with a lesson that defines key terms, introduces autonomous vehicles, and examines a real-life case study. Students will then collaborate in groups to identify potential vulnerabilities in autonomous vehicles and present their findings to the class. For homework, they will research an additional case study to further explore real-world challenges in autonomous vehicle security.

On the second day, students will briefly present their case studies to the class. Following the presentations, they will participate in a role-play simulation, dividing into two groups: the red team and the blue team. The red team will focus on devising methods to penetrate into an autonomous vehicle, while the blue team will strategize defenses against potential attacks. After a brainstorming session, the red team will "attack" by outlining their approach, and the blue team will respond with a defense strategy. This cycle will continue as time allows, concluding with a class discussion on the critical roles both teams play in ensuring vehicle security.

By the end of this lab, students will have a foundational understanding of cybersecurity in the context of autonomous vehicles. They will have explored recent attacks and gained insights into the importance of vehicle security.

3.2 CAN Bus Replay Attack Simulation

This lab was created with inspiration from the "High Tech" lab *CAN Bus Hacking with ICSim*, which will be introduced later. Recognizing the need for a version that requires no additional setup, we developed this lab as a static website[2] hosted on GitHub Pages. With minimal hardware requirements, students only need a computer with internet access to complete the activities.

In this lab, students will conduct a replay attack on a simulated CAN Bus communication network. The simulation allows students to control various components of a car, as shown in Fig. 1. They can send commands over the network to open the hood, a door, and the trunk, as well as start the engine and activate both blinkers. Additionally, students have access to a "Command Log," which enables them to record all commands transmitted over the network.

[2] https://wpi-lions-group.github.io/CAN-Bus-Replay-Attack-Lab/.

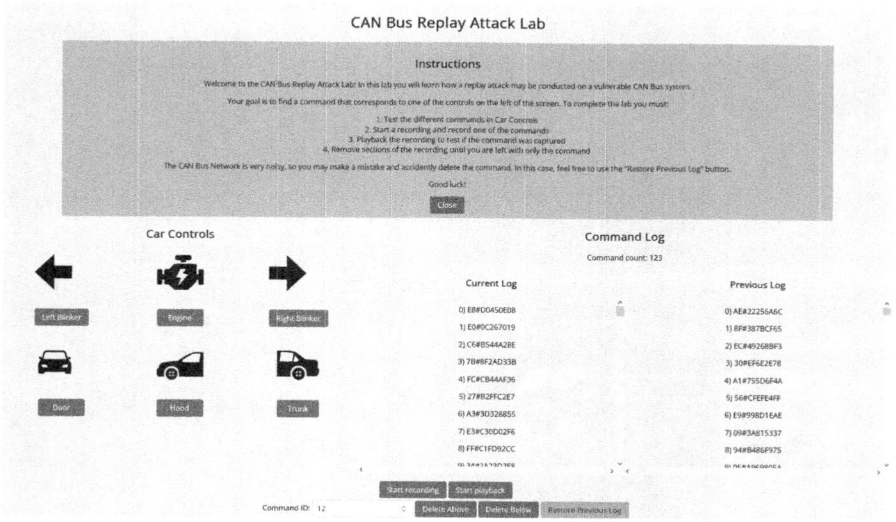

Fig. 1. Screenshot of the "CAN Bus Replay Attack Lab" website. Instructions are shown at the top in blue. Car controls are shown on the left. The command log is shown on the right. The lab control buttons are shown at the bottom of the page.

Using the command log and a set of control buttons, students can replay recorded commands and remove specific entries from the log. The objective of the lab is to narrow down the list of commands to successfully execute a replay attack on one specific car control. For instance, a student aiming to open the car door would first start a recording and trigger the door-opening command. Upon playback, they might observe that the door opens after 80 commands have been sent. To isolate the target command, the student will incrementally delete the first 80 commands using the input form. This process of playback and command elimination continues until only a handful of commands remain. The student may then test each command individually until the target command is found. If an error occurs and the target command is accidentally removed, students can restore the previous log and attempt the process again.

By the end of this lab, students will see a simulated CAN Bus in action and successfully execute a basic replay attack. They will develop an understanding of the CAN Bus's purpose, functionality, and its appeal as a target for hackers. A post-lab discussion should explore the potential risks associated with a compromised CAN Bus and examine security measures that can be implemented to safeguard vehicle systems.

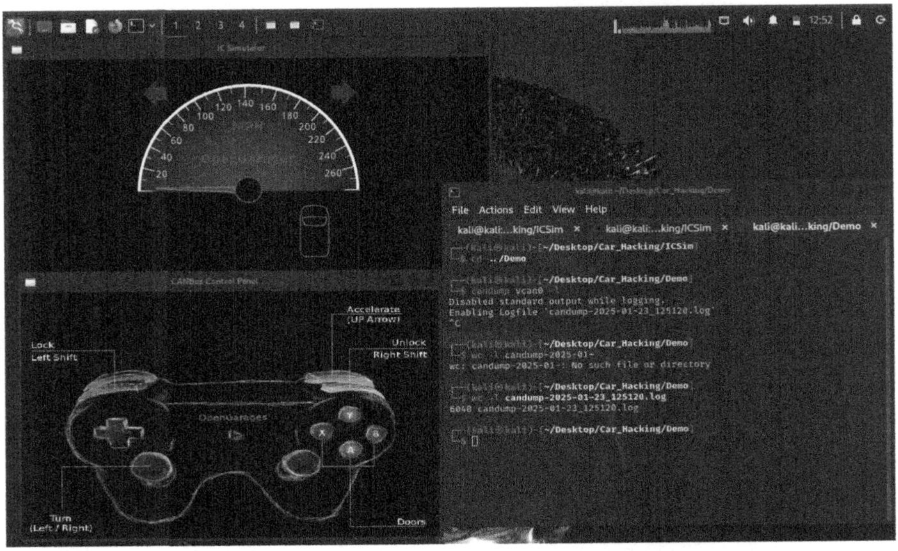

Fig. 2. Screenshot of a Kali Linux virtual machine running ICSim. The left two windows show the ICSim simulator (top) and controller (bottom). The right window shows the linux terminal.

3.3 CAN Bus Hacking with ICSim

Our adaptation of Payne's car hacking lab [13] was based on a 2022 blog post from OffSec [14]. The lab runs on Kali Linux[3] using VirtualBox[4]. However, we found that this version was outdated requiring additional setup beyond the original instructions. To simplify the process, we introduce an ISO file[5] that functions as an external hard drive for the virtual machine. This ISO contains a folder with a snapshot of most required dependencies, allowing students to complete the setup by simply attaching the ISO to the virtual machine, copying the necessary files, and installing a single additional package. We also included our own set of instructions.

Building on the previous lab, students will once again perform a replay attack on a simulated CAN Bus. However, instead of using buttons and a visual command list, they will work directly in the Linux terminal to capture and replay packets containing commands, as illustrated in Fig. 2. First, students will be prompted to record the noisy CAN Bus network and examine the length of the log file. Within just a few seconds, thousands of simulated commands may be transmitted over the network. Next, they will be asked to use a controller to execute specific actions on the car. For example, a student can press combinations of Left Shift, Right Shift, and the A, B, X, and Y keys to open and close

[3] https://www.kali.org/.
[4] https://www.virtualbox.org/.
[5] https://github.com/WPI-LIONS-Group/ADS-Labs/releases/.

the car's doors. After experimenting with multiple controls, students will select a specific target command for their attack. They will then capture and isolate that command in a recording to carry out the replay attack.

After recording a log file, students can begin isolating the target command by systematically removing commands from the file. To aid in this process, they are given access to various Linux terminal commands, including *wc*, *head*, *tail*, *cat*, and *echo*. Additionally, they can replay any log file to verify whether the target command was successfully captured. A common strategy at this stage is to iteratively remove half of the file and test whether the target command is present in either the first or second half.

By completing this lab, students will gain an understanding of the CAN Bus and its potential vulnerability to replay attacks. They will also develop hands-on experience with the Linux terminal and commands within a virtual machine.

3.4 Real-World Key Fob Cloning

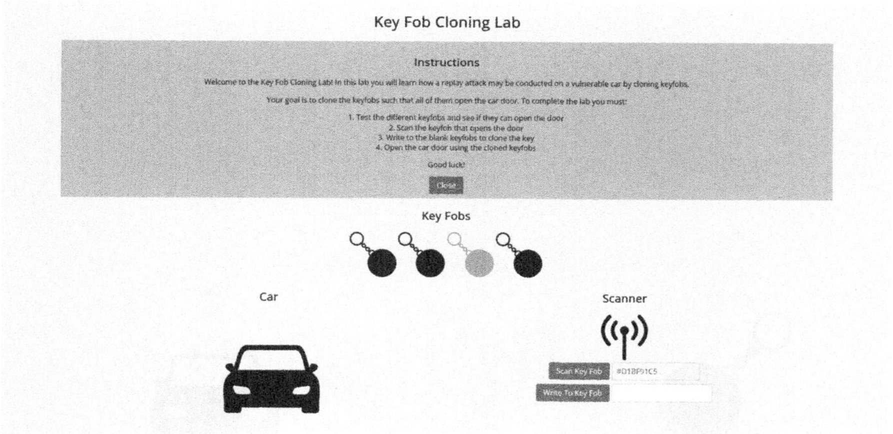

Fig. 3. Screenshot of the "Key Fob Cloning Lab" website. Instructions are shown at the top in blue. Four key fob icons are in the center. A simulated car door is shown on the left. The RFID scanner with read and write operations is shown on the right.

The most basic attack on an RFID key fob is to clone its signal onto a blank fob [7]. This process requires minimal hardware and, in its simplest form, can be accomplished using a single RFID scanner. For this lab, we selected the Flipper Zero[6] due to its ease of use and educational value. When available, this device can serve as a valuable teaching tool, enabling educators to develop a variety of lessons around its applications.

[6] https://flipperzero.one/.

In this lab, students will use a Flipper Zero device to clone a vulnerable key fob. The lab involves a few quick steps. First, the instructor pre-programs a blank key fob with an RFID signal. Students then use a Flipper Zero or an alternative RFID reader to capture the signal. Once saved, they will clone the signal onto a new key fob, successfully replicating the original access credential.

Conducting this lab with real equipment in a classroom setting may be cost-prohibitive. Hence, a free and web-based version has been developed by us and hosted on GitHub[7]. As shown in Fig. 3, this simulation includes multiple key fobs, a car, and a scanner. One key fob contains the RFID signal required to unlock the car door, while the other three are blank. Students can select a key fob, use the scanner to read or write a signal, and then test it by attempting to unlock the car door.

By completing this lab, students will show a basic understanding of RFID signals through the context of key fobs. They will understand why key fobs require basic security features to avoid simple cloning attacks.

3.5 Rolljam Attack Simulation

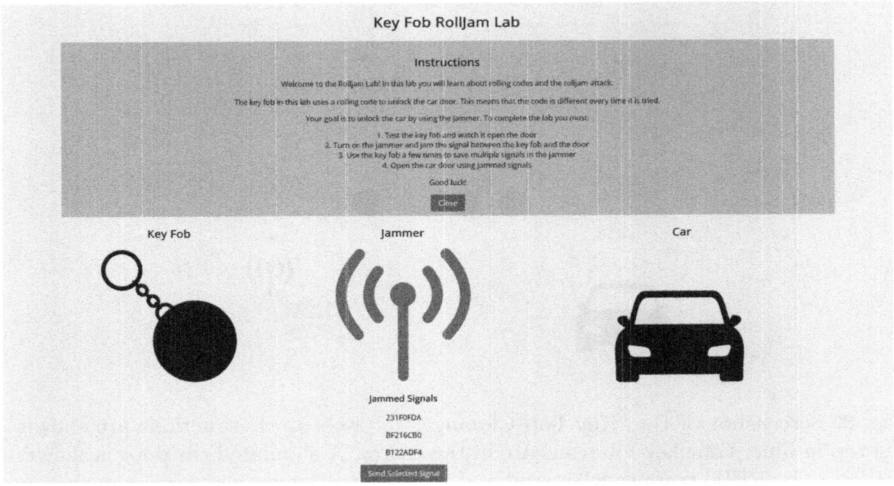

Fig. 4. Screenshot of the "Key Fob Rolljam Lab" website. Instructions are shown at the top in blue. A clickable key fob is shown on the left. The signal jammer is shown in the center with stored signals below. The simulated car is shown on the right.

The rolljam attack, first demonstrated by Samy Kamkar at DEFCON 2015 [5], exploits a jammer to bypass rolling code security in key fobs. When a key fob sends a signal, it generates a unique code that changes (or "rolls") with each use.

[7] https://wpi-lions-group.github.io/Key-Fob-Cloning-Lab/.

This dynamic code is synchronized with the receiver (such as a car or door lock). Even if an attacker intercepts a signal, the code will no longer be valid the next time it is transmitted because it will have already advanced to a new value.

To provide a learning experience with minimal cost of setup and maintenance, we developed the Rolljam Attack Simulation lab as a static website[8]. In this lab, students will seek to bypass a key fob's rolling code system using a signal jammer. As illustrated in Fig. 4, the simulation includes three interactive components: a key fob, a jammer, and a car. Selecting the key fob attempts to send an unlock signal to the car. The jammer, which can be toggled on or off with a visual indicator, intercepts these signals—either blocking them or forwarding them to the car. All blocked signals are recorded in a "Jammed Signals" list, allowing students to analyze and reuse them to bypass the rolling code security.

The objective of this lab is to unlock a car door without using the key fob. First, students will verify that the key fob successfully opens the car door when the jammer is inactive. Next, they will activate the jammer to block the key fob's signal, capturing a series of "Jammed Signals" recorded as hexadecimal strings. Students will then select a captured signal and transmit it to the car. Since the key fob operates with a rolling code system, only the correct sequential signal will successfully unlock the door.

Students who complete this lab will gain an understanding of rolling codes in key fobs and their potential vulnerabilities. After the lab, a discussion should be conducted on possible security enhancements to mitigate these risks.

3.6 Designing a Smart Key Fob Prototype

Following the completion of the previous two labs, students should have a solid understanding of common attacks on key fobs. This lab, designed for individual activity or group work, encourages creative thinking in designing a key fob prototype. Using their knowledge of attacks and security measures, students are tasked to develop a key fob that is resistant to the vulnerabilities demonstrated in earlier labs.

To complete this lab, students will develop a conceptual prototype of a key fob, presented as a detailed description rather than a physical product. This prototype is for demonstration purposes only and does not require any electronic parts. Alongside their description, students should provide design notes outlining the specific security features they have incorporated. Finally, a discussion should be conducted to assess potential vulnerabilities in the proposed key fob designs.

Students should have the opportunity to refine their designs based on the discussion. Later, they will present their prototypes to the class, highlighting their security features, initial vulnerabilities, and the modifications made after the discussion. Following the presentations, students will engage in a broader discussion on key fob technology and the importance of security in its design.

[8] https://wpi-lions-group.github.io/Key-Fob-Rolljam-Lab/.

3.7 Simulating Road Sign Attack with Adversarial Images

This is a lab activity that does not requires computer access. Students will use stickers, markers, and other materials to make subtle modifications to a printed road sign. They will then be asked to discuss how these slight alterations may affect a car's vision model, and how this can be avoided.

This lab is divided into three parts: an introduction, a simulation, and a discussion. The introduction allows a teacher to explain AI image processing in autonomous vehicles, focusing on how these systems interpret road signs. The teacher also introduces adversarial attacks, emphasizing how small modifications to a road sign can significantly impact the functionality of a car's vision model.

The second part of the lab is a simulation where students engage in road sign identification and adversarial modifications. Working in small groups or individually, they receive a printed road sign and discuss or document how an autonomous vehicle might recognize and interpret it based on its design, symbols, and text. After this initial analysis, students use stickers and markers to apply subtle adversarial changes to the sign, ensuring that while the modifications do not obscure its meaning to a human observer, they have the potential to mislead an AI model. Through this part, students explore the vulnerabilities of machine vision and gain a deeper understanding of how seemingly minor alterations can disrupt an AI system's ability to process visual information accurately.

The last part of the lab is the discussion and analysis. Each group presents their modified road sign, detailing the changes they made and how these alterations could impact an AI system's interpretation. They also discuss the potential risks associated with an autonomous vehicle misidentifying a road sign due to these modifications. The discussion will also inspire students to explore defense mechanisms against adversarial attacks, prompting students to consider potential solutions for enhancing AI robustness and reliability.

By completing this lab, students will develop a foundational understanding of image processing and adversarial attacks in the context of image-based object identification and classification. They will also become acquainted with the risks of misidentifying road signs and explore strategies for mitigating such attacks.

3.8 Road Sign Recognition with Teachable Machine

Building on the previous lab, this exercise takes students a step further by enabling them to train their own road sign image recognition model using Google's Teachable Machine[9]. After following the provided instructions to train the model, students are encouraged to creatively test its robustness by introducing adversarial changes to the road sign images. As illustrated in Fig. 5, writing a number on a poorly placed stop sign can deceive the model into misclassifying it as a speed limit sign.

For this lab, we provide a dataset of 230 images, which is divided into 210 images for training the model and 20 images for testing. The dataset consists

[9] https://teachablemachine.withgoogle.com/.

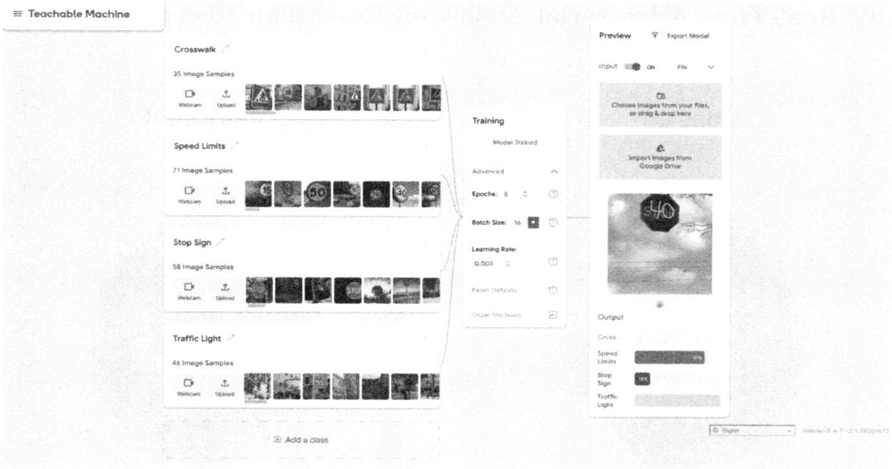

Fig. 5. Screenshot of Teachable Machine. The input data is shown on the left split into four classes. Training settings are shown in the center. The model preview is shown on the right incorrectly classifying a stop sign with adversarial markings as a speed limit sign.

of four classes: *crosswalks*, *speed limits*, *stop signs*, and *traffic lights*. The class distribution is detailed in Table 2. This dataset was curated by manually selecting images from a larger public domain Road Sign Detection dataset [8], ensuring they are suitable for this classification task. The dataset is hosted on GitHub for easy access[10], available as a ZIP file with separate folders for each class, allowing students to access the images in batch.

Table 2. Road Sign Image Dataset Classes

Class	Training Count	Test Count
Crosswalk	35	5
Speed Limit	71	5
Stop Sign	58	5
Traffic Light	46	5

By completing this lab, students will understand and be able to train and test their own computer vision models. They will also explore creative methods to deceive their models by applying subtle adversarial modifications.

[10] https://github.com/WPI-LIONS-Group/Road-Sign-Image-Dataset.

3.9 Real-Time Adversarial Attack on Road Sign Recognition

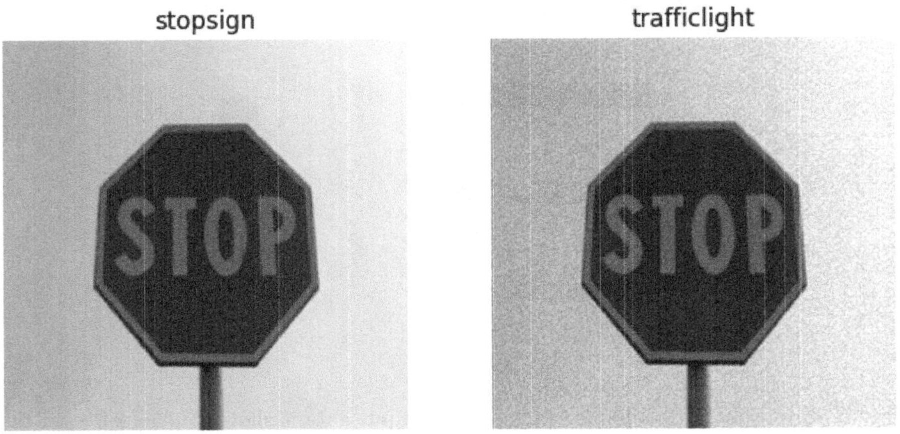

Fig. 6. Left: AI model correctly identifying a stop sign. Right: AI model misclassifying a stop sign after using applying the fast gradient method with CleverHans.

This lab allows students to experience real-time adversarial attacks on road sign recognition. A similar attack can be executed by automatically generating adversarial examples using the CleverHans library [11]. We designed this lab as a tutorial that integrates CleverHans with a Google Colab[11] notebook. Using the dataset from the previous lab, students are guided step by step to build an AI model that recognizes the images and then automatically generates adversarial examples to challenge the model (Fig. 6).

The tutorial is designed to guide students through the process of completing the lab. We assume high school students may not be familiar with the tools used, and hence all the code is provided directly in a markdown file, making it easy to copy and paste into a Colab notebook.

The lab is divided into three parts. First, students will install and import the required packages before loading the images from our dataset for use in the model. Next, they will create an AI model using TensorFlow[12], train the model, and observe its performance on the test data. After initial training, students will use the CleverHans library to generate adversarial examples for the model and analyze the results. Finally, students will have the option to adjust the model's parameters and retrain it in an attempt to improve its security.

Upon completing the lab, students will understand how images are interpreted by a computer, how an AI model can be trained to classify these images, and how small alterations to the images can generate adversarial examples that

[11] https://colab.research.google.com/.
[12] https://www.tensorflow.org/.

deceive the model. Following the lab, a discussion should focus on potential security measures for AI models and the importance of adversarial testing.

4 Evaluation Plan

This paper primarily focuses on the content introduction of the lab set. In addition, we have developed a robust evaluation plan for piloting these labs in high school environments. The project team includes five high school teachers who have been involved from the initial design phase and will play an active role in the evaluation process. The evaluation plan will include the following:

Teacher Feedback: The five participating teachers will provide feedback on the lab's clarity, engagement, and educational value. They will assess how effectively the lab content aligns with the curriculum and its ability to facilitate learning.

Student Performance: The lab's impact on student understanding will be evaluated through assessments of students' knowledge before and after completing the lab. Teachers will track students' ability to grasp concepts related to vehicle security, focusing on attacks and countermeasures.

Lab Usability: Teachers will evaluate the ease of use of the lab materials, including the clarity of instructions, the accessibility of resources, and the overall technical setup. Any challenges or obstacles encountered during the lab usage will be documented.

Student Engagement: Teachers will monitor student engagement during the lab exercises, observing how students interact with the tools, peers, and apply their learning. Feedback will be gathered through surveys and informal discussions with students.

Suggestions for Improvement: Teachers will collect suggestions from students regarding the lab's content, tools, and overall structure. This feedback will be used to refine the lab for future refinement and use.

After piloting in labs in high school classrooms, discussions with the teachers will be held to evaluate the overall success of the lab and explore areas for improvement. By integrating the teachers into the evaluation process, the plan ensures that the lab set is refined based on real-world classroom feedback and improves its educational effectiveness.

5 Conclusion

In conclusion, as technology continues to evolve, the importance of early cybersecurity education becomes ever more pressing. This paper presents a solution to the gap in high school cybersecurity resources by offering a hands-on, engaging mini-unit on autonomous vehicle security. Through practical labs that simulate real-world attacks and vulnerabilities, students gain valuable skills and insights into emerging threats. The collaboration with high school educators ensures that the labs are both relevant and effective, providing a foundation for students to explore cybersecurity careers and further studies. By fostering early awareness and critical thinking in this vital field, we empower the next generation to confront the cybersecurity challenges of an increasingly interconnected world.

Acknowledgments. Drs. Xiaoyan Sun and Jun Dai are supported by NSF DGE-2409851. Dr. Jun Dai is also supported by NSF DGE-1934285/2403603.

References

1. College Board: AP career kickstart cybersecurity pilots (2023). https://apcentral.collegeboard.org/about-ap/outreach-and-collaborations/career-kickstart/cybersecurity-pilots. Accessed 1 Feb 2025
2. Francia, G., El-Sheikh, E., Chi, H.: Vehicle security learning tools and scenarios. In: 2020 International Conference on Computational Science and Computational Intelligence (CSCI), pp. 88–92 (2020). https://doi.org/10.1109/CSCI51800.2020.00022
3. Giannaros, A., et al.: Autonomous vehicles: sophisticated attacks, safety issues, challenges, open topics, blockchain, and future directions. J. Cybersecur. Priv. **3**(3), 493–543 (2023). https://doi.org/10.3390/jcp3030025. https://www.mdpi.com/2624-800X/3/3/25
4. Grover, S., Broll, B., Babb, D.: Cybersecurity education in the age of AI: integrating AI learning into cybersecurity high school curricula. In: SIGCSE 2023, pp. 980–986. Association for Computing Machinery, New York, NY, USA (2023). https://doi.org/10.1145/3545945.3569750
5. Kamkar, S.: Drive it like you hacked it: new attacks and tools to wirelessly steal cars. Presentation at DEFCON **23**, 10 (2015)
6. Kapulica, A., Dakić, V., Morić, Z., Petrunić, R.: Key fob replay attacks on personal vehicles: vulnerabilities and mitigation strategies. In: 2024 International Congress on Human-Computer Interaction, Optimization and Robotic Applications (HORA), pp. 1–5 (2024). https://doi.org/10.1109/HORA61326.2024.10550523
7. Laurie, A.: Practical attacks against RFID. Netw. Secur. **2007**(9), 4–7 (2007)
8. Maranhão, A.: Road signs dataset. https://www.kaggle.com/datasets/andrewmvdroad-sign-detection
9. McCall, S., Yucel, C., Katos, V.: Education in cyber physical systems security: the case of connected autonomous vehicles. In: 2021 IEEE Global Engineering Education Conference (EDUCON), pp. 1379–1385 (2021). https://doi.org/10.1109/EDUCON46332.2021.9454086
10. Miller, C.: Remote exploitation of an unaltered passenger vehicle. Black Hat (2015)
11. Papernot, N., et al.: Technical report on the CleverHans v2.1.0 adversarial examples library. arXiv preprint arXiv:1610.00768 (2018)
12. Pavlitska, S., Lambing, N., Zöllner, J.M.: Adversarial attacks on traffic sign recognition: a survey. In: 2023 3rd International Conference on Electrical, Computer, Communications and Mechatronics Engineering (ICECCME), pp. 1–6 (2023). https://doi.org/10.1109/ICECCME57830.2023.10252727
13. Payne, B.R.: Car hacking: accessing and exploiting the can bus protocol. J. Cybersecur. Educ. Res. Pract. **2019**(1), 5 (2019)
14. Team, O.: Introduction to car hacking: the can bus (2022). https://www.offsec.com/blog/introduction-to-car-hacking-the-can-bus/. Accessed 24 Jan 2025
15. Xie, X., et al.: Access your tesla without your awareness: compromising keyless entry system of model 3. In: NDSS (2023)

Papers Invited from SEC

Exposing the Gaps: The State of Supply Chain Coverage in Current Security Standards

Nico Mexis[1(✉)], Bjarne Lill[2], Yousef Doleh[1,3], and Stefan Katzenbeisser[1]

[1] University of Passau, Innstraße 43, 94032 Passau, Germany
{mexis01,doleh01,katzen07}@ads.uni-passau.de
[2] University of Innsbruck, Technikerstraße 21a, 6020 Innsbruck, Austria
Bjarne.Lill@uibk.ac.at
[3] CyberShield, Julius-Hatry-Straße 1, 68163 Mannheim, Germany
doleh@cybershield-consulting.com

Abstract. Nowadays, various standards are being used to assess and even certify the security and resilience of companies all around the world. However, as most of them focus on IT and OT-related aspects, supply chain security is often forgotten or not given enough attention. This paper aims to address this limitation by using systematic mappings between four security standards, namely the ISO/IEC 27000 family, the NIST Cyber Security Framework (NIST CSF), the NIST SP 800-53 and NIST SP 800-82 standard, and the NIST SP 800-161 standard, which is dedicated to supply chain security, to determine the current state of supply chain security coverage. The results indicate that no standard covers even 50% of the baseline security aspects.

Keywords: Supply Chain Security · Security Standards · Cybersecurity · Risk Management · Vulnerability Assessment · NIST · ISO · IEC

1 Introduction

Cybersecurity is an important topic for enterprises to consider in light of continuous incidents and breaches and ever more sophisticated attack patterns and threats [24,38,40]. This is reflected in ENISA's 2024 Threat Landscape report, which outlines an increasing number of incidents, not only in terms of frequency, but also in terms of impact [14]. Today, these cybersecurity incidents not only affect large companies, but also Small and Medium-sized Enterprises (SMEs) [24,32]. In this context, cyber-attacks on SMEs can severely impact the entire supply chain in the form of other SMEs and larger organizations [31]. These observations, paired with the facts, that SMEs make up 99.8% of businesses within Europe, employ 64.4% of people, add 52.5% of value [13] and also perform worst in supply chain cybersecurity [22] make supply chain cybersecurity in enterprises of any size an increasingly important topic to consider.

Published by Springer Nature Switzerland AG 2026
L. Drevin et al. (Eds.): WISE 2025, IFIP AICT 742, pp. 203–216, 2026.
https://doi.org/10.1007/978-3-031-94924-1_14

In general, the inner structure of companies works using a top-down approach, where each layer (mobile end devices, Information Technology (IT), and Operational Technology (OT)) can only communicate with each layer directly below it. Direct communication between mobile end devices and the OT should therefore be impossible. Instead, mobile end devices use the IT in order to connect through it (using e.g., VPN services) to the OT network. This communication process is also depicted in Fig. 1. The supply chain is perpendicular to the layers within the company and corresponds to the arrows pointing in and out of the enterprise.

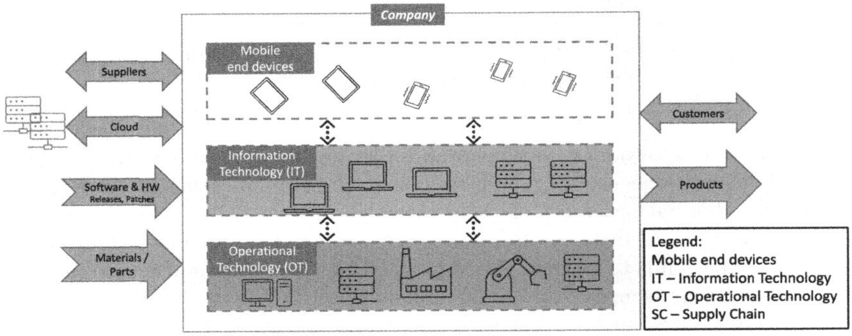

Fig. 1. General digital structure of a company in terms of the four layers *mobile end devices*, *Information Technology (IT)*, *Operational Technology (OT)*, and *Supply Chain (SC)*.

In this publication, we investigate cybersecurity standards to evaluate to which extent supply chain cybersecurity is covered within these standards. To address this research objective, we focus on three research questions:

- **RQ1**: *How do various security standards compare to each other?*
- **RQ2**: *What are the main points to consider in the context of supply chain security for companies?*
- **RQ3**: *How well do current security standards cover supply chain security for companies?*

We pursued these questions by conducting a systematic literature review and performed a systematic standards mapping and coverage calculation of the identified supply chain aspects. As a result, we identified the ISO/IEC 27000 [19] family, the NIST CSF [27], NIST 800-53 [28], and NIST 800-82 [36] as the most relevant security standards in the context of companies. Further, we uncovered that none of the standards includes even 50% of the identified supply chain aspects as outlined by the NIST SP 800-161 [4] baseline.

The rest of this work is structured as follows: In Sects. 2 and 3, the methodology behind this work and related work on its topic is summarised, respectively. Then, Sect. 4 describes the results of our study and Sect. 5 concludes the work and points out possible routes for future work.

2 Methodology

2.1 Common Security Standards

The *ISO/IEC 27000* family [19] consists of various standards, which cover the best practices for the implementation of Information Security Management Systems (ISMS). An ISMS consists of a collection of policies, procedures, and practices designed to identify, assess, and manage risks [7].

The *ISO/IEC 27001* standard is based on seven ISMS requirements, also called clauses, and is applicable to companies of any size and from all sectors. To obtain an "ISO certification," these clauses must be implemented. These clauses focus mostly on the management of a system rather than on security controls [1].

In addition, the *ISO/IEC 27002* standard covers 93 detailed security control objectives for ISMS, which are listed in Annex A. It should be mentioned that the 2013 and 2017 versions of both standards was more fine-grained and hence contained more controls, in total 114.

The *NIST Cyber Security Framework (NIST CSF)* was released as version 2.0 in February 2024 [29]. Due to its novelty, there is only very limited work regarding its mappings to other standards, such as [41]. For this reason, our work still mainly targets version 1.1 [27], but mentions the changes from version 2.0 in appropriate places. However, future work should consider fully updating these mappings to version 2.0. In general, the NIST CSF version 1.1 lists five concurrent and continuous functions: Identify, Protect, Detect, Respond, and Recover. Corresponding to these, 23 categories indicate the required cybersecurity results for each function, with 108 subcategories representing security controls to appropriately handle each category.

NIST SP 800-53 mainly targets federal agencies, contractors, and other organisations that work with government information systems. The purpose of these controls is to enhance the cybersecurity posture of information systems and facilitate the more efficient management of cybersecurity threats. The controls are divided into 20 families, each with a two-character identity and involving policy, oversight, and both manual and automated operations [28].

NIST SP 800-82 is a standard that gives recommendations for securing OT environments, while meeting the OT's particular performance, reliability, and safety needs. The guideline provides a set of controls that organisations need to use to secure OT environments and critical infrastructure [36].

Finally, the *NIST SP 800-161* standard [4] covers supply chain security. It is based on the NIST SP 800-53 standard and its controls have the exact same identifiers and names. However, the descriptions contain supply chain-specific requirements in that regard.

2.2 Supply Chain Aspects

In general, movement of goods and related data constitutes a supply-chain "flow." According to Scully and Hobig [35], the supply chain can be divided into three flows: information, material, and finance flow. The information flow is bidirectional and the content exchanged between the parties is intangible. On the other hand, the material flow is generally from source to consumer and its content is physical material. The finance flow consists mainly of money and generally flows in the opposite direction.

The digital supply chain may include parts of all three flows, which means that all three flows should be properly secured and should be part of the security certification process. Examples of goods exchanged in each of these flows include emails, hard drives, and digital currency, respectively. The aforementioned NIST SP 800-161 standard [4] aims to secure all of these flows through its controls.

2.3 Systematic Literature Review

In order to adequately answer the research questions phrased in Sect. 1, a systematic literature review according to Kitchenham [20] was conducted. The next paragraphs summarise the procedure and describe our results for each step.

The research questions have already been phrased in Sect. 1. In the next step, IEEE Xplore, Taylor and Francis, the ACM Digital Library, SpringerLink, and the AIS eLibrary have been identified as popular scientific electronic libraries that met the criteria for selection. In addition, Google Scholar and Google were utilised in order to locate grey literature and other supporting material. Since the matter of finding mappings between security standards features both contributions for the scientific and economic community, it is important to consider both white and grey literature for this work. After adjusting a preliminary boolean expression in various iterations, we ended up with the following search string:

("Information security" OR "Cyber security" OR "Security") AND ("IT" OR "OT") AND ("Standards" OR "Frameworks") AND ("Mapping" OR "Compar*") AND "ISO" AND "IEC" AND "NIST"

IT and OT occur mostly because the papers mention the main part of the digital structure, to which the standard(s) apply. On the other hand, ISO, NIST, and IEC correspond to the institutions which have published most of the relevant and common standards in the field and are hence mentioned not only in the papers on their own, but also as part of the standard's name itself. This final search string resulted in merely 2621 articles, 2321 of which come from SpringerLink. For AISeL, the filters for "ISO," "IEC," and "NIST" have been removed, though, due to leading only to very few relevant results, in contrast to the other databases.

The following expert consultation with a Lead Cybersecurity expert and a Cybersecurity Consultant identified the ISO/IEC 27000 [19] standards, the NIST CSF [27], NIST 800-53 [28], NIST 800-82 [36], and the ISA/IEC 62443 [18] as most relevant in the context of digital security. This reaffirmed the choice of the additional filters for the search string. However, it should be mentioned that the ISA/IEC 62443 standard [18] should be considered in future work on this topic as especially parts 2-1 and 3-3 were mentioned in a few articles.

Next, the inclusion and exclusion criteria were specified:

Inclusion criteria:

- Deals with mapping of requirements or controls between different security standards (at least one of the following standards and guidelines: ISO/IEC 27000, NIST CSF, NIST 800-53, or NIST 800-82)

Exclusion criteria:

- References obsolete standards
- Is written in a language other than English
- Published before 2013

Finally, the search and filter process started. As illustrated in Figure 2, in total 24 papers could be identified that are highly relevant to our paper. Section 3 summarises them accordingly and puts them into the bigger frame of our work in order to answer **RQ1**.

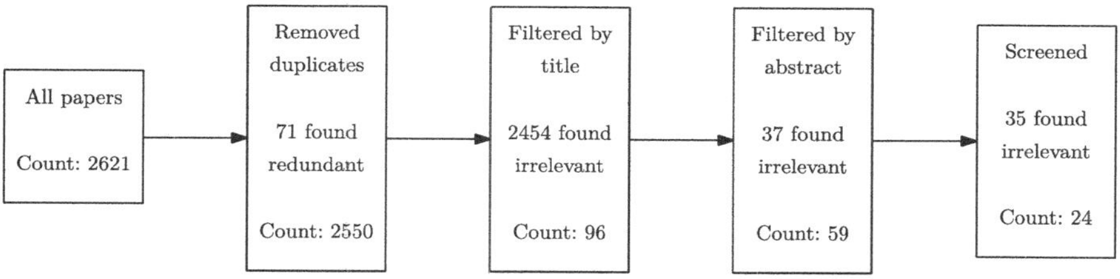

Fig. 2. Filtering process during the literature review.

2.4 Standards Mapping and Coverage Calculation

As a result of the systematic literature review, mappings between the four relevant security standards have been found and extended upon. Many mappings are already included directly in the NIST CSF [27] itself. This yields an Excel sheet that is based on the mappings of the NIST CSF Core and that lists all the aspects from the NIST CSF and maps them to different sections or controls of the other three security standards.

This Excel sheet is used as a "lookup table" to quickly find the relevant sections in the relevant security standards during the supply chain coverage calculation. For this, the NIST SP 800-161 [4] standard was used as a basis on which supply chain aspects should be considered. As described in Sect. 2.1, it is based on the NIST SP 800-53 [28] standard and hence, it can be trivially incorporated into the mapping.

Coverage scores can be calculated through various similarity measures such as the Jaccard Index, Dice-Sørensen coefficient, etc. [3]. However, in our case, the controls from the NIST SP 800-161 standard are assumed to be complete and hence both the "number of species in sample B but not sample A" (b) and "number of species absent in both samples" (d) are always 0 and $a + c$ is always equal to the number of species (i.e., controls in our case). Because of this, most measures correlate with a simple fraction calculation. In fact, the Jaccard index, Russel & Rao index and Simple Matching are all equal to a simple percentage calculation. For this reason, we have opted to simply calculate the coverage in the form of percentages as the measures do not reveal any further information in this use case.

In another Excel sheet, all the controls from the "Cybersecurity Supply Chain Risk Management (C-SCRM) Baseline" from NIST SP 800-161 [4] are listed. These are considered to be the answer to **RQ2** as they form the basis for supply chain security and are applicable to enterprises of any size. Each of these controls corresponds to a control from NIST SP 800-53 [28], whose mappings are then considered in the further analysis. When the corresponding control from a standard at least covers 50% of the points mentioned in the corresponding control from NIST SP 800-161 [4], it is considered as "covered." Otherwise, it is not covered sufficiently. Ultimately, the coverage score (and hence the answer to **RQ3**) of a standard is the percentage (or fraction) of controls that are covered sufficiently out of all the 96 controls that make up the C-SCRM baseline (see Sect. 4).

3 Related Work

3.1 Mappings Between Security Standards

A literature review of security standards mapping identified several researchers who have mapped the aforementioned standards. These different researchers have mostly mapped overarching objectives and core ideas across standards. This includes, but is not limited to, the sector in which they work, scope, and more. To systematically categorise these mappings, we classified them into distinct types, each representing a specific group of standards that were mapped together. The identified types together with all their references are presented in Table 1.

Table 1. Security standards Mapping Classification, taken from [10].

Classification	Description	References
Type 1	ISO 27001 and IEC 62443	[9]
Type 2	ISO 27001 and NIST CSF	[5,15,23,30,34]
Type 3	ISO 27001 and others	[2,6,25]
Type 4	IEC 62443 and others	[17]
Type 5	IEC 62443 and ISO 27001 and NIST CSF	[8,11,21,27,33,39]

We now summarise the most important related works out of the compendium. The least common mappings identified were between ISO 27001 and IEC 62443 and IEC 62443 with other standards. However, in 2023, Djebbar and Nordström [9], mapped all of the ISO 27001 controls to the IEC 62443-3-3 and hence discovered that the IEC 62443-3-3 standard had great matches in the physical requirements and technological requirements and none in the organization and people requirements domains of the ISO 27001.

Moving to type 2, in 2023 Malatji [23] mapped the Annex A ISO 27001:2022 controls to the NIST CSF 1.1 and found that the PROTECT function had the most mapped controls, with 82 of the ISO 27001 controls aligning with this function.

Most importantly, type 5 demonstrated the most comprehensive results, mapping all three standards together. In 2017, ENISA [11] mapped the IEC 62443, NIST CSF and IS0 27001 with the NIS Directive. This mapping offered a harmonised mapping to security measures to specific sectors such as Energy, Transport, Healthcare, and Digital Infrastructures sectors. It highlighted the correlation between measures like access control, incident management, and business continuity with standards such as ISO 27001, NIST CSF, and IEC 62443 series.

Type 4 showed limited results, with Hollerer et al. [17] mapping only the Security levels (SL) of the IEC 62443 standard to the Common Vulnerability Scoring System (CVSS).

On the other hand, type 3, Beckers et al. [2] compared the ISO 27001 with the older version 2013 and with the IT-Grundschutz. However, these mappings were only high-level, focusing on the overarching goals and scope of each standard rather than providing a comprehensive comparison.

3.2 Supply Chain Security Coverage

The literature on supply chain security coverage assessments is very sparse. However, two papers have been identified that attempt to address the issue.

In 2021, Topping et al. [37] identified 15 supply chain-related categories as the most relevant as a result of a systematic literature review and assigned a score between 1 and 3 to each, corresponding to the coverage of that aspect in the relevant standard. The results indicate insufficient coverage in almost every aspect. However, the results do not consider the different standards in isolation, but only give a coverage score when all the standards examined are combined, which hardly reflects reality. In contrast, our methodology covers a wider range of aspects, with more detail and differentiation between standards.

Hintsa [16] developed a framework for assessing supply chain security standards in 2010. A systematic approach resulted in a catalogue of 14 questions that should be consulted when evaluating existing or creating new supply chain security standards. Alas, at the time of writing, it is more than 10 years old and would need to be revised to take account of new threats arising from the constant interconnection of more and more devices.

4 Results and Discussion

This section aims to answer **RQ3**. The coverage calculation as explained in Sect. 2.4 yields the results from Table 2. The ISO/IEC 27000 family achieved the highest supply chain coverage, whilst the NIST CSF (version 1.1) performed the worst.

Table 2. Supply chain coverage of the four investigated security standards in contrast to the NIST SP 800-161 controls [4].

	ISO/IEC 27000	NIST CSF	NIST SP 800-53	NIST SP 800-82
Not covered	50	70	55	67
Covered	46	26	41	29
Percentage	48%	26%	43%	30%

The detailed Excel sheets yielding these results are published separately for space reasons. They have been exported to PDF files and uploaded externally as part of a large supplementary document [26]. It lists all the mappings between the standards as explained in Sect. 2.4 as well as all the controls from the NIST SP 800-161 [4] baseline and controls from the other standards, which address them, respectively. A X indicates that the corresponding supply chain security control is not covered adequately within the standard.

The supplementary document also contains calculations for the coverage score(s) using various similarity measures. However, as already mentioned in Sect. 2.4, they only provide rather limited additional insight, which is why a detailed discussion is omitted in this paper. The helper variables N_{00}, N_{01}, N_{10}, and N_{11} correspond to the aforementioned variables d, b, c, and a, respectively. The other variables are just combinations of these to avoid having to calculate the same values multiple times.

Initially, Table 3 was part of the supplementary document. However, the final version does not contain it since it is already included in this paper. It illustrates the coverage percentage by considering the 19 categories from the NIST SP 800-161 [4] baseline as stand-alone, each.

The NIST CSF scored so poorly mainly because the short descriptions were too broad. Supply chain aspects are only mentioned in very few categories, which in turn refer to informative references that transitively might cover supply chain aspects. However, due to the systematisation of our mapping, only the descriptions of the various controls from the NIST CSF directly are considered.

Surprisingly, the NIST SP 800-82 standard also achieved a rather low score. Since its main focus is on OT security, it was expected to perform rather good due to the high dependence on manufacturers and maintenance personnel. However, in the OT environment, availability is much more important than confidentiality and integrity and network segmentation is the key. The NIST SP 800-161 controls show exactly the opposite picture, covering confidentiality and integrity much more than availability. To address this fundamental gap, the NIST SP 800-82 standard references the NIST SP 800-161 standard in Sect. 4.2.1. However, exact mappings or detailed instructions on how to incorporate its controls within the OT environment are missing.

It is also very surprising that despite the 1:1 correspondence between the NIST SP 800-161 and NIST SP 800-53 controls, the latter did not even achieve 50% coverage. In this case, the low coverage score is due to the fact that the controls barely mention the supply chain or, if they do, they do not require systematic or documented procedures.

Each first control within each category of the NIST SP 800-161 standard is called "Policy and Procedures." It requires most often to flow down specific requirements to relevant sub-tier contractors. In addition, policies should be in place that cover specific aspects of the category. Almost none of these controls were covered by the various standards, leaving a huge gap. The ISO 27002 standard regulates the flow of "appropriate" regulations through the supply chain in Sect. 5.21. However, again, details on which requirements are omitted.

4.1 Comparison of the Categories

The obvious limitation of our approach stems from the fact that the baseline controls of the NIST SP 800-161 standard [4] contain a different amount of controls, each. This induces an imbalance between the contributions of the categories to the overall coverage score. To address this, we have calculated intermediate coverages for each category on its own and calculated another total coverage score for each standard by calculating the average across all intermediates. The results are illustrated in Table 3.

The total coverage scores changed by +3%, +2%, -2%, and +5% for the standards respectively, indicating a fairly stable score regardless of the analysis method. It was also found that the Media Protection (MP) and Planning (PL) families have 0% coverage in terms of supply chain security. In total, 13/19 families have inadequate supply chain security coverage ($< 50\%$). On the positive side, the Program Management (PM) family has 100% coverage in all four analysed standards. However, it should be noted that the PM family consists of only a single control in the NIST SP 800-161 [4] baseline.

The absence of adequate coverage in the various families leads to an increased attack surface in terms of confidentiality (e.g., Access Control (AC) or MP), integrity (e.g., MP), and availability (e.g., PL). Insufficient coverage in families such as Awareness and Training (AT) or Maintenance (MA) constitutes a vulnerability across the entire digital structure of any enterprise and supply chain.

Table 3. Supply chain coverage of the four investigated security standards in contrast to the 19 categories of the NIST SP 800-161 standard [4], sorted by total (mean) coverage across all standards.

	Total	ISO/IEC 27K	NIST CSF	NIST SP 800-53	NIST SP 800-82
MP	0%	0%	0%	0%	0%
PL	0%	0%	0%	0%	0%
AC	25%	38%	13%	50%	0%
AT	25%	50%	50%	0%	0%
CM	28%	33%	11%	67%	0%
SI	29%	43%	29%	14%	29%
SA	32%	43%	14%	71%	0%
IA	35%	80%	0%	60%	0%
CA	38%	50%	33%	17%	50%
CP	38%	25%	50%	25%	50%
SC	38%	50%	0%	50%	50%
MA	42%	67%	33%	33%	33%
SR	43%	40%	40%	50%	40%
AU	50%	60%	40%	40%	60%
PE	50%	60%	20%	60%	60%
RA	54%	33%	50%	67%	67%
IR	56%	100%	25%	50%	50%
PS	56%	100%	25%	25%	75%
PM	100%	100%	100%	100%	100%
Avg.	39%	51%	28%	41%	35%

4.2 Possible Remediation

In the future, standards should explicitly mention and detail supply chain aspects in the descriptions of each of their controls. This assures that security certifications also reflect the current state of supply chain security. The detailed results from the spreadsheets from Sect. 4 as well as Sect. 4.1 and Table 3, where each category is considered stand-alone, should be consulted to identify and subsequently fix the main issues.

In general, a dedicated supply chain security and/or risk management standard should be used in addition to a security standard for proper certification. In practice, standard mappings help to find the relevant controls in other standards fairly quickly, so the extra work involved can be kept to a minimum. In case the NIST SP 800-53 standard is consulted as the main security standard, a mapping to the relevant supply chain security-related control in NIST SP 800-161 can even be considered trivial.

5 Conclusion and Future Work

In this work, we have identified the ISO/IEC 27000 [19] family, the NIST CSF [27], NIST 800-53 [28], and NIST 800-82 [36] as the most relevant security standards in the context of enterprises. Building upon that, we have shown how these security standards compare to each other by summarising the current literature on mappings between them. Furthermore, the NIST SP 800-161 [4] baseline was identified to be appropriate for supply chain security for companies. The combination of these findings was ultimately used to identify the supply chain security coverage of the former four standards. The results indicate that no standard covers even 50% of the baseline supply chain security aspects. To remedy this situation, either the standards themselves or the certifications should be changed in the future.

Our work has a few limitations, which should be addressed as part of future work. Most importantly, the recent release of the NIST CSF version 2.0 [29] deprecates the original mappings between the security standards. A proper update, also involving recent work such as Wu et al.'s [41] should be consulted for this. In turn, some of the gaps identified in our paper may have been addressed in this new version of the NIST CSF core, potentially increasing its coverage significantly.

Also, other supply chain security frameworks, standards or even related technical reports could be used in place of NIST SP 800-161 [4] to determine different coverage scores. Furthermore, other standards such as the NIS 2 directive [12] ISA/IEC 62443 [18] – especially because of chapter 4-1 – should be reviewed for their coverage of supply chain security.

Furthermore, there may be some subjectivity in determining coverage due to manual interpretation and comparison of the various standards. We have tried to counteract this by using dedicated standard mappings and well-established scientific procedures, but complete objectivity cannot be guaranteed. Future work may consider other automated and deterministic methods to arrive at an objective scoring system.

Finally, in addition to the baseline controls from the NIST SP 800-161 standard, all its controls could be used in order to provide even more insight into the topic of supply chain security coverage of standards in the context of larger or more critical enterprises.

Acknowledgments. This work is co-funded by the European Union through INTERREG VI-A Germany/Bavaria-Austria 2021–2027 – INTERREG VI-A Bayern-Österreich 2021–2027, as part of the Project "CySeReS-KMU: Cyber Security and Resilience in Supply Chains with focus on SMEs" (project number BA0100016).

Parts of this work are based on Yousef Doleh's master's thesis [10].

Disclosure of Interests. The authors have no competing interests to declare that are relevant to the content of this article.

References

1. Alexei, A.: Ensuring information security in public organizations in the republic of moldova through the ISO 27001 standard. J. Soc. Sci. **IV**(1), 84–94 (2021). https://doi.org/10.52326/jss.utm.2021.4(1).11
2. Beckers, K., Côté, I., Fenz, S., Hatebur, D., Heisel, M.: A structured comparison of security standards. In: Heisel, M., Joosen, W., Lopez, J., Martinelli, F. (eds.) Engineering Secure Future Internet Services and Systems. LNCS, vol. 8431, pp. 1–34. Springer, Cham (2014). https://doi.org/10.1007/978-3-319-07452-8_1
3. Boyce, R.L., Ellison, P.C.: Choosing the best similarity index when performing fuzzy set ordination on binary data. J. Veg. Sci. **12**(5), 711–720 (2001). https://doi.org/10.2307/3236912
4. Boyens, J., Smith, A., Bartol, N., Winkler, K., Holbrook, A., Fallon, M.: cybersecurity supply chain risk management practices for systems and organizations. Technical Report, NIST Special Publication (SP) 800-161r1-upd1, National Institute of Standards and Technology, Gaithersburg, MD, May 2022. https://doi.org/10.6028/NIST.SP.800-161r1-upd1, includes updates as of November 1, 2024
5. Breaux, T.D., Gordon, D.G., Papanikolaou, N., Pearson, S.: Mapping legal requirements to IT controls. In: 2013 6th International Workshop on Requirements Engineering and Law (RELAW), pp. 11–20. IEEE, July 2013. https://doi.org/10.1109/relaw.2013.6671341
6. Cheng, D.C., Villamarin, J.B., Cu, G., Lim-Cheng, N.R.: Towards compliance management automation thru ontology mapping of requirements to activities and controls. In: 2018 Cyber Resilience Conference (CRC), pp. 1–3. IEEE, November 2018. https://doi.org/10.1109/cr.2018.8626817
7. Culot, G., Nassimbeni, G., Podrecca, M., Sartor, M.: The ISO/IEC 27001 information security management standard: literature review and theory-based research agenda. TQM J. **33**(7), 76–105 (2021). https://doi.org/10.1108/tqm-09-2020-0202
8. Dhirani, L.L., Armstrong, E., Newe, T.: Industrial IoT, cyber threats, and standards landscape: evaluation and roadmap. Sensors **21**(11), 3901 (2021). https://doi.org/10.3390/s21113901
9. Djebbar, F., Nordström, K.: A comparative analysis of industrial cybersecurity standards. IEEE Access **11**, 85315–85332 (2023). https://doi.org/10.1109/access.2023.3303205
10. Doleh, Y.: A Comparative Analysis of Mappings Between Information Security Standards. M.Sc. thesis, University of Passau, Passau, Germany, March 2024
11. ENISA: mapping of OES security requirements to specific sectors — enisa.europa.eu. https://www.enisa.europa.eu/publications/mapping-of-oes-security-requirements-to-specific-sectors/ (2018)
12. European commission: directive (EU) 2022/2555 of the European parliament and of the council of 14 December 2022 on measures for a high common level of cybersecurity across the Union, amending Regulation (EU) No 910/2014 and Directive (EU) 2018/1972, and repealing Directive (EU) 2016/1148 (NIS 2 Directive). http://data.europa.eu/eli/dir/2022/2555/2022-12-27, December 2022
13. European commission: eurostat: key figures on european business – 2024 edition. Publications Office of the European Union, May 2024. https://doi.org/10.2785/659794
14. European union agency for cybersecurity, ENISA: ENISA threat landscape 2024 (2024). https://doi.org/10.2824/0710888

15. Hamdani, S., et al.: Cybersecurity standards in the context of operating system: practical aspects, analysis, and comparisons. ACM Comput. Surv. **54**(3), 1–36 (2021). https://doi.org/10.1145/3442480
16. Hintsa, J.: A comprehensive framework for analysis and design of supply chain security standards. J. Transp. Secur. **3**(2), 105–125 (2010). https://doi.org/10.1007/s12198-010-0042-3
17. Hollerer, S., Sauter, T., Kastner, W.: Risk assessments considering safety, security, and their interdependencies in OT environments. In: Proceedings of the 17th International Conference on Availability, Reliability and Security, pp. 1–8. ARES 2022, ACM, August 2022. https://doi.org/10.1145/3538969.3543814
18. IEC 62443 2009-2018: security for industrial automation and control systems. Standard. International electrotechnical commission. Standard, International electrotechnical commission, Geneva, CH, February 2009
19. ISO/IEC 27001:2022: Information security, cybersecurity and privacy protection. Standard, International organization for standardization (2022)
20. Kitchenham, B.: Procedures for performing systematic reviews. Joint Technical Report TR/SE-0401, Keele University, Keele, UK, July 2004. https://www.inf.ufsc.br/~aldo.vw/kitchenham.pdf
21. Leszczyna, R.: A review of standards with cybersecurity requirements for smart grid. Comput. Secur. **77**, 262–276 (2018). https://doi.org/10.1016/j.cose.2018.03.011
22. Lill, B., Sauerwein, C., Zeisler, A., Hochstrasser, C., Mexis, N.: Assessing cybersecurity readiness among SME. In: Proceedings of the 27th International Conference on Enterprise Information Systems. INSTICC, SCITEPRESS - Science and Technology Publications (submitted for publication)
23. Malatji, M.: Management of enterprise cyber security: a review of ISO/IEC 27001:2022. In: 2023 International Conference On Cyber Management And Engineering (CyMaEn), pp. 117–122. IEEE, January 2023. https://doi.org/10.1109/cymaen57228.2023.10051114
24. Markakis, E., et al.: Acceleration at the edge for supporting SMEs security: The FORTIKA paradigm. IEEE Commun. Mag. **57**(2), 41–47 (2019). https://doi.org/10.1109/mcom.2019.1800506
25. Meriah, I., Arfa Rabai, L.B.: Comparative study of ontologies based ISO 27000 series security standards. Procedia Comput. Sci. **160**, 85–92 (2019). https://doi.org/10.1016/j.procs.2019.09.447
26. Mexis, N., Lill, B., Doleh, Y., Katzenbeisser, S.: Supplementary material for the work "Exposing the gaps: the state of supply chain coverage in current security standards". Universität Passau, OPUS Dokumentenserver, March 2025. https://nbn-resolving.org/urn:nbn:de:bvb:739-opus4-15633
27. National institute of standards and technology: framework for improving critical infrastructure cybersecurity, version 1.1. Tech. Rep. NIST Cybersecurity White Paper (CSWP) NIST CSWP 04162018, U.S. Department of Commerce, Washington, D.C., April 2018. https://doi.org/10.6028/nist.cswp.04162018
28. National institute of standards and technology: security and privacy controls for information systems and organizations. Technical Report, NIST Special Publication (SP) 800-53r5, National Institute of Standards and Technology, Gaithersburg, MD, September 2020. https://doi.org/10.6028/nist.sp.800-53r5
29. National institute of standards and technology: the NIST cybersecurity framework (CSF) 2.0. Technical Report, NIST Cybersecurity White Paper (CSWP) NIST CSWP 29, National Institute of Standards and Technology, Gaithersburg, MD, February 2024. https://doi.org/10.6028/nist.cswp.29

30. Ozkan, B.Y., Spruit, M.: Cybersecurity standardisation essentials for european SMEs, https://webspace.science.uu.nl/~sprui107/download/Cybersecurity%20Standardisation%20Essentials%20for%20European%20SMEs.pdf
31. Pfeifer, M.R.: IT security in SMEs – threats and chances for supply chains. J. Supply Chain Custom. Relationship Manage. 1–8, October 2021. https://doi.org/10.5171/2021.435883
32. Renaud, K.: How smaller businesses struggle with security advice. Comput. Fraud Secur. **2016**(8), 10–18 (2016). https://doi.org/10.1016/s1361-3723(16)30062-8
33. Rocha, F.P.D.: Cybersecurity analysis of a SCADA system under current standards, client requisites, and penetration testing. Master's thesis, Universidade do Porto (2019). https://sigarra.up.pt/feup/en/pub_geral.pub_view?pi_pub_base_id=315683
34. Roy, P.P.: A high-level comparison between the NIST cyber security framework and the ISO 27001 information security standard. In: 2020 National Conference on Emerging Trends on Sustainable Technology and Engineering Applications (NCETSTEA), IEEE, February 2020. https://doi.org/10.1109/ncetstea48365.2020.9119914
35. Scully, P., Hobig, M.: Exploring the impact of blockchain on digitized supply chain flows: a literature review. In: 2019 Sixth International Conference on Software Defined Systems (SDS), pp. 278–283. IEEE, Rome, Italy, June 2019. https://doi.org/10.1109/SDS.2019.8768573
36. Stouffer, K. et al.: Guide to Operational Technology (OT) security. Technical Report, NIST Special Publication (SP) 800-82r3, National Institute of Standards and Technology, Gaithersburg, MD, September 2023. https://doi.org/10.6028/NIST.SP.800-82r3
37. Topping, C., Dwyer, A., Michalec, O., Craggs, B., Rashid, A.: Beware suppliers bearing gifts!: analysing coverage of supply chain cyber security in critical national infrastructure sectorial and cross-sectorial frameworks. Comput. Secur. **108**, 102324 (2021). https://doi.org/10.1016/j.cose.2021.102324
38. U.S. Small business administration: stay safe from cybersecurity threats (2021), https://www.sba.gov/business-guide/manage-your-business/strengthen-your-cybersecurity, Accessed 13 Dec 2024
39. Wang, B.: Rethinking existing cybersecurity frameworks: how to incentivise companies to better defend against cyber threats. Master's thesis, University of London, Royal Holloway, University of London (United Kingdom) (2020), https://www.proquest.com/docview/2447994765
40. World economic forum: global cybersecurity outlook 2022 – insight report (2022), https://www3.weforum.org/docs/WEF_Global_Cybersecurity_Outlook_2022.pdf
41. Wu, F.T., Lee, W.B., Ku, C.C.Y., Wu, Y.S., Shih, C.Y.: Integrating ISO 27001, NIST CSF 2.0, and cyber defense matrix for enhancing organizational cybersecurity governance. SSRN, October 2024. https://doi.org/10.2139/ssrn.4991340

Integrating Security Concepts Into Introductory Programming Courses

Alina Torbunova(✉) and Ivan Porres

Åbo Akademi University, Turku, Finland
{alina.torbunova,ivan.porres}@abo.fi

Abstract. This article proposes a method to help students develop a security mindset by incorporating security concepts into a university-level introductory programming course. The method is based on a mapping of introductory programming topics to relevant security concepts. The mapping is used to modify lecture materials and programming projects to incorporate security-related information and requirements. These modifications are added gradually, with minimal impact on existing learning outcomes and expected student effort. We evaluated our method in a case study on the introduction of security concepts in an introductory programming course in Python. For this, we analyzed student programming projects and conducted a post-course survey. The results show improved security implementation in student projects and increased awareness of the importance of security in programming.

Keywords: Cybersecurity · Secure programming · Teaching · University · Introductory programming course

1 Introduction

Software developers should prioritize security from the start of the software development lifecycle [24]. Identifying potentially exploitable defects early is crucial for programmers [21], as it enhances the overall security of the software [25] by ensuring information confidentiality, integrity, and availability. To achieve this, programmers need to develop a security mindset [21], which should be fostered through continuous learning and practice. In a university context, it is essential to teach students about security [20,24], ensuring they are equipped to defend against cyber threats and, in turn, contribute to a more secure and resilient digital environment.

Programming students should be aware of security problems and relevant countermeasures from the start of their studies [5,25], as understanding the importance of secure coding and forming secure habits early is beneficial [25]. Additionally, this helps prevent students from developing insecure coding habits [22] and fosters a security mindset early on [20]. Introductory programming courses can also be taken by students from different majors, making these courses the only opportunity for some students to study security [20].

Published by Springer Nature Switzerland AG 2026
L. Drevin et al. (Eds.): WISE 2025, IFIP AICT 742, pp. 217–233, 2026.
https://doi.org/10.1007/978-3-031-94924-1_15

The security concepts taught to beginner programmers should be simple, as they may not yet have a strong understanding of programming or software-based security exploits [25]. To apply relevant countermeasures in practice, security requirements should be included in course projects [25]. However, integrating security concepts into a course can be challenging due to the already dense curriculum, especially in introductory courses that focus on fundamental programming topics [21].

This paper presents two contributions towards improving security education. First, we propose a method to integrate security concepts into an introductory programming course, covering both lectures and assignments. Our goal is to gradually incorporate security topics without affecting other learning outcomes. We create a concept map linking programming topics with their prerequisites and relevant security concepts, and provide recommendations to implement these changes. Second, we demonstrate our method through a case study, illustrating its practical implementation and evaluating its effectiveness. Our method enables students to learn programming with a security mindset from the start, without detracting from the primary focus of the course.

This article is structured as follows. In Sect. 2, we describe background and previous research on the integration of security concepts into programming courses. Section 3 provides a description of our method. Section 4 presents a case study where we applied the proposed method and its evaluation. Finally, we present and discuss our conclusions in Sect. 5.

2 Background and Related Work

An effective pedagogical approach is an important factor of the success of a course. One example of such approach is Constructive Alignment [2], which aligns teaching activities and assessment tasks with the intended learning outcomes, ensuring that students engage in meaningful learning experiences [3]. In programming courses, this approach may help students to effectively translate theoretical knowledge into practical skills.

In terms of integrating security concepts into introductory programming courses, existing research suggests incorporating them into lecture materials, assignments, or both. This integration can be achieved in various ways.

Some studies propose modifying lecture materials through separate course modules [8,22,25,26]. These modules can be classroom lectures [8,25,26] or e-learning content [22], followed by programming assignments [8,22], code refactoring assignments [26], and questions [22,26]. Furthermore, security concepts can be incorporated into existing classroom lectures [1,6,12]. These lectures can be complemented by programming assignments that focus on both programming and security concepts or exclusively on security-related topics [12]. Alternatively, security concepts can be integrated into existing courses through hands-on use cases [19]. Besides lectures, [6] incorporate a security-related course project, whereas [1] utilize lab assignments to enhance practical understanding. Another existing study [10] proposes a step-by-step process for introducing the topic of buffer overflow, which includes real-life examples of attacks, a code example illustrating the issue, and secure coding guidelines, all of which are later applied in coding assignments.

Key topics among code defects covered in the aforementioned studies include improper input validation [1,19,22,26], buffer overflow [1,10,19,22,25], integer errors [1,22,25,26], and insecure general coding practices [1,6,19]. Some studies also address the negative effects of these defects [6,10,12,19,22]. Recommended countermeasures include input validation [1,10,12,19,22,25,26], output validation [19,26], cryptographic practices [1,6,12], error handling [1,6], secure file and memory management [1,6,10,19], and general programming practices [1,6,8,12,19,25]. These contributions cover programming languages such as Java [1,6,8,22,25,26], C [10,19], C++ [10,22], and Python [22]. A common limitation in studies that propose course modules is that adding a new module to a course may not be feasible. In contrast, some studies focus on integrating security concepts into existing courses [1,6,19], but these are tied to specific programming languages.

Alternatively, [4,7,20,21] focus exclusively on security-related programming assignments where students can practice both security and general programming concepts. Among these, [4,7] propose one or more assignments, while [20] focus on teaching security through a course project that is developed incrementally throughout the course. [21] suggest a structured process for teaching security in practice via assignments. These studies address various categories of code defects, including authentication and password practices [20], memory and file management [4,20,21], input validation [20], and general coding practices [4,20,21]. Each study discusses the negative effects of these defects and proposes applicable countermeasures that should be included in assignments. These contributions cover programming languages such as C [4], C++ [4,20,21] and Python [7]. While practical assignments help students learn to program with security in mind, there is a need for a holistic approach that combines both theoretical and practical materials and is not dependent on any specific programming language.

In our method, we integrate security aspects into both theoretical and practical materials of an existing programming course. The approach is not tied to any specific programming language and is supported by a mapping of topics recommended for introductory programming courses to their corresponding security concepts, based on existing curriculum guidelines. For the practical materials, we suggest incorporating relevant security concepts into existing exercises and projects.

3 Method: Integrating Security Concepts Into an Existing Course

We propose a systematic method to integrate security concepts into an existing introductory programming course. The main idea behind our method is to update the course materials to include relevant security concepts in both theoretical and practical components. The method is based on a mapping between programming topics and relevant security concepts. We present the mapping in Sect. 3.1 and describe how to apply our method in Sect. 3.2.

3.1 Mapping: From Programming Topics to Relevant Security Concepts

We present a mapping between programming topics and relevant security concepts to be used when updating course content. For the list of programming topics, we utilized the new curriculum recommendations for Computer Science recently published by The Association for Computing Machinery (ACM) [9]. One of the recommended knowledge areas, Software Development Fundamentals (SDF), includes the Fundamental Programming Concepts and Practices (SDF-Fundamentals) unit, which covers essential concepts for introductory programming courses. We use topics from this unit as the basis for our mapping. The SDF-Fundamentals unit includes a topic called Develop a security mindset, related to the Foundational Security (SEC-Foundations) unit from the Security knowledge area, highlighting the importance of teaching security in introductory courses. The security topics we use in our mapping correspond to the following SEC-Foundations topics: developing a security mindset, vulnerabilities, threats, and protection practices.

Our mapping applies to both theoretical materials and practical tasks in a course and is independent of any programming language. For lecture materials, security concepts can be added as text, code examples, or demonstrations. For practical tasks, security concepts can be incorporated as requirements.

We categorize related security concepts as security issues, negative effects, and countermeasures [23]. The security issues category refers to code problems leading to negative consequences, negative effects include these consequences, and countermeasures specify methods to prevent them. Relevant security issues and negative effects are identified using CWE [11], OWASP materials [13–18], and our analysis. Countermeasures are categorized using OWASP Secure Coding Practices [17].

We present the list of programming topics that can be mapped to security-related ones in Table 1. Since topics require prior knowledge, we analyzed and noted their dependencies as prerequisites. Some topics, while useful for teaching subsequent concepts, are not strictly necessary and are indicated in parentheses as optional prerequisites. By leveraging these prerequisites, related security concepts can be gradually integrated into the course materials.

We show the mapping between programming topics and relevant security concepts in Table 2. The majority of topics can be mapped to all three categories of related security concepts. For security issues, we specify which exact issues are relevant for introductory programming courses. For negative effects, we define six categories: unauthorized access, unauthorized modification, availability problems, information leak, runtime error, and unexpected modification. Additionally, for libraries (topic 15), the related negative effects are context-dependent,

Table 1. Programming topics from SDF-Fundamentals [9] and their prerequisites.

#	Programming topics	Prerequisites
1	Variables	2
2	Primitive datatypes	–
3	Logical expressions	(1), 2
4	Arithmetical operations	(1), 2
5	Conditional statements	1–3, (8, 9)
6	Iteration based on condition	1–5, (8, 9)
7	Iteration based on collection	1, 2, (9, 13)
8	Input from the user	1, 2
9	Output from the program	(1), 2, (3, 4)
10	Parameter passing	1, 2
11	Scope of variables	1, 2
12	Files: input and output	1, 2, (7), 9, 10
13	Structured datatypes	1, 2
14	Operations with strings	1, 2
15	Libraries	1, 2, 9
16	Recursion	1–5, 9, 10
17	Exception handling	1, 2, 8, 9
18	Testing and debugging	each topic
19	Comments in a code	–

as they depend on security issues specific to each library. In this table, we specify relevant negative effects which are suitable for beginners. For countermeasures, in addition to the mentioned categories from [17], we specify concrete countermeasures if OWASP Secure Coding Practices do not provide enough information about the relevant one. For example, in the category General coding practices, we have a number of topics that are not directly listed by OWASP, and we could not map those topics to any other category. Some programming topics are mapped solely to countermeasures, indicating that these topics are necessary to apply the specified countermeasure. The security issues, negative effects, and countermeasures noted for the programming topic of exception handling (topic 17) are applicable to any programming topic where a runtime error is mentioned as a negative effect. For each programming topic, we provide links to relevant sources if applicable. These sources are also suitable for students as additional learning materials.

3.2 The Step-by-Step Method for Introducing the Changes

To introduce changes to course materials, we recommend following this step-by-step method:

Table 2. Mapping of programming topics and security concepts.

#	Security issues	Negative effects	Countermeasures	Sources
1	-	-	Needed to apply countermeasures	-
2	-	-	Needed to apply countermeasures	-
3	-	-	Input validation, general coding practices: reachable exit condition	-
4	Incorrect calculation	Unauthorized access/ modification, runtime error	Input validation, general coding practices	CWE-682 [11], [17]
5	-	-	Input validation, general coding practices: reachable exit condition	-
6	Infinite loop	Availability problems	General coding practices: reachable exit condition	CWE-835 [11]
7	Accessing a non-existing value	Runtime error	General coding practices: correct values in loop condition and body	CWE-606 [11]
8	Unexpected/ malicious input	Unauthorized access/ modification, availability problems, runtime error	Input validation	CWE-20 [11], [15], [17]
9	Improper encoding/ escaping of output	Unauthorized access/ modification	Input validation, output encoding	CWE-116 [11], [17]
10	Input errors in functions	Runtime error, unexpected modification	General coding practices: correct parameter passing	CWE-628 [11]
11	Incorrect variable scope	Unexpected modification, runtime error	General coding practices: correct scope of variables	CWE-1108, 1109, 1126 [11]
12	Not closing the file, not handling exceptional conditions	Unexpected modification, availability problems, runtime error	Memory management, error handling and logging	CWE-404 [11], [17]
13	Null pointer dereference	Unauthorized access/ modification, runtime error	General coding practices: correct values for elements in structured datatypes	CWE-476 [11]
14	-	-	Input validation, output encoding	-
15	Vulnerable libraries	Context-dependent	General coding practices: review libraries	CWE-1395 [11]
16	Infinite recursion	Availability problems	General coding practices: reachable exit condition	CWE-674 [11]
17	Unhandled errors	Information leak, runtime error	Error handling and logging	CWE-755 [11], [14], [17]
18	-	-	General coding practices: vulnerability testing	[18]
19	Sensitive information in comments	Information leak	Data protection	CWE-615 [11], [17]

Step 1: Analyze which course materials are used in the course (e.g., lecture materials, assignments, and exams).
Step 2: Based on the list of programming topics presented in Table 1, determine which programming topics are covered during the course and in which order they are introduced.
Step 3: Identify which of the relevant security concepts listed in Table 2 are already covered in the course and which are missing.
Step 4: Define intended learning outcomes (ILOs) for security topics that will be covered at your course. For example, "Identify potentially exploitable defects in code" and "Apply relevant secure coding practices to avoid these defects".
Step 5: Determine which teaching activities (TLAs) and assessment tasks (ATs) are aligned with defined ILOs, and thus which course materials are suitable for modification. These changes should have minimal impact on the existing learning outcomes of the course and should not require a significant increase in the effort required from students. We recommend to update lecture materials and course assignments, as these TLAs help to translate theoretical knowledge into practical skills. For example, if lecture materials include slides, consider adding relevant security information as 1–3 additional slides for each corresponding programming topic. Alternatively, integrate the relevant information into existing slides, if it does not overload them. For course assignments, we recommend incorporating a few security-related requirements. This will enable students to practice programming while considering security aspects and will also serve as an AT. Another ATs that can be utilized are, for example, surveys and quizes.
Step 6: Based on the decisions in Steps 2–5, decide to which programming topics the relevant security concepts can be added and utilize the prerequisites mentioned in Table 1 to integrate these concepts at a suitable time.
Step 7: To update lecture materials, for each chosen programming topic, add information about related security issues, negative effects, and countermeasures by utilizing the information and references provided in Table 2. For course assignments, add security-related requirements, for example, based on the relevant countermeasures that can be mapped to programming topics already present in the assignment. If a topic is introduced only in this assignment, add theoretical information about the relevant security concepts too. Plan how the introduced requirements will be graded and add other ATs if needed.

4 Case Study

We present experiences in the transformation of an introductory programming course as a case study. This course is offered at Åbo Akademi University in Finland. The course is taught in Python, which is often chosen for teaching beginners [22]. The course is held in-person. In-person sessions consist of lectures where the lecturer presents the course material, as well as labs where the students work on course tasks and can ask questions from the lecturer or course assistants. The course is for degree students majoring in Computer Science and Computer Engineering, but it can also be taken by students studying other subjects and adult learners.

We conducted our case study in two editions of the course: 2023 and 2024. In 2023, we familiarized ourselves with the course materials, planned changes, and analyzed submitted student code for security aspects. In 2024, we implemented changes, analyzed student code, compared the results to those of 2023, and conducted a post-course survey. We adhered to the ethical principles of research outlined by the Finnish National Board on Research Integrity (TENK) and obtained the students' consent to analyze their code.

We present how we applied the method proposed in this paper in Sects. 4.1, 4.3, and 4.4. We introduce additional programming topics explored through the case study, along with relevant security concepts, in Sect. 4.2. Finally, to evaluate our contribution, we analyzed the submitted code for programming projects, compared the results to those from the course version before our intervention, and analyzed the results of the post-course survey. The evaluation can be found in Sect. 4.5.

4.1 Applying the Method

To apply our method to the chosen case study, we followed the recommendations defined in Sect. 3.2:

Step 1: The course materials include lecture slides presented during classroom lectures, practical exercises comprising after-lecture training programming tasks and automatically graded programming exercises, larger programming projects, and an automatically graded programming exam.
Step 2: When utilizing the list of programming topics presented in Sect. 3.1, we identified that all programming topics were covered in the course. We also found some additional topics, see Sect. 4.2 for more details. Details about the order of these programming topics that influenced our modifications are described in Sect. 4.3.
Step 3: We observed that such countermeasures as input validation, exception handling, encryption, and logging were already present in the course but were not emphasized as security-related. Therefore, relevant security information was required for each programming topic explored in the previous step.
Step 4: We defined the following ILOs: 1) Identify potential security issues in basic programming constructs (e.g., infinite loops, unexpected or malicious inputs, and unhandled errors); 2) Understand which negative impacts these security issues can cause; and 3) Apply secure coding practices to mitigate the identified security issues.
Step 5: We discussed with the course lecturer where changes could be made in the course materials to align TLAs with ILOs. We agreed to modify the lecture materials by adding a few slides to each programming topic selected in

steps 2 and 3, covering related security issues, potential negative effects, and countermeasures. Additionally, we included a few security-related requirements into larger programming projects. Since these changes are minimal, they do not affect other learning outcomes or increase the effort required from students. See Sects. 4.3 and 4.4 for more details. Modifications to the lecture materials align with ILOs 1) and 2), while the additional requirements in the programming projects align with ILO 3). As ATs, modifications in programming projects served these purposes, and we also distributed a survey at the end of the course. See Sect. 4.5 for more details.
Step 6: We utilized the prerequisites mentioned in Table 1 and additional ones identified in Sect. 4.2 to determine when to add the related security concepts. Information about the added security concepts is presented in Sects. 4.3 and 4.4 .
Step 7: We updated the lecture slides to include information about relevant security concepts and added security-related requirements to course programming projects. These details are described in Sects. 4.3 and 4.4.

4.2 Additional Programming Topics and Related Security Concepts

We identified some additional topics that were taught in the course: encryption and decryption, and logging. The former was present both in the lecture materials and in one course project, while the latter was present in one course project only. The encryption and decryption programming topic belongs to the Cryptography knowledge (SEC-Crypto) unit in the ACM curriculum recommendations for Computer Science [9], while logging belongs to Software Construction (SE-Construction). We show these topics, their prerequisites, and the relevant security concepts in Tables 3 and 4. These tables are a continuation of Tables 1 and 2.

Table 3. Additional programming topics from SEC-Crypto and SE-Construction [9] and their prerequisites.

#	Programming topics	Prerequisites
20	Encryption and decryption	1, 2, 4, 9
21	Logging	1, 2, (5), 9, 10, (12, 15)

4.3 Modification of Lecture Materials

In the lecture materials, we updated slides and added corresponding security-related information in the form of text or code examples for nearly every programming topic listed in Table 3. The exception is recursion (topic 16), where we did not add any security-related information since this topic is usually perceived

Table 4. Mapping of additional programming topics and security concepts.

#	Security issues	Negative effects	Countermeasures	Sources
20	No encryption, weak encryption	Unauthorized access/ modification	Data protection	CWE-310, 311 [11], [13], [17]
21	No logging, logging sensitive or malicious data	Unauthorized modification, information leak, forensic analysis problems	Logging	CWE-117, 532, 778 [11], [16], [17]

as difficult and was not required in the course projects or the exam. Additional programming topics listed in Table 3 are covered without exception.

At the beginning of the course, topics such as variables, datatypes, logical expressions, and arithmetical expressions (topics 14) were taught to students. We did not add any explicit security-related information to these topics since they were utilized when we explained input validation and exception handling. For input from the user (topic 8), we added some theoretical information about security issues, negative effects, and countermeasures first. When the students learned how to write conditional statements, we showed code examples of how to use these to validate input.

Structured datatypes (topic 13) were initially taught early in the course, but we added security-related information at a later stage when some additional information about lists was provided to the students. For libraries (topic 15), we considered the Python built-in module random. As extra information, we mentioned to students that this module provides insecure random number generation, which can lead to unauthorized access and modification of data if applied in cryptography. We suggested using the Python module secrets to generate secure random numbers and provided [13] as a reference. Security-related information about logging (topic 21) was added to the course project only, see Sect. 4.4.

4.4 Modification of Programming Projects

To modify the programming projects, we applied the mapping presented in Tables 2 and 4 to identify which security-related requirements could be added. We discussed our ideas with the lecturer. Since these projects involve user interaction and it is important for the students to apply secure programming practices, we chose to add requirements for countermeasures such as input validation (specifically, range validation), exception handling, and input sanitization. The students already had knowledge of these security concepts from lectures.

To gradually incorporate the selected changes, we did not add any explicit security requirements to the first programming project, allowing students to focus on basic programming topics. In the second project, we added only a range validation requirement to one user input, to see if the students would validate other inputs and apply exception handling. In the third programming project, we required both range validation and exception handling, while in the last one, we added input sanitization, as this was relevant to the nature of the project. It should be noted that for the first and second programming projects in the second course edition, some general functional requirements were changed. Thus, we refer to the functional requirements that are common to both editions.

The first project is a game where the user plays against the computer by providing inputs according to the rules of the game. The user can choose the number of points required to win the game, and the flow of the game is controlled by a while loop.

The goal of the second project is a quiz with arithmetic questions. The user chooses the number of questions and enters the answer for each one. Asking the chosen number of questions is governed by a for loop. A new functional requirement is that the user inputs positive integers for an arithmetic operation chosen randomly by the program. For this input, we added an explicit range validation requirement.

The third project focuses on the encryption and decryption of a text provided by the user. We added requirements for range validation and exception handling for the encryption key chosen by the user.

In the fourth project, the students implement a program that simulates a conversation, which is logged in a file. We added a requirement to sanitize user input by removing punctuation marks to eliminate potentially dangerous characters, to process it, and provide a corresponding answer. Since logging was not covered in the lecture materials, we explained its importance for monitoring security and asked the students to consider whether to log user input before or after sanitization.

4.5 Evaluation

In this section, we present our evaluation of the impact of the course changes. We show the analysis of programming projects and a post survey. As described earlier in this section, we performed a case study in two editions of the chosen introductory programming course: one before we applied our method and the other after. We refer to the course version before our intervention as V1 (version 1) and the version after our changes as V2 (version 2). For the programming projects, we compare the scores for certain requirements between these two versions. The evaluation of the projects and the results of the post survey are shown later in this section.

Evaluation of Updated Student Projects. We assessed the code submitted by the students for the four programming projects included in the course. For each project, we identified specific aspects to examine. Each aspect was evaluated for implementation, assigning a score of 1 (implemented, meaning present in the code) or 0 (not implemented). In this section, we compare the scores assigned to each chosen aspect.

Student projects were typically completed in pairs. Due to consent restrictions, we analyzed only those submissions where both the participating students provided consent. The number of analyzed submissions varies for each project, depending on the number of students who submitted solutions and any changes in group composition. In Table 5, we present the evaluation of all four student projects.

Table 5. Comparison: projects 1–4.

Project	Aspects	Explicit	Accepted solutions		
			V1	V2	p-value
1	1.1 Exception handling is present		7/32	10/32	0.57
	1.2 Range validation is present		6/32	7/32	1
	1.3 No infinite while loop		32/32	32/32	1
2	2.1.1 Exception handling is present		7/32	7/30	1
	2.1.2 Range validation is present		9/32	12/30	0.42
	2.2.1 Exception handling is present		3/32	8/30	0.10
	2.3.1 For loop executes without errors		32/32	30/30	1
	2.4.1 Exception handling is present		N/A	8/30	N/A
	2.4.2 Range validation is present	✓	N/A	29/30	N/A
3	3.1 Exception handling is present	✓	9/31	29/30	**<0.0001**
	3.2 Range validation is present	✓	6/31	28/30	**<0.0001**
4	4.1 Input is sanitized	✓	22/31	30/30	**0.002**
	4.2 Sanitized user input is logged	✓	0/31	17/30	**<0.0001**

In Project 1, we examined the implementation of the following functional requirements: 1) a user can choose the number of points required to win the game, and 2) the flow of the game is controlled by the while loop. For the user input, we analyzed whether students implemented exception handling for possible non-numerical values and whether they implemented input validation to verify that the provided value fell within an acceptable range (see aspects 1.1 and 1.2 in the table). For the while loop, we analyzed whether there was an infinite loop present in the code. There was a small increase in the implementation of exception handling and range validation between V1 and V2. In both course versions, no submissions had infinite loops. In both V1 and V2, more groups applied exception handling than range validation.

In Project 2, we compared the implementation of the following functional requirements: 1) allowing a user to choose the number of questions, 2) handling user input for arithmetic questions, 3) using a for loop to control the quiz flow, and 4) allowing a user to choose positive integers to generate an arithmetic question. For the first user input, we compared the same two security aspects as in Project 1. For the second user input, we focused on exception handling, as range validation is not applicable to the user answer. For the for loop, we assessed its correct implementation to ensure it does not cause any runtime errors. We observed a small increase in range validation for the first user input, while the number of groups applying exception handling remained unchanged. Exception handling implementation increased for the second input. The for loop was implemented correctly. For the third user input added in V2, 29 out of 30 groups applied range validation, an explicit security requirement, and 8 groups implemented exception handling that was not explicitly required.

In project 3, there was a large increase in implemented exception handling and range validation between V1 and V2. This indicates that security aspects are more likely to be implemented when explicitly required in the project guidelines.

In project 4, we compared the students' projects between V1 and V2 for implementation of input sanitization and logging. The sanitization of user input increased between V1 and V2, reaching 100%. In V2, 17 out of 30 groups logged the sanitized input, whereas in V1, all the groups logged the input immediately.

For each aspect compared in Table 5, we computed a p-value using two-tailed Fisher's exact test and compared it to the significance level of 0.05. The results show that differences for aspects 3.1–4.2 are statistically significant, whereas the differences for other aspects are not. This can be explained by the fact that requirements 3.1–4.2 were explicitly stated in V2, while the others were not.

Evaluation of Post Survey. At the end of the course, we distributed an anonymous post survey to the participants. The students evaluated each statement with a score on a scale ranging from 1 (Strongly disagree), 2 (Disagree), 3 (Neutral), 4 (Agree), to 5 (Strongly agree). We included statements related to the security topics that were emphasized most during the course. We received 34 responses to the survey. Since no students assigned a score of 1 to any of the questions, this value is not present in the table with the results of the post survey.

Table 6. Post survey

Statement	2	3	4	5	Mean
Programmers play an important role in protecting applications against cyberattacks.	0	1 (3%)	13 (38%)	20 (59%)	4.6
All input must be validated, as the application can receive unexpected and even harmful input.	0	3 (9%)	16 (47%)	15 (44%)	4.4
Unhandled errors pose a security risk, and error handling must be implemented to protect applications against cyberattacks.	0	1 (3%)	14 (41%)	19 (56%)	4.5
The programmer must ensure that an infinite loop cannot occur in the application, as it poses a security risk.	1 (3%)	3 (9%)	11 (32%)	19 (56%)	4.4
Data must be protected from unauthorized access, and one of the measures that can be applied is encryption.	0	1 (3%)	11 (32%)	22 (65%)	4.6

The post survey results presented in Table 6 show that students understand the importance of security in the scope of programming. The majority of respondents selected *Agree* or *Strongly agree* for each statement, with mean values ranging from 4.4 to 4.6. This indicates that the students understand the importance of security in programming.

4.6 Summary of the Case Study

We applied the method described in Sect. 3 to update course materials, incorporating security information into lecture slides and adding security requirements to programming projects. We confirmed with the lecturer that these modifications had minimal impact on the learning outcomes and did not significantly increase student effort. Additionally, we explored two programming topics not originally included in the mapping presented in Sect. 3. By leveraging the prerequisites of each topic, we introduced related security concepts gradually.

To evaluate the effectiveness of our method, we assessed student programming projects and conducted a post survey. We compared the implementation of security aspects in projects from two course versions: before and after our intervention. The comparison shows an improvement, especially when security aspects were explicitly required. Post-course survey results indicate that the students now recognize the importance of security in programming.

5 Discussion and Conclusions

In this paper, we propose a method that helps students develop a security mindset starting in their first programming course. The core idea is to integrate security concepts into an introductory programming course by updating materials to include these concepts in both theory and practice. Our method is supported by mapping existing programming topics to relevant security concepts, which are introduced gradually. The method should be applied in a way that has minimal impact on other learning outcomes of the course and does not increase the effort required from the students. To apply the proposed method, one should identify and assess the course materials and programming topics, determine gaps in security concepts, decide on modifications, plan the integration of additional security concepts, and implement the changes.

We implemented the proposed method in a case study within a selected introductory programming course, modifying both lecture materials and programming projects. This supported students in transforming theoretical knowledge into hands-on skills which is a key principle of Constructive Alignment. We confirmed with the lecturer that our planned modifications would minimally impact the learning outcomes of the course and not significantly increase student effort. For the lecture materials, we identified which programming topics could be mapped to security-related ones by comparing them to the proposed mapping. For each of these topics, we added relevant information about security issues, negative effects, and countermeasures, depending on the applicable categories and the feasibility of adding security-related information. We considered the appropriate timing for introducing this information, ensuring the students had sufficient knowledge to understand it based on the identified prerequisites. Additionally, we explored other programming topics taught in the course and added relevant security information to these. In the programming projects, we incorporated explicit security-related requirements where possible, starting from the second project. These requirements were added gradually. A comparison of submitted solutions between the course versions before and after our intervention shows an improvement in the implementation of security-related aspects, particularly when these were explicitly required. The results of a post-course survey indicate that the students recognize the importance of security in programming.

Overall, we believe that the proposed method helps raise awareness among students in introductory programming courses about the importance of security in programming. Although we based our list of programming topics on generalized curriculum guidelines, there are limitations to our approach, as it was evaluated within the context of a single programming course. Future research should explore variations across different student populations, course structures, programming languages, and the range of topics covered in introductory programming courses. We plan to conduct additional studies at other universities.

Acknowledgments. This work has received funding from the Finnish Ministry of Education and Culture under grant agreement OKM/60/522/2022. We would like to thank Annamari Soini for providing the opportunity to perform a case study on the method proposed in this paper.

Disclosure of Interests. The authors have no competing interests to declare that are relevant to the content of this article.

References

1. Bandi, A., Fellah, A., Bondalapati, H.: Embedding security concepts in introductory programming courses. J. Comput. Sci. Coll. **34**(4), 78–89 (2019)
2. Biggs, J.: Enhancing teaching through constructive alignment. High. Educ. **32**(3), 347–364 (1996). https://doi.org/10.1007/BF00138871
3. Biggs, J., Tang, C.: Constructive alignment: an outcomes-based approach to teaching anatomy. In: Chan, L.K., Pawlina, W. (eds.) Teaching Anatomy, pp. 23–30. Springer, Cham (2020). https://doi.org/10.1007/978-3-030-43283-6_3
4. Bishop, M.: Some "Secure Programming" exercises for an introductory programming class. In: Dodge, R.C., Futcher, L. (eds.) Information Assurance and Security Education and Training, pp. 226–232. Springer, Berlin Heidelberg (2013)
5. Doss, C., Yuan, X., Chennakeshva, V., Abernathy, A., Ford, K.: Modules for teaching secure in Android application development. J. Colloquium Inf. Syst. Secur. Educ. (CISSE) **6**(2), 1–13 (2019)

6. Earwood, B., Yang, J., Kim, Y.R.: Effective learning of cybersecurity concepts with model-eliciting activities. In: 2021 IEEE International Conference on Engineering, Technology & Education (TALE), pp. 01–07 (2021). https://doi.org/10.1109/TALE52509.2021.9678713
7. Fiesler, C., Dalal, S., Paup, J.: Passwords and python: introducing security concepts in lower-division programming. Assoc. Comput. Mach. (2023). https://doi.org/10.1145/3631988
8. Haywood, A., Yu, H., Yuan, X.: Teaching java security to enhance cybersecurity education. In: 2013 Proceedings of IEEE SoutheastCon, pp. 1–6. IEEE SoutheastCon-Proceedings, IEEE; UNF Student Branch, April 2013. https://doi.org/10.1109/SECON.2013.6567447
9. Kumar, A.N., et al.: computer science curricula 2023. ACM, New York, NY, USA (2024). https://doi.org/10.1145/3664191
10. Mano, C.D., DuHadway, L., Striegel, A.: A case for instilling security as a core programming skill. In: Proceedings. Frontiers in Education. 36th Annual Conference, pp. 13–18 (2006). https://doi.org/10.1109/FIE.2006.322347
11. MITRE: Common weakness enumeration, https://cwe.mitre.org/, Accessed 01 Aug 2024
12. Null, L.: Integrating security across the computer science curriculum. J. Comput. Sci. Coll. **19**(5), 170–178 (2004)
13. OWASP: cryptographic storage cheat sheet, https://cheatsheetseries.owasp.org/cheatsheets/Cryptographic_Storage_Cheat_Sheet.html, Accessed 01 Aug 2024
14. OWASP: improper error handling, https://owasp.org/www-community/Improper_Error_Handling, Accessed 01 Aug 2024
15. OWASP: input validation cheat sheet, https://cheatsheetseries.owasp.org/cheatsheets/Input_Validation_Cheat_Sheet.html, Accessed 01 Aug 2024
16. OWASP: logging cheat sheet, https://cheatsheetseries.owasp.org/cheatsheets/Logging_Cheat_Sheet.html, Accessed 01 Aug 2024
17. OWASP: OWASP secure coding practices-quick reference guide, https://owasp.org/www-project-secure-coding-practices-quick-reference-guide/, Accessed 16 Sep 2024
18. OWASP: OWASP web security testing guide, https://owasp.org/www-project-web-security-testing-guide/, Accessed 01 Aug 2024
19. Pawelczak, D.: Teaching security in introductory C-programming courses. In: 6th International Conference on Higher Education Advances (HEAd 2020), pp. 595–603 (2020). https://doi.org/10.4995/HEAd20.2020.11114
20. Pournaghshband, V.: Teaching the security mindset to CS1 students. In: Proceeding of the 44th ACM Technical Symposium on Computer Science Education, SIGCSE 2013, pp. 347–352. Association for Computing Machinery, New York, NY, USA (2013). https://doi.org/10.1145/2445196.2445299
21. Pournaghshband, V., Pournaghshband, H.: Entailing security mindset in foundational CS courses: an interactive approach. In: 2024 IEEE World Engineering Education Conference (EDUNINE), pp. 1–6 (2024). https://doi.org/10.1109/EDUNINE60625.2024.10500581
22. Taylor, B., Kaza, S.: Security Injections@Towson: integrating secure coding into introductory computer science courses. ACM Trans. Comput. Educ. **16**(4) (2016). https://doi.org/10.1145/2897441
23. Torbunova, A., Ashraf, A., Porres, I.: A systematic mapping study on teaching of security concepts in programming courses. In: 2024 50th Euromicro Conference on Software Engineering and Advanced Applications (SEAA), pp. 288–295 (2024). https://doi.org/10.1109/SEAA64295.2024.00052

24. Weiss, R., Mache, J.: Teaching security labs with web applications, buffer overflows and firewall configurations. J. Comput. Sci. Coll. **27**(1), 163–170 (2011)
25. Williams, K.A., Yuan, X., Yu, H., Bryant, K.: Teaching secure coding for beginning programmers. J. Comput. Sci. Coll. **29**(5), 91–99 (2014)
26. Yu, H., Jones, N., Bullock, G., Yuan, X.Y.: Teaching secure software engineering: writing secure code. In: 2011 7th Central and Eastern European Software Engineering Conference (CEE-SECR), pp. 1–5, October 2011. https://doi.org/10.1109/CEE-SECR.2011.6188473

Discussions

Advancing Digital Privacy Education: A Global Curriculum Initiative

Gurvirender P. S. Tejay[1(✉)], Tamara Bonaci[2], Travis Breaux[3], Ümit Cali[4], Ernesto Cuadross-Vargas[5], Sara Foresti[6], Andrew McGettrick[7], Rajendra Raj[8], Kai Rannenberg[9], and Andrew Seely[10]

[1] Zarb School of Business, Hofstra University, New York, USA
tejay@ieee.org
[2] Northeastern University, Washington, USA
t.bonaci@northeastern.edu
[3] Carnegie Mellon University, Pennsylvania, USA
tdbreaux@andrew.cmu.edu
[4] University of York, York, UK
umit.cali@york.ac.uk
[5] National University of Engineering, Lima, Peru
ecuadros@spc.org.pe
[6] Università degli Studi di Milano, Milano, Italy
sara.foresti@unimi.it
[7] University of Strathclyde, Glasgow, Scotland
andrew.mcgettrick@strath.ac.uk
[8] Rochester Institute of Technology, New York, USA
rkr@cs.rit.edu
[9] Goethe University, Frankfurt, Germany
kai.rannenberg@m-chair.de
[10] Hillsborough Community College, Florida, USA
andrew.seely@ieee.org

Abstract. As digital privacy becomes a critical concern across industries, structured education in this field is urgently needed. To address this gap, ACM, IEEE, and IFIP have launched a collaborative initiative to develop a Privacy Curricular Guideline for graduate programs. This framework defines core knowledge areas and aligns academic training with real-world needs. A Joint Taks Force of global experts identified eight foundational pillars for digital privacy education: (1) Privacy Body of Knowledge, (2) Privacy Foundations, (3) General Computer Science Concepts for Privacy, (4) Privacy-Preserving Computer Science/Software Engineering, (5) Information Systems/Technology, (6) Privacy Development Lifecycle, (7) Applied Domains, and (8) Privacy-related Industry Perspective. These are now being refined by dedicated Working Groups. This work is highly relevant to IFIP TC11 WG11.8, as privacy complements security but requires distinct focus areas addressing issues of user autonomy, data governance, and ethical considerations. Currently, privacy topics are often scattered across computer security and information security courses, leaving graduates unprepared for specialized privacy technologist roles. The initiative aims to bridge the education-practice gap and equip students with skills for emerging privacy challenges.

L. Drevin et al. (Eds.): WISE 2025, IFIP AICT 742, pp. 237–240, 2026.
https://doi.org/10.1007/978-3-031-94924-1_16

Keywords: Privacy Education · Digital Privacy · Privacy Body of Knowledge

1 Introduction

As privacy regulations evolve and data protection becomes a priority across industries, there is an urgent need to define a structured approach to privacy education within technology programs. Recognizing this gap, the Association of Computing Machinery, IEEE Computer Society, International Federation for Information Processing (IFIP), and IEEE Digital Privacy Initiative have launched a collaborative effort to develop a Privacy Curricular Guideline for university graduate programs. This initiative aims to establish a comprehensive digital privacy curriculum that defines the boundaries of the field, identifies key knowledge areas, and aligns with industry needs.

A Joint Task Force composed of global experts met in December 2024 to define the core knowledge areas essential for a structured privacy curriculum. The knowledge areas identified include:

Privacy Body of Knowledge
Privacy Foundations
General Computer Science Concepts for Privacy
Privacy-Preserving Computer Science/Software Engineering
Information Systems/Technology
Privacy Development Lifecycle
Applied Domains
Privacy-Related Industry Perspective

These areas have been operationalized into dedicated Working Groups that contribute to shaping the curricular framework.

2 Digital Privacy Knowledge Areas

A robust digital privacy curriculum requires mastery of key competencies across eight critical domains. This section provides a brief overview of the essential knowledge areas that prepare professionals to address modern privacy challenges in technology and business.

Privacy Body of Knowledge. A structured compilation of core concepts, human right perspectives, social norms, and practices that define the discipline of digital privacy. This knowledge area includes legal frameworks, ethical considerations, and standardized terminology.

Privacy Foundations. Fundamental theories and philosophies underpinning privacy including privacy principles, levels of privacy, and historical context. This knowledge area covers cultural differences in privacy expectations, and the societal impact of surveillance and data collection.

General Computer Science Concepts for Privacy. This area focuses on essential computer science topics that support privacy engineering, including data flow analysis, algorithms, networking, distributes systems, cybersecurity and machine learning/artificial intelligence. It provides the technical groundwork for understanding how privacy mechanisms are implemented in digital systems.

Privacy-preserving Computer Science/Software Engineering. This knowledge area covers advanced techniques for embedding privacy into systems, including privacy enhancing technologies (PETs), database protection, privacy computations, dark patterns, encryption, and anonymization methods. It focuses on designing software and architectures that minimize data exposure.

Information Systems/Technology. This area examines how privacy integrates with IT infrastructure along with privacy management. It addresses challenges like data governance, access control, and audit logging in enterprise environments. This area emphasizes designing privacy systems and privacy operations including risk management and privacy usability.

Privacy Development Lifecycle. A systematic approach to incorporating privacy at every stage of software and product development – from requirements gathering and design to deployment and decommissioning. This knowledge area aligns with established frameworks like Privacy by design (PbD) and threat modeling for proactive risk mitigation.

Applied Domains. This knowledge area examines specialized privacy concerns in high-impact sectors like healthcare, energy, finance, and connected vehicles. It covers domain-specific regulations, real-world applications and emerging challenges – such as facial recognition and genomic privacy.

Privacy-related Industry Perspective. This knowledge area bridges curriculum elements with industry demands, offering practical insights into real-world privacy operations. It explores emerging privacy job roles and current market needs.

3 Relevance to IFIP TC11 WG11.8

Privacy is inherently linked to security, as effective privacy protections rely on strong security controls, risk management, and compliance measures. However, privacy extends beyond security by addressing issues of user autonomy, data governance, and ethical considerations, which require specialized frameworks. From an academic standpoint, privacy is often integrated into information security courses but lacks a dedicated, structured educational approach. Given that privacy professionals are in high demand, a well-defined curriculum will help bridge the knowledge gap and provide students with the skills needed to tackle real-world privacy challenges. Engaging WG11.8 members in this initiative will ensure the curriculum reflects the latest advancements in privacy education.

Goals to be Achieved During WISE. This working group session at WISE aims to:

1. **Present the foundational structure** of the Privacy Curricular Guideline, including the rationale behind the knowledge areas, key topics, and learning outcomes.
2. **Engage WG11.8 members in discussions** to refine and enhance the curriculum based on their expertise and experience.
3. **Gather constructive feedback** from conference attendees to ensure the curricular framework aligns with both academic and industry needs.

Plans for Continued Collaboration. Following WISE, attendees will be invited to join one of the initiative's Working Groups to contribute to the ongoing development of the Privacy Curricular Guideline. Their expertise will be critical in finalizing a global privacy education framework that supports both academic institutions and industry professionals. By fostering continued collaboration, WG11.8 members will play a vital role in shaping the future of privacy education and preparing students for emerging privacy-related roles.

4 Conclusion

This initiative is a critical step toward addressing the growing need for structured privacy education. By developing a comprehensive curricular framework, this initiative will ensure that future professionals are equipped with the necessary expertise to navigate complex privacy challenges. By working together, we can strengthen privacy education, support interdisciplinary learning, and empower next generation of privacy and security professionals.

Cybersecurity Awareness via Physical Games

Steven Furnell[1](✉), James Todd[1], Simon Castle-Green[1], and Lucija Šmid[2]

[1] School of Computer Science, University of Nottingham, Nottingham, UK
steven.furnell@nottingham.ac.uk

[2] School of Management, University of Bath, Bath, UK

Abstract. This short paper (supporting an invited presentation at the WISE 2025 conference) summarises a series of cybersecurity awareness activities, which have been designed to offer short but meaningful opportunities for layperson users to build basic cybersecurity awareness. The three activities – Password Strength Meter, Hacker Whacker game, and Cyber Defence Dice game – have been used in various public-facing events, and collectively demonstrate success in delivering cybersecurity awareness in a fun and engaging manner.

Keywords: Awareness · Cyber Games · Gamification · User Engagement

1 Introduction

Today's technology-dependent society calls for an increasingly digitally literate population, which includes awareness of security threats and related protection. However, while numerous resources are available to support cyber awareness and literacy, cybersecurity is rarely something that users will consider exciting, and so it is desirable to involve them in ways that are more fun and engaging. There have been various prior examples of cybersecurity games, in both online and physical formats. With the latter, the most common modes appear to be board games (e.g. [1, 2]) and card games (e.g. [3, 4]). However, many of these games are relatively long form, potentially requiring a non-trivial degree of setup and explanation of the rules, followed by a prolonged period of actual play. It is also common for the games to be aimed at players who are already somewhat knowledgable about cybersecurity at the outset (e.g. one of the card games referenced above uses terminology such as 'Local Privilege Escalation' and 'Application Shimming', which is unlikely to feel like accessible language for novices seeking to understand the basics). Moreover, some of the games require facilitators to run the session, adding to the level of organization and overhead involved in playing. Such requirements may, of course, be fine in the context of running a pre-planned awareness and training session within an organization or classroom, but the games consequently lend themselves less well to quick use in more casual and informal contexts. With this in mind, there is role for something quicker that helps to reinforce basic lessons, focused around aspects such as basic cyber hygiene and awareness of related threats and safeguards.

Published by Springer Nature Switzerland AG 2026
L. Drevin et al. (Eds.): WISE 2025, IFIP AICT 742, pp. 241–244, 2026.
https://doi.org/10.1007/978-3-031-94924-1_17

2 Physical Cybersecurity Awareness Activities

The authors haves designed a series of physical engagement activities, each promoting different aspects of cybersecurity awareness and/or decision making. These are depicted in Fig. 1 and summarized as follows:

- **Password Strength Meter**: Taking its cue from a fairground-style 'test your strength' machine, this device allows users to enter a candidate password and test its strength. Pressing the large red button initiates the testing and feedback, with the latter occurring via the progressive reveal of the number of lights that are lit as the strength rating. The meter raises awareness of password strength as an issue of importance, and clearly illustrates to players how well their choice has scored. The progressive reveal of the score adds an element of suspense to the process, and helps to promote competition between players.
- **Hacker Whacker**: Based on the concept of another fairground-style game, Whack-a-Mole, this device requires the player to differentiate between attacks and defences, hitting a 'mole' lit in red if the screen displays an attack, or one lit in green if the screen displays a defence (see Fig. 2). The game raises awareness of basic threat and defence types. Players have 3 lives, and score based upon the number of correct decisions against a timer (with speed gradually increasing to heighten the difficulty).
- **Cyber Defence Dice:** Players are provided with two sets of five dice, a red set in which all of the die faces are forms of attack, and a blue set in which the faces are defences. Following an initial throw, players select which dice to keep or throw again in order to mount a good attack/defence (depending on which side starts), and then to combat the combination that previous player has thrown. The game raises awareness of threats and defences, and builds on this with related decision-making in order to determine which side wins.

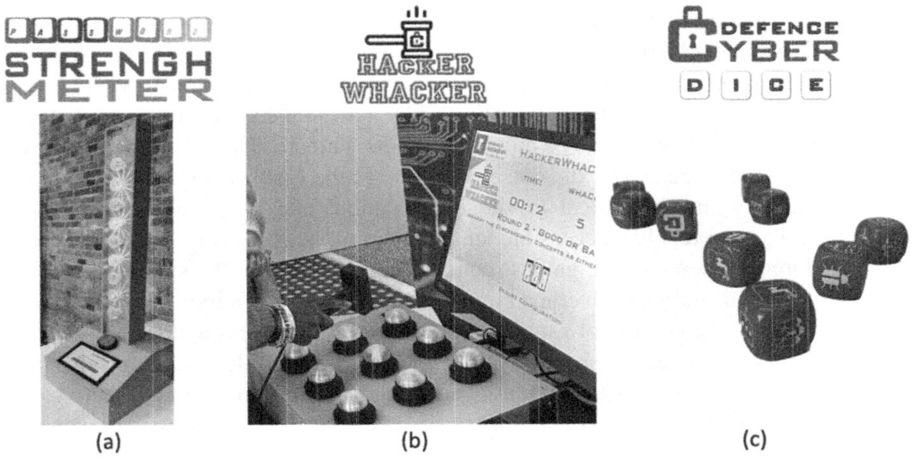

Fig. 1. Images of (a) Password Meter, (b) Hacker Whacker, and (c) Cyber Defence Dice games

The Hacker Whacker and Dice games are underpinned by a series of attack and defence types, as depicted in Fig. 2. The related symbols are displayed on-screen for Hacker Whacker, to cue the player as to whether they should hit red or green lights. Meanwhile, in the dice game the images form the faces on the two sets of dice, and the accompanying game rules (see stepintocyber.org/dice) explain how to use them.

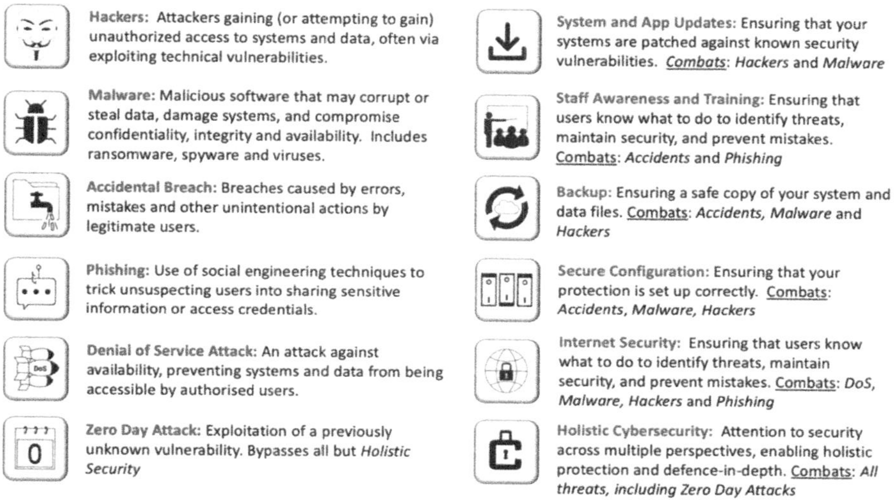

Fig. 2. Images used for attack and defence types

3 Discussion and Conclusion

Each of the games is designed to offer a short but meaningful interaction that supports a level of cybersecurity awareness raising in an engaging manner. All require only brief explanation in order for players to understand what they are expected to do, with the Password Meter and Hacker Whacker proving very easy for new players to pick up simply from observing previous ones. The Cyber Defence Dice require some brief explanation of the rules, but players can get underway within a minute or two, using a cribsheet of the attack and defence types to guide their decisions.

The games have been used in practice in a variety of public-facing contexts, including a series of awareness-raising events for post-16 students (see www.stepintocyber.org). These experiences have demonstrated that prospective players are keen to engage with the activities, and that those who play enjoyed the experiences. While all three games could be implemented virtually/online (and many readers will already be familiar with seeing password meters offered in this manner on websites), the physical aspect is considered to add to the attraction and resulting engagement. Indeed, from the experience of using them at events, all of the games act as a provocation of interest, with the Password Meter and Hacker Whacker being particularly able to draw crowds on the basis of their physical size and audio-visual components.

All of the physical implementations provide foundations for further development. For example, the software for both Password Meter and Hacker Whacker is being further developed to offer new game variations. Meanwhile, the Cyber Defence Dice readily lend themselves to the design of new game variants beyond the three for which rules were initially offered. Overall, the experience of creating the games and watching them in use has prompted further ideas, and the team plans to further develop the existing games and complement them with a range of additional ones.

Acknowledgments. The authors would like to acknowledge the supporting contributions of Lewis Brand (for implementing the original version of the Password Meter) and Xavier Carpent (for proposing one of the game variants for the Cyber Defence Dice).

Disclosure of Interests. The authors have no competing interests to declare that are relevant to the content of this article.

References

1. Riskio. Riskio: A Serious Game for Cyber Security Awareness and Education. https://www.riskio.co.uk. Accessed 14 Apr 2025
2. Threats and Trade-offs. Describe Hub. https://www.discribehub.org/boardgame-threats-tradeoffs. Accessed 14 Apr 2025
3. Cyber Threat Defender: University of Texas at San Antonio. https://cias.utsa.edu/ctd. Accessed 14 Apr 2025
4. Backdoors & Breaches. Black Hills Information Security. https://www.blackhillsinfosec.com/tools/backdoorsandbreaches. Accessed 14 Apr 2025

Author Index

Published by Springer Nature Switzerland AG 2026
L. Drevin et al. (Eds.): WISE 2025, IFIP AICT 742, pp. 245–246, 2026.
https://doi.org/10.1007/978-3-031-94924-1

The manufacturer's authorised representative in the EU is Springer Nature Customer Service Centre GmbH, Europaplatz 3, 69115 Heidelberg, Germany. If you have any concerns regarding our products, please contact ProductSafety@springernature.com

Printed and bound by CPI Group (UK) Ltd, Croydon, CR0 4YY
30/09/2026
02225570-0003